BELL ON

MISSISSIPPI FAMILY LAW

THIRD EDITION

2025 SUPPLEMENT

by
Deborah H. Bell

THE NAUTILUS PUBLISHING COMPANY
OXFORD, MISSISSIPPI
www.nautiluspublishing.com

BELL ON MISSISSIPPI FAMILY LAW

Citations to cases and statutes are current through December 31, 2025.

Printed in United States.

Library of Congress Cataloging-in-Publication Data

Bell, Deborah H. (1953 -

Bell on Mississippi Family Law/By Deborah H. Bell

3rd Edition (2025 Supplement)

ISBN

To subscribe to the annual supplement or to order additional copies, contact:

The Nautilus Publishing Company

Tel: 662-513-0159

E-mail: info@nautiluspublishing.com • Web: www.msfamilylaw.com

FROM THE AUTHOR

The 2025 Supplement updates the Third Edition of *Bell on Mississippi Family Law* with cases and legislative developments from January 1, 2020 through December 31, 2025. The supplement follows the headings used in the Third Edition. You should be able to locate any new developments by checking the heading and page number that corresponds to the main volume. If a heading or subheading is not included in the supplement, no new information has been added to that topic.

The supplement begins with "Highlights of the Year," a short summary of the most significant developments of the years covered by the supplement.

Thanks to Carroll Moore for formatting the book and to Nautilus Publishing Company and Neil White, III for making *Bell on Mississippi Family Law* and the annual supplement possible.

I appreciate comments and suggestions from readers on how to improve the book and supplement. Thank you, as always, for using *Bell on Mississippi Family Law*.

Debbie Bell
April, 2026

SUMMARY OF CONTENTS

TABLE OF CONTENTS

HIGHLIGHTS OF 2025

PROPERTY DIVISION

Tax consequences of division. The court of appeals reversed a chancellor's division of marital assets for failure to consider the tax consequences to the wife. She was awarded 47% of the $627,884 marital estate. All but $20,000 of her share consisted of a Vanguard retirement account. The chancellor should have considered that she would have to deplete the retirement account to meet expenses. The resulting 10% penalty and 30% in taxes made her award significantly less valuable. *Begnaud v. Begnaud,* 409 So. 3d 604 (Miss. Ct. App. 2025). § 6.08[1][6].

Burden of proof. The court of appeals held that a chancellor erred in classifying a husband's defined benefit retirement plan as all marital even though he presented no evidence to identify the value of the separate premarital portion. In *Arthur v. Arthur,* 691 So. 3d 997, 1003-04 (Miss. 1997), the supreme court reversed a chancellor's marital classification of a husband's retirement benefit even though the parties presented "no evidence at trial as to what portion of the [retirement account] was accumulated prior to the marriage." The court of appeals stated that the supreme court "apparently concluded that a spouse should not forfeit his separately earned retirement despite a failure to present evidence on the point at trial." *Matter of Dissolution of Tauzin*, 2025 WL 2317673 (Miss. Ct. App. Aug. 12, 2025). §§ 6.03[4][a], 6.04[2].

Insurance to secure property division payments. In a case of first impression, the court of appeals held that a husband's agreement to maintain a $1 million insurance policy to secure property division and child support payments was nonmodifiable. The chancellor reduced the required amount to $400,000 because four of his five children were emancipated. The court of appeals held that while a provision for securing child support is modifiable, a provision for securing property payments is not. Because the entire policy protected the wife's property division award it could not be modified. *J.T.S. v. M.L.S.*, 2025 WL 12206928 (Miss. Ct. App. Dec. 16, 2025). § 6.12[9].

ALIMONY

The court of appeals heard an unusual case in which a former wife's estate sued her deceased husband's estate for alimony in arrears at his death. The court affirmed the chancellor's finding that the estate had standing to sue for arrearages. She was not required to file a contempt action during her lifetime to preserve that right to the estate. However, the chancellor should have given the husband's estate credit for partial payments made by the husband and for a lump sum transfer of life insurance proceeds to her estate. The court also affirmed the chancellor's ruling that the seven-year statute of limitations had run on all but one year of the arrearages. The court rejected the payor's estate's argument that interest should not have been awarded because the property settlement agreement did not provide for interest. Alimony payments are vested as they become due. Each payment bears interest at the legal rate from its due date. *In re Estate of Brent*, 417 So. 3d 114 (Miss. 2025). §§ 14.02[3], 14.04[5], 14.06[1][a].

CUSTODY

Visitation rights of nonparents. A divided court of appeals reversed a chancellor's decision that a nonparent must prove parental unfitness, abandonment, or desertion as a prerequisite to visitation. The biological mother's same-sex partner, who acted in loco parentis to her partner's child for two years, sought visitation after they separated. The chancellor denied the petition, reading *Brownlee v. Powell*, 368 So. 3d 1268 (Miss. 2023) to hold that a nonparent must overcome the natural parent presumption to be awarded visitation. The court of appeals reversed, holding that under *Brownlee*, a nonparent may be granted visitation based on proof that they acted in loco parentis, that "special, unique, limited" circumstances exist, and that "justice requires and the child's well-being demands" an ongoing relationship with that person. The court remanded the case for the chancellor to determine whether the petitioner acted in loco parentis and whether the necessary special circumstances existed. *Edwards v. Johnson,* 2025 WL 2837431 (Miss. Ct. App. Oct. 7, 2025). § 11.06[2][c].

Modification of joint legal custody. The court of appeals reversed a court's modification of custody from sole legal custody in the mother to joint legal custody. The father sought modification based on the mother's alleged interference with his visitation. Evidence showed that she regularly interfered with his custodial time by calling repeatedly, interfering with his attendance at the boy's events, calling security when he visited the child in the hospital, failing to allow him phone visitation, and withholding visitation for seven months prior to the modification hearing. The chancellor held that an adverse material change in circumstances supported changing to joint legal custody, noting the hardship the mother's conduct caused to the father. The court of appeals reversed, holding that the chancellor did not sufficiently identify a material change that adversely affected the child. In addition, the chancellor did not address the *Albright* factors to determine whether the change was in the child's best interest. The court remanded for the chancellor to articulate how the m. *Hopkins v. Perry,* 420 So. 3d 354 (Miss. Ct. App. 2025). § 12.12[6].

Modification of durable legal custody. The court of appeals affirmed a youth court judge's order modifying custody of a child from durable legal custody with his maternal grandparents to his mother, based on her improved circumstances. After she was released from four years of incarceration, the mother completed supervised probation, secured employment and had a suitable home. She provided primary care for her son for two years after her release when she and her son lived with her parents. The chancellor found that there had been a material change in circumstances based on her release, employment, and housing and that it was in her son's best interest to live with her. *Interest of A.B.,* 419 So. 3d 976 (Miss. Ct. App. 2025). § 12.13[2].

Child Support

Deductions from gross income. In a case of first impression, the court of appeals held that a chancellor erred in reducing a husband's $931 a month child support by $350 to reflect the custodial mother's receipt of a $700 a month adoption subsidy for the child. Child support may be reduced when a child receives Social Security funds tied to a payor's disability. Support may not be reduced to reflect Social Security disability payments based on the child's disability. The adoption assistance, which provided funds intended to meet the child's needs, was more like a child's disability benefits than to a payor's. The court noted that other states to consider the issue have reached the same result. *Begnaud v. Begnaud,* 409 So. 3d 604 (Miss. Ct. App. 2025). § 6.05[3][b]. § 13.04[2][d].

Escalation clauses. The court of appeals held that a couple's agreed child support escalation clause was ambiguous and unenforceable. Their agreement set support at $3,500 a month for two children and stated that the father would provide a complete copy of his federal tax return each year and that "child support will be increased if appropriate based upon statutory guidelines." In 2024, the mother filed a contempt petition, alleging that he had failed to increase support as required by the clause. The chancellor increased the father's support to 20% of his adjusted gross income. The court of appeals reversed, holding that the words "if appropriate under the guidelines" made the provision unclear. The support guidelines instruct chancellors that, for payors whose annual adjusted income exceeds $100,000, a court may order support above or below the statutory percentages, based on the facts. In those cases, there is no presumptively correct percentage. As worded, the agreement did not clearly establish a percentage by which the support should be increased. *Cole v. Fish,* 2025 WL 2450130 (Miss. Ct. App., Aug. 26, 2025). §13.10[2].

Paternity

A woman was barred from inheriting from her presumed grandmother because she failed to file a petition for determination of heirs within one year of her father's death, even though the defendants failed to affirmatively plead the one-year statutes. Miss. Code Ann. δ 91-1-15a provides that a nonmarital child "shall inherit from and through the illegitimate's natural father and his kindred" if there has been an adjudication of paternity. "However, no such claim of inheritance shall be recognized unless the action . . . is filed within one (1) year after the death of the intestate . . . ." The statute also states that the one-year period "may not be tolled for any reason." The court of appeals held that the one-year period is a self-executing "nonclaim" statute, which may not be waived. *Matter of Estate of Lewis,* 422 So. 3d 484 (Miss. Ct. App. 2025). § 2.08.

The court of appeals affirmed a chancellor's finding that a 1974 adoption action established a nonmarital child's paternity for purposes of inheritance. The administrator argued that the petitioner was not an heir because there was no determination of paternity within one year of the father's death, as required by MISS. CODE ANN. δ 93-1-15(3)(c). The chancellor found, and the court of appeals agreed, that the adoption proceedings adjudicated paternity and legitimacy – the petition identified the deceased as the child's father; he was properly notified; the decree stated that he was properly before the court; and the judgment terminated his parental rights. The court of appeals also affirmed the chancellor's finding that equity barred the administrator from asserting the one-year statute of limitations. He delayed challenging the appellant's legitimacy for three years after the family listed him in the obituary as a child of the decedent. *Estate of Dorsey*, 2025 WL 3524732 (Miss. Ct. App. Dec. 9, 2025). § 2.08.

TERMINATION OF PARENTAL RIGHTS

The court of appeals reversed a county court judge's finding that DCPS had made reasonable efforts to reunify an incarcerated father with his two children. DCPS policy requires that the department develop a service plan tailored to a family's needs. No service agreement was introduced. It was not clear that the father received one. CPS policy requires staff to work with an incarcerated parent's social worker to identify programs and to make efforts to arrange visitation. The policy also allows them to extend the time for completing a service plan. The court held that CPS failed to follow its own policy regarding incarcerated parents. *Interest of J.S.*, 422 So. 3d 1055 (Miss. Ct. App. 2025). § 16.04[2].

CHILD'S NAME CHANGE

The supreme court affirmed a chancellor's dismissal without prejudice of a sixteen-year-old's petition for a name change. The minor, who was born female but identified as male, petitioned for the name change with the support of both parents. After an unrecorded bench conference, the chancellor entered an order dismissing the petition without prejudice and stating that the petitioner should mature before the name change would be considered. The petitioner appealed, arguing that chancellors have no discretion to deny an uncontested petition for name change. MISS. CODE ANN. δ 93-17-1(1) provides that chancellors have jurisdiction "upon the petition of any person to alter the names of such person." Language formerly requiring "good cause shown" for the name change was removed many years ago. The supreme court held that a chancellor may deny a minor's uncontested request for name change based on the child's best interest. The court acknowledged that, ordinarily, a person is entitled to a name change in the absence of a fraudulent purpose. However, in *Marshall v. Marshall,* 93 So. 2d 822 (Miss. 1957), the Mississippi Supreme Court distinguished name change cases involving minors, holding that a chancellor properly refused to change a boy's name to that of his stepfather over his father's objections because it was not in his best interest. *Matter of the Petition of S.M.-B.*, 407 So. 3d 1050 (Miss. 2025). § 12.16.

Procedure

Judgment for damages. The court of appeals rejected an ex-wife's argument that she could not be held in contempt for nonpayment of a judgment for property damages that was included in a divorce settlement. The husband filed an action against her in county court for damages she caused to his property after their separation. The action was consolidated with their divorce. The court of appeals affirmed the finding of contempt. Ordinarily, a civil judgment cannot be collected through a contempt proceeding. However, the award of damages was part of the court's judgment of divorce, which is enforceable by contempt. In addition, the chancellor gave her a year to satisfy her obligation, something that would not be available in an ordinary civil suit. *Martin v. Martin*, 2025 WL 1741578 (Miss. Ct. App. June 24, 2025). §§ 14.05[1][a].

HIGHLIGHTS OF 2024

PROPERTY DIVISION

Commingling separate and marital funds. The Mississippi Supreme Court has long held that commingling separate property with marital property converts it to marital, without regard to whether the separate property can be traced. In a significant shift, the court held that a husband's practice of depositing separate and marital income in a single bank account did not convert it to marital. The chancellor properly classified land that the husband purchased with funds from the commingled account as separate property, based on his testimony that he used separate funds for the purchase. The decision appears to align Mississippi with the majority of states, allowing tracing of commingled accounts. *Cassell v. Cassell,* 389 So. 3d 305 (Miss. 2024). § 6.05[3][b].

Burden of proof. The supreme court clarified who has the burden of proving that assets are separate, an issue that has produced conflicting decisions in the past. The court held that property acquired during marriage is presumed to be marital, placing the burden on a husband to prove that land purchased during marriage was bought with separate funds. However, the marital property presumption does not apply to premarital property, placing the burden on his wife to prove that his premarital business was converted to marital property. *Cassell v. Cassell,* 389 So. 3d 305 (Miss. 2024). § 6.03[4][b].

ALIMONY

Lump sum alimony. The supreme court overruled a 1988 case, *Cheatham v. Cheatham,* 537 So. 2d 435 (Miss. 1988) that created factors for awarding lump sum alimony prior to adoption of equitable distribution. In recent years, chancellors have made lump sum awards using either the *Cheatham* factors or the general alimony factors set out in *Armstrong v. Armstrong*, 618 So. 2d 1278 (Miss. 1993). The supreme court in 2024 overruled *Cheatham,* stating that in the future all alimony awards should be analyzed under *Armstrong. Cassell v. Cassell,* 389 So. 3d 305 (Miss. 2024). § 9.02[2][c].

De facto marriage. For the first time in almost twenty years, an appellate court addressed termination of alimony based on *de facto* marriage. Four years after a 1988 divorce, an ex-wife began living with a man who remained her partner until his death in 2020. Her former husband stopped paying alimony when he learned of the relationship. After her partner's death, she filed a petition for contempt for nonpayment of alimony. The court of appeals affirmed the chancellor's grant of summary judgment to the husband, holding that alimony automatically terminates upon entry into a *de facto* marriage. The court distinguished cohabitation, which may or may not justify modification, depending on whether the cohabitation reduces the need for alimony. *Collins v. Collins*, 397 So. 3d 856 (Miss. Ct. App. 2024). § 9.10[2].

Custody

Modification of joint physical custody. The court of appeals agreed with a joint custodial father that reducing his parenting time from fifteen nights a month to eight constituted a modification to sole custody in the mother, regardless of the label. The chancellor erred in changing their parenting time without first finding a material change in circumstances adverse to the child. *Briggs v. Weary*, 396 So. 3d 1246 (Miss. Ct. App. 2024). § 12.04[1][b].

Child Support

Private school tuition. The court of appeals reversed a chancellor's order that a father should pay $400 a month in tuition and one half of his children's enrollment or activity fees in addition to basic monthly support. Private school tuition should be calculated as part of the support award under the guidelines. If the award of basic support plus private school tuition and expenses exceeds the guidelines, the court must support the deviation based on statutory criteria. The fact that a father agreed that children should stay in private school is not in itself sufficient to support a deviation. There must also be a finding that the expense is reasonable under the current circumstances. *Chapman v. Chapman*, 395 So. 3d 447 (Miss. Ct. App. 2024). § 13.05[2][b].

Effective date of support modification. The legislature amended Miss. Code Ann. δ 43-19-34(4) to comply with federal law and DHS policy. The statute now provides, "Any order for the support of minor children, whether entered through the judicial system or through an expedited process, shall not be subject to a retroactive modification except from the date that notice of such petition to modify has been given, either directly or through the appropriate agent, to the obligee or to the obligor where the obligee is the petitioner." Previously, an upward modification of support could be made retroactive prior to the date of filing, back to the date of the event that justified modification. § 13.11[10].

Emancipation. The court of appeals rejected a father's argument that his youngest child should be emancipated because she lived with her older boyfriend over the father's objections. The chancellor held that the girl was not emancipated – she was nineteen, attending college, and not employed. The emancipation statute allows, but does not require, a chancellor to find emancipation when a child cohabits without a payor's consent. The chancellor had discretion to determine that the girl was not emancipated even if she was living with her boyfriend. *Stewart v. Stewart*, 382 So. 3d 531 (Miss. Ct. App. 2024). § 13.09[2].

Inheritance by posthumously conceived child

The Mississippi Legislature enacted a statute providing posthumously conceived children of a deceased a partial right of inheritance. Miss. Code Ann. δ 91-1-33 provides that a child who is born through assisted reproduction within forty-five months of a biological parent's death is entitled to a child's share of the parent's personal property, if certain conditions are met. The statute also provides that the legislature intended, by passing the statute, that children meeting the requirements for inheritance would be eligible for Social Security benefits as the decedent's child. § 15.05[1], [3].

Termination of parental rights

The Mississippi Legislature made significant changes to termination of parental rights statutes in 2024, including

- Providing a right to counsel for indigent parents in termination of parental rights proceedings;
- Providing a right to counsel in abuse and neglect proceedings for custodial parents and noncustodial parents with a significant custodial relationship with a child;
- Clarifying that children should be represented in all proceedings, from disposition hearings through termination of parental rights;
- Removing the grace period that allowed parents to revoke an agreement to termination until a court accepts their agreement;
- Providing that neglect does not include failure to provide based on financial inability;
- Changing the ground for termination based on a parent's mental illness; and
- Providing that all orders leading up to a termination of parental rights are interlocutory.

§§ 16.03, 16.04[3][a], [d], 16.06[4], 16.08.

Jurisdiction and procedure

Void judgments. The supreme court reversed a decision of the court of appeals that had found a twenty-year-old paternity and support order void for lack of service of process. The Rule 81(d) summons provided the father with twenty-nine, rather than thirty days, of notice prior to the hearing. He did not appear. The court entered a judgment of paternity and an order requiring that he pay child support. When his driver's license was suspended for nonpayment, he signed a stipulated agreement of support setting a schedule for payment. Twenty years later, he petitioned to set aside the judgment as void. The supreme court agreed that under Rule 60(b)(4), a party may seek to set aside a void judgment at any time – "no amount of time or delay may cure a void judgment." Because service was not proper and the defendant did not appear, the court lacked jurisdiction to enter the order. However, the supreme court held that the father waived the issue of jurisdiction by signing a stipulation that acknowledged the judgment without raising the issue. *Mississippi Dep't of Human Servs. v. Johnson*, 396 So. 3d 1151, 1156 (Miss. 2024). § 19.11[5][a].

Service of process for contempt matters in pending litigation. The court of appeals resolved an issue that has produced conflicting decisions over twenty years.

Some decisions held that a contempt petition must always be noticed through a Rule 81(d) summons. Others held that when a contempt petition is filed in pending litigation, notice is appropriate through Rule 5. The court of appeals overruled the latter cases, holding that a contempt action in pending litigation must be noticed through a Rule 81(d) summons. *Bolivar v. Bolivar,* 378 So. 3d 433 (Miss. Ct. App. 2024). § 19.04[1][c].

Collaborative law

The Mississippi Supreme Court on July 26, 2024, granted the petition of the Mississippi Bar to approve the Mississippi Collaborative Law Rules allowing parties and their lawyers to resolve family law matters through a collaborative law process. Parties in a collaborative law process agree to forego court intervention during the process except in certain emergencies, to hire neutral experts, and to make "timely, full, candid, and informal" disclosure without formal discovery. They also commit that if the process is terminated, a collaborative lawyer or his or her firm cannot continue as the lawyer in litigation except in defined emergencies. The rules contains detailed provisions discussing the information a lawyer must provide to a party considering collaborative law as an option. *In re Rules for Collaborative Law,* No. 89-R-99044-SCT (Miss. July 26, 2024). § 19.14.

Torts arising out of marriage

The court of appeals affirmed a chancellor's grant of summary judgment to a wife in her husband's tort action against her arising out of their separation and divorce. The court agreed that she was precluded from arguing that their prenuptial agreement waived all tort claims – she did not raise the issue as an affirmative defense. However, his claims failed, nonetheless. The court held that a spouse's decision to leave a marriage does not rise to the level of outrageous conduct required for intentional infliction of emotional distress. Nor is a spouse who expresses love during the marriage liable for fraudulent misrepresentation upon leaving the marriage. *Herbert v. Herbert,* 2023 WL 3069523 (Miss. Ct. App. April 25, 2023). §§ 1.06[1], 1.08[3][e].

Property division

The court of appeals rejected a wife's argument that assets accumulated by her husband while they lived together between marriages were marital assets. The couple lived separately for only two months after their first divorce, cohabited for fourteen years, and then remarried. The court held that assets accumulated by a former spouse during a period of post-divorce cohabitation are not subject to equitable distribution in the absence of joint financial contribution. The court distinguished cases in which both cohabitants worked and contributed to the accumulation of assets. Because the wife in this case did not contribute financially, there was no basis for treating the cohabitation as a business partnership. *Chambliss v. Chambliss,* 2023 WL 7317109 (Miss. Ct. App. Nov. 7, 2023). § 2.02[3][b][i].

Alimony

Reimbursement alimony. Reimbursement alimony appeared in a reported case for the first time since its adoption in 1999. A chancellor properly ordered that a divorcing wife of ten years repay her husband for $125,879 in separate property funds that he used to pay off her nursing school student loans. Four years after she graduated, she sought a divorce and custody of their two children. The court of appeals affirmed, citing *Guy v. Guy*, 736 So. 2d 1042 (Miss. 1999), in which the supreme court recognized "reimbursement alimony" – a lump sum award to one who supports a spouse through school, and whose spouse seeks divorce before the payor realizes the benefit of the investment. *Whittington v. Whittington,* 2023 WL 7318777 (Miss. Ct. App. Nov. 7, 2023). § 9.02[4].

Termination based on cohabitation. The court of appeals rejected an alimony payor's argument that a chancellor should have terminated his former wife's alimony based on her cohabitation. Her cohabitant shared some expenses, such as utilities, and provided some in-kind work that reduced her expenses. Upon proof of cohabitation, there is a presumption of mutual support, which the alimony recipient must rebut. If the recipient does not rebut the presumption, the chancellor should consider the *Armstrong* factors to determine whether alimony should be modified or terminated. The chancellor appropriately modified rather than terminating alimony upon finding that cohabitation reduced, but did not eliminate, her need for financial support. *Gillenwater v. Redmond*, 359 So. 3d 232 (Miss. Ct. App. 2023). § 9.10[1].

Custody and Visitation

Temporary orders. The court of appeals held that an out-of-court agreement giving a father temporary custody for thirteen months should not have been treated as a de facto permanent order. The chancellor erred in treating the agreement as permanent custody and requiring the mother to prove a material change in circumstances to modify the order. The court should have conducted a de novo, *Albright*/best interests test to determine custody. The court distinguished cases involving court-ordered temporary custody orders that remained in place for three to four years and which were treated as permanent orders. *Hendrix v. Whitt,* 373 So. 3d 778 (Miss. Ct. App. 2023). § 12.01[7][b].

Non-parent visitation. The appellate courts in 2023 issued two significant decisions dealing with grandparent visitation and one dealing with other non-parents. The court of appeals affirmed a chancellor's finding that a girl's parents reasonably denied visitation with her paternal grandfather – he refused to abide by their request that he treat his daughter-in-law's children equally with his biological grandchild. They testified that his preferential treatment for the younger child was causing problems within their family. *Hutson v. Hutson,* 2023 WL 6418777 (Miss. Ct. App. Oct 3, 2023). §§ 19.09[3][b], [6][d]. In another grandparent visitation case, the court of appeals held that a grandmother was entitled to seek visitation against her son, who was awarded sole custody when the child's mother died, under Miss. Code Ann. § 93-16-3(1). This section (Type 1 visitation) provides that when one parent of a child is awarded custody, one parent's rights are terminated, or one parent dies, "*either parent of the child's parents*" may seek visitation. The statute previously provided that "either parent of the child's parent *who was not awarded custody* or whose parental rights have been terminated or who has died may petition" for visitation. Under the amended statute, the parents of a custodial parent may also sue for visitation, rather than being required to proceed under Type 2 visitation, which has more stringent requirements. *Poole v. Poole,* 2023 WL 5922110 (Miss. Ct. App. Sept. 12, 2023). §§ 12.09[3][a], [5].

And in a significant decision expanding visitation rights, the supreme court held that nonparent visitation is not limited to grandparents and legal fathers who believed themselves to be a child's biological parent. The court reversed a chancellor's dismissal of a same-sex cohabitant's request for visitation with her former partner's biological children. The supreme court held that the plaintiff could be awarded visitation, if she could prove she that she came within certain narrow, unique circumstances that rebut the natural parent presumption. The court cited

Griffith v. Pell, 881 So. 3d 184 (Miss. 2004) as setting out those circumstances: (1) a petitioner stood *in loco parentis* to a child; (2) they supported, cared for, and treated the child as their own; (3) they could have been required to pay child support; and (4) the biological father of the child was not in the picture. *Brownlee v. Powell,* 368 So. 3d 1268 (Miss. 2023). §§ 11.06[2][a], [b].

CHILD SUPPORT

Incarcerated payors. The Legislature enacted MISS. CODE ANN. § 43-19-105 addressing child support payments by incarcerated payors. The new statute provides, "The court may not consider incarceration as intentional or voluntary unemployment or underemployment when establishing or modifying a child-support order." § 13.04[4][b][vi].

Support for college. The court of appeals reversed and remanded an order that a father of three pay one half of the expenses of his children "attending and completing" college. The chancellor should have made findings of fact regarding the children's aptitude for college, the father's ability to pay, and the children's relationship with him. The father alleged that he lacked the ability to pay and that his sons refused to have a relationship with him. The court also held that the chancellor lacked authority to extend the father's duty for college support past majority unless he agreed. *Capocaccia v. Capocaccia,* 372 So. 3d 1106 (Miss. Ct. App. 2023). §§ 13.05, 13.07[3][c], [i].

Agreements to terminate support prior to majority. The court of appeals affirmed a chancellor's order finding a father in contempt for nonpayment of child support and orthodontic expenses in the amount of $53,825. The couple's property settlement agreement, incorporated into the judgment of divorce, ended support when the youngest child turned eighteen. The father argued that the chancellor erred in finding that he was obligated to pay support until the youngest was twenty-one. The court of appeals affirmed, holding that parents may not contract away the duty to support a child until majority. The fact that an agreement was judicially approved is given great weight; however, an agreement ending support prior to twenty-one is against public policy and unenforceable. *White v. White*, 357 So. 3d 1165 (Miss. Ct. App. 2023). § 13.09[3].

CONTEMPT

The supreme court affirmed a chancellor's order incarcerating a father for five years based on contempt stemming from his failure to pay child support and failure to comply with the court's order to complete psychological testing. The majority held that he defied the chancellor's order to complete a mental health examination and failed to prove inability to pay child support. The majority noted that a defendant may be incarcerated indefinitely until he complies with a court's order and emphasized that the father held the key to his release. Four justices dissented, urging that contempt should be enforced using the least possible power to accomplish the desired result and that the father substantially complied with the order by submitting to an interview which led to a nine-page report with recommendations. *McPhail v. McPhail,* 357 So. 3d 602 (Miss. 2023). § 14.06[6][a].

Abuse and Neglect Proceedings

The legislature enacted substantial changes to youth court abuse and neglect and permanency proceedings. Miss. Code Ann. § 43-21-201 was amended to provide that a child in an abuse and neglect proceeding is a party to the proceedings and is entitled to an attorney at all stages. Courts are to appoint an attorney for an unrepresented child. The guardian ad litem may act in a dual role as guardian and as the child's attorney; however, if a conflict arises, the guardian must report the conflict to the youth court. The guardian should continue to serve in that role and the court should appoint a new attorney to represent the child. The amendments also provide that DCPS is a party to all proceedings and must be served with a summons, Miss. Code Ann. § 43-21-501. §§ 16.01A, 16.02[2].

Termination of Parental Rights

Youth court jurisdiction. The Mississippi Legislature amended Miss. Code Ann. § 93–15–105(1) to clarify that a youth court's exclusive jurisdiction over termination of parental rights in cases pending before it extends to both voluntary and involuntary termination actions. This amendment overrides the supreme court's 2020 decision, *In re Adoption of C.C.B. and S.R.B.*, 306 So. 3d 674, 679 (Miss. 2020) (holding that the exclusive jurisdiction of youth courts does not apply to adoptions based on consent, which do not involve a petition to terminate parental rights). §§ 16.01[1]; 17.01[1]. However, the exclusive jurisdiction applies only to county courts sitting as a youth court. It does not apply to youth court proceedings presided over by a youth court referee. *In re Adoption of Jane,* 360 So. 3d 286 (Miss. Ct. App. 2023) (also holding that a grandmother/guardian did not have standing to challenge termination of the parents' rights.) §§ 16.01[1], 17.01[1].

Right to counsel. The court of appeals rejected an argument that parents are entitled to effective assistance of counsel in termination proceedings. Mississippi appellate courts have held in other contexts that the Sixth Amendment does not apply in civil proceedings. Furthermore, even if the right applied, the mother failed to demonstrate prejudice because of her attorney's performance. Two judges dissented, arguing that cases discussing the right to counsel in other civil contexts were not applicable and that new procedures established by the 2016 Termination of Parental Rights Law should impose a right to effective counsel. *Denham v. Lafayette County Dep't of Child Protection Services,* 356 So. 3d 173, 183-84 (Miss. Ct. App. 2023). § 16.06[4].

Jurisdiction and Procedure

The court of appeals held that a 2002 judgment of paternity and child support was void for lack of proper service of process under Rule 81(d), setting it aside two decades later and ordering DHS to return any support collected under the order.

The putative father was served on January 21, 2002, with a Rule 81(d) summons setting a hearing for February 19, 2002, twenty-nine days later. He did not appear. The court entered a judgment of paternity and an order requiring that he pay $285 a month in child support. The court of appeals held that a Rule 81(d) summons must be served thirty days prior to a paternity hearing. As a result, the judgment was void for lack of personal jurisdiction and could be set aside at any time. The father did not waive the issue by signing two stipulations regarding his arrearages. Waiver occurs when a party appears and defends a case on the merits without preserving the issue of jurisdiction. Agreements made after the judgment did not amount to defenses on the merits of the case. *Mississippi Dep't of Human Services v. Johnson*, 2023 WL 8592891 (Miss. Ct. App. Dec. 12, 2023). § 19.04[3].

Divorce grounds

The court of appeals emphasized the importance of using a subjective test to determine the impact of spousal domestic abuse on a plaintiff rather than an objective test. A chancellor erred in stating that it was reasonable to assume a wife did not fear her husband because she went voluntarily to his house. She went there, and was sexually assaulted, after he threatened her with the release of nude photographs. The impact of spousal abuse should be tested by its effect on the individual victim, not based on an objective reasonable person standard. The court also emphasized that a single incident of violence can be sufficient to satisfy the test for spousal domestic violence. *Baughman v. Baughman,* 350 So. 3d 271 (Miss. Ct. App. 2022). § 4.03[8][b].

Property division

Findings of fact. In several cases, the court of appeals reversed a chancellor's division of assets or award of alimony for failure to classify or value assets or to address specific *Ferguson* factors. For example, the court held that a chancellor erred in failing to classify a Mazda, a fifteen-year-old tractor, personal clothing, a four-wheeler, tools and equipment, bank accounts, and the wife's mother's wedding ring as separate or marital. *Brown v. Brown,* 350 So. 3d 1169 (Miss. Ct. App. Nov. 15, 2022). §§ 6.02[1], 6.07[2]. In another case, the court held that a chancellor erred in determining property division and alimony without considering the wife's separate property assets, including a diamond ring valued at $14,000, a golf cart, a piano, and jet skis and failing to consider debt assigned to the husband. *Warner v. Warner,* 341 So. 3d 152 (Miss. Ct. App. 2022). § 7.07.

Foreign judgments. A husband's attempt to enforce a Texas divorce and property division judgment in Mississippi failed. He obtained a divorce in Texas after a Mississippi court dismissed his and his wife's divorce petitions with prejudice. The supreme court held that the Mississippi court lacked jurisdiction to divide assets because the divorce action was dismissed. Although the Texas judgment might have provided an independent basis for recovery, he failed to register the foreign judgment as required by statute. *Ellis v. Ellis,* 334 So. 3d 1148 (Miss. 2022). § 18.05[2].

Alimony

Rehabilitative alimony. The court of appeals clarified that rehabilitative alimony need not always be used to support a spouse returning to school or reentering the workplace. It may be used to assist a lower income employed spouse to transition financially. The court rejected a husband's argument that rehabilitative alimony was inappropriate because his wife was already employed. *Denham v. Denham,* No. 2020-CA-00675-COA, 2022 WL 290890 (Miss. Ct. App. Feb. 1, 2022), *reversed in part on other grounds*, 351 So. 3d 954 (Miss. 2022). § 9.02[3][a].

Social Security benefits. The court of appeals rejected a husband's argument that an alimony award to his sixty-two-year-old wife should have been reduced because she could have drawn Social Security at sixty-two. The court stated, "We know of no precedent under which a party to a divorce can be required to apply for Social Security benefits." In keeping with *Alford v. Alford*, 298 So. 3d 983 (Miss. 2020), the husband could petition for modification when she did begin receiving benefits. *Phang v. Phang,* 350 So. 3d 1154, 1163-64 (Miss. Ct. App. 2022). §§ 9.02[1][g], 9.07[4][c], 9.08[2][a].

Custody and Visitation

Albright factors. In an unusual case, a father was awarded custody of his sons even though none of the *Albright* factors favored him. The court found that most factors were neutral. The mother was favored on continuity of care and moral fitness. However, the guardian ad litem and expert witness recommended custody to the father based on the mother's ongoing, unsubstantiated claims of abuse against the father and her animosity to him. Two judges dissented, arguing that a custody award was error when no factors favored the father. *Lambes v. Lambes,* 345 So. 3d 592 (Miss. Ct. App. 2022). § 12.03.

Testimony of children. The supreme court provided direction for determining whether children should be allowed to testify in divorce or custody proceedings. The court emphasized that calling children to testify is "highly disfavored." However, because of the due process right to call witnesses, a *per se* rule excluding children as witnesses is unconstitutional. When presented with a request for children to testify, a chancellor must first determine through an *in camera* interview whether the child is competent to testify and whether the child's best interest will be served by allowing them to testify. The chancellor must make a record of the interview and if testimony is not allowed, state the reasons for denying the request. *Denham v. Denham,* 351 So. 3d 964 (Miss. 2022). § 19.08[1].

"Primary" physical custody. The court of appeals disagreed with a chancellor's interpretation of a couple's custody agreement, finding that it provided for joint physical custody rather than sole physical custody in the mother. Their agreement provided that they would share joint legal custody "with primary physical custody to the mother . . . with custody for the father . . . as set out herein." The father had "custody with the minor children every other week" from Friday to Friday. The agreement used the word visitation to describe both parents' holiday and special occasion time. The agreement also provided that because the parents had closely equal time, neither would pay child support. The order stated that the parents "have equal opportunity in decisions affecting the children." *Lamy v. Lamy,* 2022 WL 17259752 (Miss. Ct. App. Nov. 29, 2022). § 12.04[1][c], [4], *cert. granted*, 368 So. 3d 814 (Miss. Aug. 23, 2023).

Parental decision-making. The supreme court held that a chancellor, as the guardian of children of divorce, may override a decision-maker parent's choice of schools without finding a material change in circumstances. A chancellor did not err in finding that it was in the children's best interest to attend school in the town where they lived with their mother rather than thirty miles away where the father lived, even though their divorce agreement provided that the father was the decision-maker in the event of disagreement. *Bryant v. Bryant,* 348 So. 3d 309 (Miss. 2022). §§ 12.04[1][a], 12.12[6].

CHILD SUPPORT

Low-income payors. The Mississippi Legislature amended MISS. CODE ANN. § 43-19-101, the child support guidelines, to address child support orders involving low-income payors. The amendments require that a court take into consideration the basic subsistence needs of payors with limited resources. The amendment also provides that a court may not automatically impute income to an unemployed or under-employed payor at a standard amount. Imputed income should be based on facts applicable to the payor, including their work history, "assets, residence, job skills, educational attainment, literacy, age, health, criminal record and other employment barriers, and record of seeking work," as well as the local job market and earnings in the local community. Laws 2022, Chp. 365 (H.B. 1067), § 1, eff. July 1, 2022. § 13.04[4].

Modification. A father was not entitled to a reduction in child support when his job was terminated for violation of company policy. The chancellor found that the father's job loss was in bad faith because he voluntarily violated company policy. The court of appeals affirmed. To obtain a reduction in support, a payor must prove a material, unforeseeable change and that the change was not caused by bad faith. The court stated that bad faith is a voluntary act that reduces income – it does not require an intent to harm the child's interests. *Tolliver v. Tolliver,* 334 So. 3d 1228 (Miss. Ct. App. 2022). § 13.04[4][b][ii].

Out-of-court agreements. A chancellor properly refused to enforce parents' out-of-court agreement to reduce the father's child support. The noncustodial father sought to reduce his monthly $800 support obligation based on an agreement with the mother to reduce his support to $550 a month and that he would pay the daughter's cheerleading and orthodontic expenses. The court of appeals held that the chancellor properly refused to recognize the agreement and ordered him to pay $8,750 in arrearages. Child support is for the benefit of the child, not the parents – an out-of-court agreement between parents is not enforceable. The court also denied his request for a credit against arrearages for the cheerleading payments he made, holding that they were a voluntary undertaking. *Kelley v. Zitzelberger,* 342 So. 3d 499 (Miss. Ct. App. 2022). § 13.11[5][b].

Retroactivity. The court of appeals affirmed a chancellor's increase of child support retroactive to a date eighteen months prior to the mother's petition for modification. When the parents changed from joint custody to custody in the mother, they agreed that the unemployed father would pay no support for ninety days. Eighteen months later she petitioned for support. The chancellor ordered him to pay $451 a month retroactive to the date on which the ninety-day suspension ended. The father appealed, arguing that the court lacked authority to increase support prior to the date of filing. The court of appeals disagreed. A chancellor has discretion to make an order retroactive prior to the filing date based on Miss. Code Ann. § 43-19-34 (allowing upward modification retroactive "to the date of the event justifying the upward modification"). *Ponder v. Ponder*, 349 So. 3d 212 (Miss. Ct. App. 2022). § 13.11[10].

Termination of Parental Rights

The court of appeals affirmed a chancellor's termination of parents' rights based on the mother's mental disability and the father's unwillingness or inability to provide adequate care for their newborn. The court of appeals affirmed the youth court's holding that reunification was not proper because of the parents' mental limitations. Reunification efforts are not required if the parent has subjected the child to "aggravated circumstances, *including, but not limited to*, abandonment, torture, chronic abuse and sexual abuse." Miss. Code Ann. § 43-21-603(7)(c)(i) (emphasis added). The court of appeals held that a parent's severe intellectual disability can be an aggravating circumstance under the "including but not limited to" phrase. However, the court noted that ordinarily a parent's mental limitations should not be considered as an aggravating circumstance, distinguishing the severe limitations present in this case. *C.P. v. Lowndes County Dep't of Child Protective Services*, 349 So. 3d 1209 (Miss. Ct. App. 2022). §§ 16.04[2], [3][a].

HIGHLIGHTS OF 2020-2021

Divorce grounds

The court of appeals overruled a 1940 Mississippi case which held that a husband has the right to determine family residence and that a wife's refusal to follow him is desertion. A chancellor properly rejected a husband's argument that his wife deserted him by failing to follow him when he moved for job-related reasons. The court relied on *Orr v. Orr*, 440 U.S. 268 (1979) which stated that old notions of a man's responsibility to provide a home do not justify family law doctrines that discriminate based on gender. *Stephenson v. Stephenson*, 2021 WL 5459386 (Miss. Ct. App. Nov. 23, 2021); § 4.03[5].

Property division

Retirement benefits. Several cases clarified issues related to retirement benefits. The court of appeals for the first time characterized a state employee's direct payment of PERS benefits to a former spouse as property division rather than as a form of alimony. A husband's court-ordered obligation to pay his ex-wife a share of his monthly retirement benefit was a form of deferred distribution of the marital share of his retirement. *Sullivan v. Sullivan,* 302 So. 3d 1280 (Miss. Ct. App. 2020); § 7.04[1][a]. The court of appeals also addressed valuation of PERS retirement benefits, holding that a chancellor properly valued a wife's pension by its cash-out value rather than its value as a stream of payments, when she had in fact cashed it out. *Gaskin v. Gaskin,* 304 So. 3d 641, 646-47 (Miss. Ct. App. 2020); § 7.04[3]. And the supreme court affirmed a court's division of the marital portion of military benefits using a formula dividing the number of months the husband served during the marriage by the total number of months he served in the military. *Gerty v. Gerty,* 296 So. 3d 704, 707-09 (Miss. 2020); § 7.07.

Family use doctrine. The court of appeals clarified that the test for marital property is not based on the definition of homestead property. The court rejected a wife's argument that the marital home should have included her husband's premarital forty acres because they filed homestead exemption on the forty acres. *Dean v. Dean*, 304 So. 3d 156, 168-69 (Miss. Ct. App. 2020); § 6.05[1][b].

Alimony

The court of appeals affirmed an award of $2,500 a month in permanent alimony to a thirty-eight-year-old wife of ten years with no income and serious mental health issues, even though she dissipated assets and received substantial property in the divorce. The court acknowledged that permanent alimony is not usually awarded in short marriages but held that her need for treatment and her inability to work justified the award. *In re Conservatorship of Geno,* No. 2018-CA-01767-COA, 2021 WL 1184583 (Miss. Ct. App. March 30, 2021); § 9.04[5][a].

Agreements

The supreme court held that a husband's divorce settlement agreement was signed under duress and unenforceable, making it one of a few Mississippi cases in which agreements have been set aside after a judgment of divorce. The unemployed and bankrupt husband, incarcerated for contempt for nonpayment of temporary expenses, agreed to pay substantial amounts in property division, alimony, attorneys' fees and expert's fees. The court of appeals held that he signed the agreement under duress, facing return to jail for months if he did not reach an agreement. *Lindsay v. Lindsay*, 303 So. 3d 770, 785-87 (Miss. Ct. App. 2020); § 23.10[2].

Parenthood

The court of appeals affirmed a chancellor's order finding that a husband was the legal father of his wife's child conceived during their separation and reconciliation attempts. The husband challenged the child's paternity in divorce but did not submit to the court-ordered genetic testing or appear at trial. A chancellor may resolve the issue of paternity against a party who refuses to submit to genetic testing. *Greer v. Greer*, 312 So. 3d 414, 416 (Miss. Ct. App. 2021); § 11.02[4].

Custody and visitation

Grandparent visitation. The appellate courts issued two significant decisions dealing with grandparent visitation rights. The Mississippi Supreme Court held that a statutory provision allowing parents to recover attorneys' fees from grandparents in visitation actions applies only to actions brought by the petitioner's own parents ("Type 2" visitation). A chancellor erred in awarding attorneys' fees to a mother in litigation with the child's paternal grandparents. *Battise v. Aucoin,* 311 So. 3d 588, 590-92 (Miss. 2021); § 12.09[6][d]. And the court of appeals held that grandparents seeking visitation must prove strict compliance with the statutory requirements. The court reversed a chancellor's ruling that a grandmother's ten months of visitation with a child substantially met the statutory requirement of a year of visitation. The court also held that the test for visitation must be met for each grandchild with whom visitation is sought. *Greer v. Akers,* No. 2019-CA-00745-COA, 2021 WL 248051, at *4 (Miss. Ct. App. Jan. 26, 2021); § 12.09[3][b].

Modification of joint legal custody. The court of appeals affirmed a chancellor's modification from joint legal custody to sole custody – the parents' three years of litigation showed their inability to work cooperatively to make decisions regarding the children's education and activities. In the same case, the court approved the chancellor's modification of the father's agreement to pay for extracurricular activities on which both parents agreed, providing instead that his obligation was capped at a set amount without requiring approval of both parents. *Smith v. Smith*, 318 So. 3d 484, 493 (Miss. Ct. App. 2021); § 12.12[6].

Guardians ad litem. In a case of first impression, the supreme court held that courts need not appoint mandatory guardians ad litem in actions that involve only visitation. The statute requires appointment when allegations of abuse and neglect arise in matters involving *custody* – here, the mother attempted to limit the father's visitation in her petition for a domestic abuse protection order. Custody was not at issue. *Barton v. Barton,* 306 So. 3d 682, 685-86 (Miss. 2020); § 12.10[1].

Child support

High income payors. The court of appeals addressed the standard for awarding child support in high-income cases, affirming an award of $7,500 a month in child support from a payor with $71,000 a month in net income, though the children's expenses were listed as $2,194 a month on the mother's 8.05 Financial Statement. The court stated that child support is not capped at the amount of expenses stated in an 8.05 financial statement – a chancellor may consider the family standard of living in determining what is a reasonable amount of child support. *Descher v. Descher,* 304 So. 3d 620 (Miss. Ct. App. 2020); § 13.06[1].

Deviation based on shared parenting. The court of appeals held that a chancellor erred in failing to deviate downward from the statutory guidelines where the noncustodial father had more extensive visitation than usual (forty-two percent of the time). The court remanded the case with instructions to reduce the support order below the guidelines. *Doe v. Doe,* No. 2020-CA-00853-COA, 2021 WL 5193082 (Miss. Ct. App. Nov. 9, 2021); § 13.05[3].

Medical costs. The court of appeals reversed and remanded a chancellor's child support order because it did not address health insurance and payment of uncovered medical expenses as required by the child support statutes. *Savell v. Manning,* 325 So. 3d 1208 (Miss. Ct. App. 2021); § 13.07[1].

Modification based on involuntary income loss. The court of appeals held that a chancellor should have granted a father's petition to reduce child support based on income loss. The court disagreed with the chancellor's position that the father's loss of income from in-patient treatment for addiction and his subsequent loss of revenue from board-imposed limits on practice was voluntary. *Braswell v. Braswell,* No. 2020-CA-01090-COA, 2021 WL5193751 (Miss. Ct. App. Nov. 9, 2021); § 13.04[4][b][3].

Obligations of adoptive parents. The court of appeals addressed the child support obligations of adoptive stepparents, reversing a chancellor's order awarding custody of a girl to her biological mother but failing to order support from her stepfather who adopted her. An adoptive parent has the same duties to a child as a biological parent. *Hackler v. Hackler,* 296 So. 3d 773 (Miss. Ct. App. 2020); § 13.03[2].

Support for adult disabled children. The court of appeals held that a mother's suit for support for her adult disabled son was properly denied – the son, who was living with his mother, was not a party to the litigation or under a guardianship or conservatorship. The court distinguished *Ravenstein v. Ravenstein*, 167 So. 3d 210 (Miss. 2014), a case involving support for an adult disabled son who was under his mother's guardianship. *Burrell v. Burrell,* 289 So. 3d 749 (Miss. Ct. App. 2020); § 13.02[4].

Adoption

Finality of consent to adoption. The supreme court confirmed that the 2016 Termination of Parental Rights Law changed the prior rule that a parent's written consent to adoption was final absent proof of coercion or duress. Under the new statute, a consent may be withdrawn until it is accepted by court order. A chancellor properly allowed a mother to withdraw her consent to adoption prior to acceptance by the court. *Adoption of A.M.*, 323 So. 3d 509, 513-17 (Miss. 2021); § 16.03[2].

Finality of judgment of adoption. In a case with implications for the finality of adoptions, the supreme court held that a chancery court may set aside a judgment of adoption for failure to name a known biological father, as fraud on the court, after the six-month statute of limitations for challenging the adoption. The court also held that failure to join a child's known parent is a jurisdictional defect that can be raised after the six-month period has run. *Stacks v. Smith*, 291 So. 3d 809, 816-18 (Miss. 2020); § 17.08[4].

I
THE MARRIAGE RELATIONSHIP

§ 1.01 The Evolution of marriage

[3] Marriage equality for same-sex couples

Page 5. Insert in text after sentence ending in footnote 35:

In 2022, Congress repealed the Defense of Marriage Act and enacted the Respect for Marriage Act. The new act provides that no person acting under color of state law may deny full faith and credit to a marriage recognized in another state on the basis of the sex of the spouses. Nor may a person acting under color of state law refuse to enforce a right available on the basis of marriage because that state would not recognize the marriage. The act provides for enforcement by the Attorney General in federal court as well as providing a private right of action for persons injured by nonrecognition. The act further provides that to determine marital rights under federal law a marriage will be recognized if it was valid in the state in which it was entered.[35.1]

[35.1] Respect for Marriage Act, Pub. L. No. 117-228, 136 Stat. 2305 (2022).

§ 1.03 Property rights between spouses

[3] Joint ownership

[d] Joint tenancy with rights of survivorship

Page 19. Add to footnote 185:

Cf. Hatton v. Hatton, 323 So. 3d 1149, 1152 (Miss. Ct. App. 2021) (couple's premarital agreement provided that property held in joint title with right of survivorship would continue to be held jointly at divorce and go to the survivor).

[g] Effect of divorce on common ownership

Page 20. Insert in text after sentence ending in footnote 200:

A divorce agreement may sever a joint tenancy even though the spouses do not transfer their interests through a deed. The court of appeals held that a couple's joint tenancy with right of survivorship in two mineral interests was severed by their agreement to "divide equally all mineral rights" in one field and that the husband "shall have exclusive rights to" the other field. When the husband died, his will leaving his mineral interests to his son was effective even though the title to the property was never changed out of joint title with his former wife; their intent to divide the property was clear.[200.1]

[200.1] *In re* Estate of Callender, 309 So. 3d 131, 137-38 (Miss. Ct. App. 2020).

§ 1.04 Rights of inheritance between spouses

[4] Waiver through premarital agreement

Page 22. Insert in text after sentence ending in footnote 220:

And a husband was precluded from taking from his wife's estate by a premarital agreement providing that each spouse could transfer property as though there were no marriage. [220.1]

[220.1] Estate of Bell v. Estate of Bell, 372 So. 3d 1008, 1017-18 (Miss. Ct. App. 2023) (agreement waived automatic revocation under Miss. Code Ann. § 91-5-27 as well as election to renounce under Miss. Code Ann. § 91-5-25, even though agreement specifically mentioned only the latter statute).

§ 1.06 Contracts and Conveyances between spouses

[1] Contracts for labor or services

Page 25. Insert in text after sentence ending in footnote 244:

And a former wife's alleged contract to decorate her husband's condominium was unenforceable under the statute.[244.1]

[244.1] Herbert v. Herbert, 374 So. 3d 562, 578 (Miss. Ct. App. 2023).

§ 1.08 Tort actions

[1] Tort actions between spouses

[c] Jurisdiction over tort actions

Page 28. Add to footnote 270:

See also Woodard v. Miller, 326 So. 3d 439, 442 (Miss. 2021) (tort action against minister husband and Methodist church brought in circuit court).

[3] Heart balm actions

[a] Alienation of affection

Page 31. Add to footnote 291:

Cf. Dew v. Harris, 343 So. 3d 387, 391 (Miss. Ct. App. 2022) (reversing a circuit court's grant of summary judgment to the defendant; the parties presented conflicting testimony as to whether marriage was over prior to affair).

[i] Statute of limitations

Page 31. Add to footnote 298:

See also Davis v. Davis, 360 So. 3d 196, 201-202 (Miss. 2023) (former husband's suit for alienation of affection decades after their divorce barred by statute of limitations).

Page 34. Insert in text after section [d]:

[e] Other actions arising out of the marriage [NEW]

In 2023, the supreme court upheld a circuit court's dismissal of a husband's tort claims arising out of his wife's decision to leave their marriage. His claim for intentional infliction of emotional distress was properly dismissed. The action requires conduct that "evokes outrage or revulsion in society" – conduct that is "beyond all possible bounds of decency." An adult's choice to leave a relationship is not actionable under this standard. Nor did he provide authority that she should be liable for fraudulent misrepresentation for saying "I love you." The court also held that he failed to sufficiently plead his claim that she defamed or slandered him in talking to friends and family about his conduct – he did not specify the content of the remarks, when or to whom the statements were made, or how he suffered concrete harm.[317.1]

[317.1] Herbert v. Herbert, 374 So. 3d 562, 577-78 (Miss. Ct. App. 2023).

§ 1.12 Choice of residence

Page 36. Replace text of paragraph after footnote 342 with the following:

In 1979, the United States Supreme Court in *Orr v. Orr* invalidated gender-based distinctions in family law, holding that old notions of a man's duty to provide a home do not justify discriminatory family law doctrines.[343] In 2021, the court of appeals relied on *Orr* to overrule the 1940 Mississippi case stating that a husband has the right to determine the family residence. The couple in question separated after a few months of marriage when the husband was transferred to a work site an hour's drive from their home. He chose to move to be close to his job. His wife did not want to relocate. Four years later, the husband filed for divorce arguing that his wife's failure to follow him was desertion. The court held that *Outz* was no longer good law and that a wife's refusal to follow her husband is not desertion.[344]

---

[343] Orr v. Orr, 440 U.S. 268, 282-83 (1979).

[344] Stephenson v. Stephenson, 332 So. 3d 360, 363 (Miss. Ct. App. 2021) (also holding that even if she had a duty to follow, his unilateral decision to move was not in good faith).

§ 1.13 Separate Maintenance

[2] Basis for award

Page 38. Add to footnote 361:

Cf. Hasley v. Hasley, 385 So. 3d 1258, 1264-65 (Miss. Ct. App. 2024) (a court erred in converting a temporary separate maintenance order to a permanent order based on the six-year passage of time; separate maintenance must be based on proof that the recipient was not materially at fault).

Page 39. Add to footnote 363:

See also Baughman v. Baughman, 350 So. 3d 271, 284 (Miss. Ct. App. 2022) (separate maintenance denied to husband whose abusive conduct caused the parties' separation; rejecting his argument that wife's affair caused separation).

[3] Amount of award

[d] Attorneys' fees and temporary support

Page 42. Add to footnote 391:

See also Hasley v. Hasley, 385 So. 3d 1258 (Miss. Ct. App. 2024) (a court erred in converting a temporary separate maintenance order to a permanent order based on the six-year passage of time; separate maintenance must be based on proof that the recipient was not materially at fault).

[5] Child custody and support

Page 43. Add to footnote 409:

See Colbert v. Colbert, 403 So. 3d 729, 736 (Miss. Ct. App. 2025) (reversing chancellor's order of $7,000 combined separate maintenance and child support for findings of fact to support separate award of child support).

[8] Res judicata effect at divorce

Page 45. Insert in text following sentence ending in footnote 424:

Similarly, a husband was barred from introducing evidence of habitual cruelty that predated his wife's award of separate maintenance. However, he was not barred from proving adultery of which he was unaware at the time of the separate maintenance action. Nor was he barred from presenting evidence of habitual cruelty that occurred after the judgment and aggregating that conduct with prior conduct to prove his ground.[424.1]

[424.1] Turner v. Turner, 385 So. 3d 827, 834 (Miss. Ct. App. 2024).

II
RIGHTS BETWEEN UNMARRIED PARTNERS

§ 2.02 Financial rights between cohabitants

[1] Rights between never-married cohabitants

Page 51. Insert in text after sentence ending in footnote 35:

A 2023 case suggests that cohabitants who contribute financially to the accumulation of assets during cohabitation may be entitled to a division of assets in the other's name. The court rejected a homemaker's argument that she was entitled to division of retirement funds acquired by her husband in the fourteen years that they cohabited between their first and second marriages. The court distinguished earlier cases in which a non-owning partner worked and contributed financially, allowing the court to treat the relationship as a business partnership. In this case, the woman did not contribute financially during their cohabitation. The decision does not seem to limit its scope to cohabitants who were formerly married.[35.1]

[35.1] Chambliss v. Chambliss, 385 So. 3d 1246, 1254-55 (Miss. Ct. App. 2023); *see also* McGee v. McGee, 399 So. 3d 163, 168 (Miss. 2024) (wife was not entitled to division of retirement account accumulated during cohabitation between first and second marriage; there was no evidence that they accumulated property together during the period of dating and cohabitation). See discussion in § 2.02[3][b][i] of the supplement, *infra*.

Page 52. Insert in text after section [c]:

[d] Return of property [NEW]

Cohabitants have used various legal actions to obtain a return of property held by a cohabitant. A circuit court judge properly entered a replevin order requiring a man's former girlfriend to return items (guns, equipment, clothing) that he had left in her trailer and that she failed to return to him despite her agreement to do so. The trial court found that the items in question belonged to the plaintiff, rejecting his former partner's argument that they were inter vivos gifts to her.[43.1] And in a case in which a woman obtained a deed naming her as a joint owner of her boyfriend's house, the chancellor reformed the deed based on unilateral mistake. The couple separated shortly after the boyfriend purchased the house. Ten years later, he discovered that at the signing that she handled on his behalf, his girlfriend had the deed issued in their joint names. The chancellor found that the plaintiff met the proof required to reform a deed by proving a unilateral mistake in combination with inequitable conduct on the part of his former girlfriend.[43.2]

[43.1] Massey v. Neely, 309 So. 3d 138, 143 (Miss. Ct. App. 2021).

[43.2] White v. Brown, 301 So. 3d 750, 758-59 (Miss. Ct. App. 2020).

[3] Rights between once-married cohabitants
[b] Rights between former spouses
[i] Division of assets

Page 54. Insert in text after sentence ending in footnote 49:

A 2023 case appears to both limit and possibly expand the earlier cases. The court of appeals held that a homemaker wife who cohabited with her husband for fourteen years between their first and second marriages had no claim to assets he acquired during cohabitation. The court held that the division in the earlier cases was limited to situations in which both parties worked and contributed financially during their cohabitation. The decision does not appear to allow division based on homemaker contributions. On the other hand, the holding did not seem to be limited to former spouses who cohabit, possibly opening the door for never-married cohabitants to seek division of assets when both worked and contributed financially.[49.1]

[49.1] Chambliss v. Chambliss, 385 So. 3d 1246, 1254-55 (Miss. Ct. App. 2023); *see also* McGee v. McGee, 399 So. 3d 163, 168 (Miss. 2024) (wife was not entitled to division of retirement account accumulated during cohabitation between first and second marriage; there was no evidence that they accumulated property together during the period of dating and cohabitation).

§ 2.08 Rights between nonmarital children and their parents

Page 57. Insert in text after sentence ending in footnote 81:

A nonmarital child may inherit from the biological father and his relatives if there was an adjudication of paternity during the father's lifetime or an heirship proceeding is filed within one year of the father's death or 90 days after first publication of notice to creditors, whichever is less. The statute provides that the one-year period "shall be self-executing and may not be tolled for any reason, including lack of notice." The father and relatives of a nonmarital child may inherit from the child if the requirements for adjudication of paternity are met and if "the father has openly treated the child as his, and has not refused or neglected to support the child."[81.1]

Nonmarital children and their mothers are wrongful death beneficiaries of each other. Nonmarital children and fathers are wrongful death beneficiaries if they meet the requirements for inheritance.[81.2] A father who failed to acknowledge and support his daughter was not a wrongful death beneficiary of her estate.[81.3]

[81.1] Miss. Code Ann. § 91-1-15(3)(c), (d). *See* Matter of Estate of Lewis, 422 So. 3d 484, 493 (Miss. Ct. App. 2025) (alleged grand-daughter who failed to file petition within one year was not entitled to inherit; other heirs did not waive argument by failing to cite the statute as an affirmative defense – the one-year requirement "is incapable of waiver"). *But cf.* Estate of Dorsey, 2025 WL 3524732, at *8 (Miss. Ct. App. Dec. 9, 2025) (estate administrator who listed the petitioner as a child of the deceased in the obituary, then waited three years to open the estate and object to his claim as untimely, could not raise issue of one-year limitation).

[81.2] Miss. Code Ann. § 11-7-13.

[81.3] Matter of Estate of Tate, 409 So. 3d 1179, 1187 (Miss. Ct. App 2025).

IV
GROUNDS FOR DIVORCE

§ 4.01 History and overview

[7] Challenges to Mississippi divorce law

Page 70. Insert in text following sentence ending in footnote 32:

The issue was addressed in 2022 by the federal district court for the southern district of Mississippi, which found the statute to be constitutional. The court began by rejecting the notion that there is any fundamental right to divorce. No-fault divorce, which was not available until the 1970s, is not "deeply rooted" in our traditions. The court did not find support for the husband's arguments that the requirement of consent violated his right to privacy or association. Regarding the impact on his right to marry, the court noted that he did not assert that he intended to `marry and did not present any argument that the right to marry included a right to multiple marriages.

Applying the rational basis test, the court found that the state asserted legitimate interests in support of the statute, including "protecting children by making divorce more thoughtful by both parents, protecting economically dependent spouses, encouraging amicability and settlement of disputes in divorce actions, incentivizing spouses to make decisions during the relationship that will increase the likelihood it will be successful, and preventing premature divorce actions."[32.1]

[32.1] Watson v. Watson, 2022 WL 18688901 (S.D. Miss. March 3, 2022).

§ 4.02 Irreconcilable differences divorce

[2] Consent

[b] Withdrawal of contest or denial

Page 72. Insert in text after sentence ending in footnote 49:

The filing of a joint complaint for irreconcilable differences divorce constitutes a withdrawal of any earlier contest or denial.[49.1]

[49.1] Hodge v. Hodge, 2025 WL 2837224, at *6 (Miss. Ct. App. Oct 7, 2025) (also stating that there was no contest because the husband never responded to the wife's fault-based petition).

[c] Withdrawal of consent

Page 72. Add to footnote 51:

See also Osing v. Osing, 392 So. 3d 442, 448 (Miss. Ct. App. 2024) (husband was not entitled to withdraw consent without leave of court after the court approved the consent, held two hearings, and issued a temporary order).

[5] No divorce before all matters resolved

Page 74. Insert in text after sentence ending in footnote 68:

A grant of divorce in a bifurcated trial was not a final and appealable judgment.[68.1]

[68.1] Williams v. Williams, 415 So. 3d 1011, 1013 (Miss. Ct. App. 2025).

§ 4.03 Fault-based grounds for divorce

[1] General considerations

[f] Standard of review

Page 79. Add to footnote 110:

The de novo standard was declared in *Potts v. Potts*, 700 So. 2d 321, 322 (Miss. 1997) (determining whether habitual cruelty has occurred is a determination of law and will be reversed if the chancellor applied an erroneous legal standard).

Page 79. Insert in text after sentence ending in footnote 110:

In two recent cases, however, the court of appeals applied the abuse of discretion standard to review a chancellor's findings on habitual, cruel, and inhuman treatment.[110.1] The court stated that the case cited by the supreme court for the principle that the ground is reviewed as a matter of law did not make that statement.[110.2] And in 2021, the supreme court, without overruling *Potts,* appeared to apply the abuse of discretion standard. The supreme court reinstated a chancellor's denial of divorce, holding that the court of appeals failed to apply the abuse of discretion standard.[110.3]

[110.1] *See* Roley v. Roley, 329 So. 3d 473, 491 (Miss. Ct. App. 2021); Gwathney v. Gwathney, 208 So. 3d 1087, 1091 n.1 (Miss. Ct. App. 2017).

[110.2] *See* Gwathney v. Gwathney, 208 So. 3d 1087, 1091 n.1 (Miss. Ct. App. 2017).

[110.3] Rankin v. Rankin, 323 So. 3d 1073, 1080 (Miss. 2021) (two justices dissented, arguing that the conflict was not over the facts but over the spouses' subjective interpretations of the husband's actions).

[3] Adultery

[d] Circumstantial proof

Page 81. Add to footnote 146:

See Schaubhut v. Schaubhut, 373 So. 3d 802, 808 (Miss. Ct. App. 2023) (a wife presented sufficient proof of adultery including documents, a video, and a corroborating witness in addition to her own testimony).

Page 82. Add to footnote 150:

See also Guinn v. Claiborne, 352 So. 3d 646, 650 (Miss. Ct. App. 2022) (adultery not proved by testimony of plaintiff's son that his mother was "in a relationship with a man" and possibly living together).

[f] Same-sex relationships

Page 83. Add to footnote 159:

In re Matter of Blaisdell, 261 A.3d 306, 312-13 (N.H. 2021) (husband granted divorce based on his wife's relationship with another woman; expanding the definition of adultery to include intimate sexual contact between persons of the same sex).

[5] Desertion for one year

[b] Wilful and obstinate

[i] Intent to abandon the marriage

Page 85. Insert in text after sentence ending in footnote 175:

A husband was properly granted divorce against his wife who left the marital home, taking her belongings, and who testified that she had no intention of returning and would not consider reconciling if asked.[175.1]

[175.1] Thornhill v. Thornhill, 421 So. 3d 626, 635 (Miss. Ct. App. 2025).

[d] Constructive desertion

Page 87. Add to footnote 197:

See Watson v. Watson, 306 So. 3d 800, 802-05 (Miss. Ct. App. 2020) (wife's alleged erratic behavior, combative outbursts, irrational accusations, failure to take care of herself and house, was not sufficiently extreme to constitute constructive desertion).

[ii] Dispute over location of residence

Page 88. Replace second paragraph in the section with the following:

In 1979, the United States Supreme Court in *Orr v. Orr* invalidated gender-based distinctions in family law, holding that old notions of a man's duty to provide a home do not justify discriminatory family law doctrines.[209] In 2021, the court of appeals relied on *Orr* to overrule the 1940 Mississippi case stating that a husband has the right to determine the family residence. The couple in question separated after a few months of marriage when the husband was transferred to an office an hour's drive from their home. He chose to move to be close to his job. His wife did not want to relocate. *Four* years later, the husband filed for divorce, arguing that his wife's failure to follow him was desertion. The court held that *Ouzts* was no longer good law and that a wife's refusal to follow her husband is not desertion. The court of appeals also agreed with the chancellor that even if *Ouzts* was good law, the husband's unilateral decision to move from their debt-free home was not made in good faith. Two judges dissented, arguing that the issue should be whether one spouse's refusal to move with the other is unreasonable, regardless of gender. They stated that the husband was the family wage-earner, his decision to move was in good faith, and his wife's refusal to follow him was unreasonable.[210]

---

[209] Orr v. Orr, 440 U.S. 268, 279-80 (1979).
[210] Stephenson v. Stephenson, 332 So. 3d 360, 365 (Miss. Ct. App. 2021).

[6] Habitual drunkenness

Page 89. Add to footnote 220:

See also Garrison v. Courtney, 304 So. 3d 1129, 1138-39 (Miss. Ct. App. 2020) (husband drank up to a six pack most days, became argumentative when drinking, belittled his wife, and punched furniture; repeatedly texted and called during separation, leaving abusive messages).

[8] Habitual, cruel, and inhuman treatment: History and overview

[a] The defendant's conduct: Cruelty defined

Page 92. Insert in text after sentence ending in footnote 240:

For example, a husband was granted divorce after his wife threw him out of the house and threatened to kill him. He testified that he feared for his life, particularly since there were guns in the house.[240.1]

[240.1] Montgomery v. Montgomery, 339 So. 3d 819, 828 (Miss. Ct. App. 2022) (husband's testimony corroborated by neighbor who said wife told her she wished she could shoot him).

[b] Causal connection

Page 93. Insert in text after sentence ending in footnote 251:

The court of appeals emphasized the importance of the subjective test in a 2022 case, reversing a chancellor's denial of a wife's request for divorce. The chancellor found it reasonable to assume that the wife did not fear her husband because she voluntarily went to his house after he threatened to publish nude photographs of her if she did not come to his house. The court held that the chancellor used an improper test by asking what a reasonable person would do – the question is how a woman in the plaintiff's position would react, not how an objective, reasonable person would respond.[251.1]

[251.1] Baughman v. Baughman, 350 So. 3d 271, 283 (Miss. Ct. App. 2022).

Page 93. Add to footnote 253:

See also Moss v. Moss, 361 So. 3d 140, 148-49 (Miss. Ct. App. 2022) (wife was treated for depression, was anxious, lost sleep, developed hair-pulling disorder); Dickinson v. Dickinson, 293 So. 3d 322, 329 (Miss. Ct. App. 2020) (wife suffered from depression, weight loss, and low self-esteem) (sister corroborated control and abuse).

Page 94. Add to footnote 257:

See also Lindsay v. Lindsay, 303 So. 3d 770, 782 (Miss. Ct. App. 2020) (wife testified that she had a heart attack but did not show that it was related to husband's behavior).

Page 94. Insert in text after sentence ending in footnote 258:

However, the court of appeals rejected a husband's argument that expert medical testimony was required to establish that his conduct impacted his wife's health. She presented sufficient evidence for the chancellor to determine that her husband's explosive anger, extreme uncleanliness and lack of personal hygiene directly affected and endangered her and the children's physical health and well-being.[258.1]

[258.1] Roley v. Roley, 329 So 3d. 473, 487 (Miss. Ct. App. 2021) (wife testified that she was afraid of her husband, that their house became rat-infested, and that she was revolted by his lack of personal hygiene).

[d] Corroboration

Page 96. Add to footnote 271:

See Thornton v. Thornton, 324 So. 3d 345, 350 (Miss. Ct. App. 2021) (wife's testimony regarding husband's violence sufficiently corroborated by daughter's testimony regarding one incident); Dickinson v. Dickinson, 293 So. 3d 322, 329 (Miss. Ct. App. 2020) (wife's sister corroborated husband's control and abuse).

Page 96. Add to footnote 276:

See also Kerr v. Kerr, 323 So. 3d 462, 471 (Miss. 2021) (denying wife's request for divorce based on husband's alleged violence; no witness, including her father, supported her testimony; municipal judge denied her request for a restraining order, finding no violence).

[f] Standard of review

Page 97. Add to footnote 283:

See also Roley v. Roley, 329 So. 3d 473, 491 (Miss. Ct. App. 2021) (applying abuse of discretion standard).

Page 97. Insert in text after sentence ending in footnote 283:

And in 2021, the supreme court appeared to apply the abuse of discretion standard, reinstating a chancellor's denial of divorce. The supreme court held that the court of appeals failed to apply the abuse of discretion standard.[283.1]

[283.1] Rankin v. Rankin, 323 So. 3d 1073, 1080 (Miss. 2021) (two justices dissented, arguing that the conflict was not over the facts but over the spouses' subjective interpretations of the husband's actions).

[9] Habitual, cruel, and inhuman treatment: Specific conduct

[a] Physical violence

[i] Pattern of violence or one or more incidents of severe violence

Page 97. Add to footnote 287:

See also Kerr v. Kerr, 323 So. 3d 462, 471 (Miss. 2021) (witnesses testified that they observed wife's physical violence toward her husband and toward her father).

[ii] Isolated acts of violence

Page 98. Add to footnote 289:

See also Thornton v. Thornton, 324 So. 3d 345, 348-50 (Miss. Ct. App. 2021) (husband was violent on several occasions, one corroborated by their daughter; he called his wife the devil, refused to allow her to get an education or work; refused to help support the household when she did so without his permission; disabled appliances in their home).

Page 98. Insert in text after sentence ending in footnote 289:

In a case tried on the ground of spousal domestic abuse, a wife was granted divorce against a husband who sexually assaulted her, threatened to shoot her, stated that he wished she were dead, destroyed valuable personal belongings and keepsakes, and blocked her from accessing accounts.[289.1]

[289.1] Williams v. Williams, 309 So. 3d 560, 564-65 (Miss. Ct. App. 2020); *see also* Brownlee v. Brownlee, 419 So. 3d 453, 465 (Miss. Ct. App. 2025) (affirming divorce to wife whose husband was explosive and violent, fathered three nonmarital children, struck her her and broke her tooth and slammed a car trunk on her arm.

Page 99. Insert in text after sentence ending in footnote 296:

[iii] Threats of violence [NEW]

The spousal domestic abuse subsection of habitual cruelty defines physical violence as causing bodily injury or attempting by physical menace to put the plaintiff in fear of imminent serious bodily injury.[296.1] In a 2022 case, the court of appeals noted that a husband's intimidation of his wife with property destruction and threats could be sufficient to meet this standard even in the absence of physical violence. The court also held that the chancellor erred by finding that the wife did not fear her husband since she went voluntarily to his house after he threatened to publish nude photographs of her. [296.2]

[296.1] MISS. CODE ANN. § 93-5-1.

[296.2] Baughman v. Baughman, 350 So. 3d 271, 283 (Miss. Ct. App. 2022) (dicta - case also involved an incident of sexual assault) (stating that the test for impact on the plaintiff is subjective, not a reasonable person standard).

[iv] Sexual assault [NEW]

Marital rape is a form of physical violence. In a recent case, the court of appeals addressed a chancellor's skepticism about a wife's allegation that her estranged husband forced her to have sex. The wife testified that her husband intimidated and threatened her during their marriage. She testified that after their separation, he threatened to publish nude photographs of her unless she came to his house to discuss whether she was seeing someone. When she did, he forced her to have sex over her stated objection. The chancellor found it questionable that the wife stayed there for the night and did not report the assault. The court of appeals reversed and rendered, holding that the single incident could be sufficient to satisfy the test for spousal domestic violence. The court also stated that the chancellor's findings were at odds with research on domestic violence, which shows that most victims do not report assault.[296.3]

[296.3] Baughman v. Baughman, 350 So. 3d 271, 284 (Miss. Ct. App. 2022).

[b] Verbal or emotional abuse

[i] Unfounded accusations

Page 100. Add to footnote 303:

See also Johnson v. Johnson, 357 So. 3d 1168, 1174 (Miss. Ct. App. 2023) (allegations of infidelity combined with outbursts of rage, property destruction, threats of suicide, cursing and abusive language); Moss v. Moss, 361 So. 3d 140, 149 (Miss. Ct. App. 2022) (divorce properly granted to wife based on verbal abuse, controlling behavior, unfounded accusations of infidelity and paternity of children, husband's inappropriate behavior with a minor, stalking, and threats of suicide at separation); Dickinson v. Dickinson, 293 So. 3d 322, 328 (Miss. Ct. App. 2020) (husband accused wife of affairs with relatives and her daughter's boyfriend).

Page 100. Insert in text after sentence ending in footnote 305:

And, in a case tried under the spousal domestic abuse ground, a husband's accusations of infidelity toward the end of the couple's marriage did not rise to the level of constant and long-term accusations that constitute habitual cruelty.[305.1]

[305.1] Wangler v. Wangler, 294 So. 3d 1138, 1147 (Miss. 2020) (husband also attempted to isolate wife from family by taking keys and phone; physically forced her to go to bed; kept her up for hours in the night screaming at her).

[iii] Abusive sexual behavior

Page 101. Add to footnote 316:

For a discussion of whether a petitioner adequately proved that her spouse transmitted a sexual disease to her, see Doe v. Doe, 341 So. 3d 953, 964-69 (Miss. Ct. App. 2021) (considering STD infection as factor in property division; chancellor erred in finding causation based in part on judicial notice regarding HPV and improperly shifted burden of proof to husband).

Page 101. Add to footnote 317:

Cf. Moss v. Moss, 361 So. 3d 140, 148-49 (Miss. Ct. App. 2022) (husband's inappropriate behavior with minor, causing the family's required return from a mission trip, considered in awarding divorce based on habitual cruelty).

[iv] Treatment of children

Page 101. Insert in text after sentence ending in footnote 320:

A husband was entitled to divorce based on his new wife's treatment of his children as "unnatural and infamous" conduct. She stated that she "hated" his children; she belittled and embarrassed them, became angry over insignificant incidents, and criticized his eight-year-old daughter's weight, damaging her self-confidence. Her conduct significantly impacted his relationship with his children and caused him to suffer from depression and high blood pressure.[320.1]

[320.1] Cannon v. Cannon, 375 So. 3d 697, 709-10 (Miss. Ct. App. 2023).

[c] Factors in combination

Page 101. Add to footnote 323:

See Moss v. Moss, 361 So. 3d 140, 148-49 (Miss. Ct. App. 2022) (divorce properly granted to wife based on thirty-plus years of verbal abuse, criticism, shaming, control, isolating her from friends, unfounded accusations of infidelity and paternity of children, inappropriate behavior with minor, stalking, and threats of suicide at separation).

Page 102. Add to footnote 328:

Johnson v. Johnson, 357 So. 3d 1168, 1174 (Miss. Ct. App. 2023) (outbursts of rage, allegations of infidelity, property destruction, threats of suicide, cursing and abusive language); Dickinson v. Dickinson, 293 So. 3d 322, 327 (Miss. Ct. App. 2020) (husband exploded into anger if wife or her daughters disobeyed his rules on gum chewing, noise, or water use).

Page 102. Add to footnote 333:

See Dickinson v. Dickinson, 293 So. 3d 322, 328 (Miss. Ct. App. 2020) (husband refused to speak to wife for a year).

Page 102. Add to footnote 334:

See Thornton v. Thornton, 324 So. 3d 345, 349 (Miss. Ct. App. 2021) (husband refused to allow his wife to go to school or work; when she did, he refused to provide any support for the household).

Page 103. Add to footnote 337:

See Montgomery v. Montgomery, 339 So. 3d 819, 828 (Miss. Ct. App. 2022) (divorce properly granted to husband whose wife asked him to leave, threw things at him, threatened to kill him, exhibited bizarre behavior, and tried to file rape charges against him).

Page 103. Add to footnote 338:

Cf. Johnson v. Johnson, 357 So. 3d 1168, 1174 (Miss. Ct. App. 2023) (allegations of infidelity combined with outbursts of rage, property destruction, threats of suicide, cursing and abusive language); Moss v. Moss, 361 So. 3d 140, 148-49 (Miss. Ct. App. 2022) (husband made multiple threats of suicide during separation, which chancellor found to be manipulative).

Page 103. Add to footnote 339:

Cannon v. Cannon, 375 So. 3d 697, 709-10 (Miss. Ct. App. 2023) (wife stated that she hated husband's children, belittled them, criticized his daughter's weight; her conduct affected his relationship with his children).

Page 103. Add to footnote 341:

Cf. Montgomery v. Montgomery, 339 So. 3d 819, 828 (Miss. Ct. App. 2022) (divorce properly granted to husband whose wife asked him to leave, threw things at him, threatened to kill him, exhibited bizarre behavior, and tried to file rape charges against him).

Page 103. Add to footnote 344:

Dickinson v. Dickinson, 293 So. 3d 322, 329 (Miss. Ct. App. 2020) (husband's extreme hoarding made house unlivable).

Page 103. Add to footnote 346:

Moss v. Moss, 361 So. 3d 140, 144 (Miss. Ct. App. 2022) (husband controlled what wife wore, forced her to stop activities).

[d] Revolting and unnatural conduct

Page 104. Insert in text after sentence ending in footnote 354:

The court of appeals rejected a husband's argument that his wife was required to provide expert medical testimony to prove that his behavior impacted her. She presented sufficient evidence for the chancellor to determine that her husband's explosive anger, extreme uncleanliness and lack of personal hygiene directly affected and endangered her and the children's physical health and well-being.[354.1]

[354.1] Roley v. Roley, 329 So. 3d 473, 487 (Miss. Ct. App. 2021) (wife testified that she was afraid of her husband, that their house became rat-infested, and that she was revolted by his lack of personal hygiene).

Page 104. Insert in text after sentence ending in footnote 358:

A chancellor granted divorce on this ground based on evidence of the husband's uncontrolled anger, verbal abuse, extreme hoarding and lack of personal hygiene that made the marriage revolting to the wife and made it impossible for her to remain in the marriage.[358.1]

[358.1] Roley v. Roley, 329 So. 3d 473, 487 (Miss. Ct. App. 2021) (husband did not bathe with soap or brush his teeth; retrieved expired food from trash and fed it to children; screamed at wife for minor incidents; allowed ten-year-old son to watch pornography).

Page 104. Add to footnote 361:

See also Cannon v. Cannon, 375 So. 3d 697, 709-10 (Miss. Ct. App. 2023) (divorce based on wife's verbally abusive treatment of her stepchildren that damaged husband's relationship with them); Kerr v. Kerr, 323 So. 3d 462, 474 (Miss. 2021) (child ingested Klonopin in mother's care).

[e] Incompatibility

Page 105. Insert in text after sentence ending in footnote 365:

A wife's testimony that her husband was condescending, mean-spirited, and belligerent did not rise to the level of habitual, cruel, and inhuman treatment.[365.1] And in a case tried under the ground of spousal domestic abuse, the court of appeals held that a husband's accusations of infidelity, physically forcing his wife to go to bed on occasion, keeping her up for hours into the night arguing, and taking her keys and phone to prevent her from contacting her family did not rise above the level of incompatibility and unkindness.[365.2]

[365.1] Lindsay v. Lindsay, 303 So. 3d 770, 781 (Miss. Ct. App. 2020) (husband left the house rather than participating in family time; screamed in wife's face; sometimes threw dinner in the trash).

[365.2] Wangler v. Wangler, 294 So. 3d 1138, 1144-45 (Miss. 2020) (court noted that accusations occurred late in marriage, that the physical removal to bed only happened once a month or so, and that in spite of husband's attempts, wife was in contact with her family; also considering that wife posted positive things about her husband on social media and had planned to move with him shortly before separating).

[10] Spousal domestic abuse

Page 106. Insert in text after sentence ending in footnote 381:

A chancellor properly awarded divorce based on spousal domestic abuse based on proof that a wife took almost a million dollars from her elderly husband "by threats, intimidation, emotional or verbal abuse and forced isolation," including threats of imprisonment. She forced isolation on him by putting him in a rental house without a vehicle or phone and in a deteriorated mental state.[381.1]

[381.1] Brodie v. Brodie, 2025 WL 1741866, at *9 (Miss. Ct. App. June 24, 2025).

Page 106. Add to footnote 382:

See Brodie v. Brodie, 2025 WL 1741866, at *8 (Miss. Ct. App. June 24, 2025) (plaintiff's testimony is sufficient); Moss v. Moss, 361 So. 3d 140, 151 (Miss. Ct. App. 2022) (wife's testimony alone sufficient to establish spousal domestic abuse); Williams v. Williams, 309 So. 3d 560, 565 (Miss. Ct. App. 2020) (corroboration not required for spousal domestic abuse ground).

Page 106. Insert in text after sentence ending in footnote 383:

And in a 2022 case, the court of appeals held that a husband's sexual assault of his estranged wife could be sufficient to meet the test for spousal domestic abuse, reversing a chancellor's denial of divorce. The court also held that the chancellor erred in applying an objective, reasonable person test to judge the wife's response to her husband's threats, rather than a subjective test. The court disagreed with the chancellor's skepticism about the wife's claim of sexual assault because she did not report the assault, noting that only a small percentage of victims report sexual assault.[383.1]

[383.1] Baughman v. Baughman, 350 So. 3d 271, 283 (Miss. Ct. App. 2022) (case also involved multiple threats and intimidation).

Page 106. Replace the last two sentences in the section with the following:

At least with regard to temporary orders of protection, that issue was resolved in a recent case. The court of appeals held that a justice court temporary protection order did not bar a woman's tort action against her abuser based on res judicata, for two reasons. The tort action, seeking damages based on the defendant's abuse, lacked identify of subject matter with the justice court matter, which sought injunctive relief from abuse. And, res judicata applies only to final judgments, not to temporary orders.[383.2]

In cases involving non-physical violence, it is not clear whether the new ground will permit divorce on a less demanding standard than habitual, cruel, and inhuman treatment. In a 2020 case, the court of appeals denied divorce to a wife who testified that her husband took her keys and phone to prevent her from contacting her family, kept her up hours into the night with screaming and arguments, physically forced her to bed on occasion, and made unfounded accusations of infidelity. The court held that the conduct alleged did not rise above unkindness and incompatibility.[383.3]

The court of appeals held in 2021 that the new ground applied in an action that was filed before the effective date of the amendment but tried after the effective date.[383.4] The supreme court noted in a 2021 case that a divorce petition requesting divorce based on habitual, cruel, and inhuman treatment includes a petition for divorce based on spousal domestic abuse, which is a subset of habitual cruelty.[383.5]

[383.2] Griffin v. Adams, 291 So. 3d 825, 828-29 (Miss. Ct. App. 2020).

[383.3] Wangler v. Wangler, 294 So. 3d 1138, 1147 (Miss. 2020) (court noted that the accusations occurred late in marriage, the physical removal to bed only happened once a month, and that in spite of husband's attempts, wife was in weekly contact with her family; also considering that she posted positive things about her husband on social media and had planned to move with him shortly before separating).

[383.4] Roley v. Roley, 329 So. 3d 473, 509 n. 11 (Miss. Ct. App. 2021).

[383.5] Wangler v. Wangler, 294 So. 3d 1138, 1141 (Miss. 2020) (specific pleading of the new ground is not necessary).

§ 4.04 Defenses to Fault-Based Divorce

[1] Knowledge of condition

Page 109. Add to footnote 416:

But cf. Garrison v. Courtney, 304 So. 3d 1129, 1145-46 (Miss. Ct. App. 2020) (wife not barred from divorce based on habitual drunkenness by premarital knowledge of husband's drinking, which had increased significantly during the marriage).

[6] Condonation

[a] Of adultery

Page 112. Insert in text after sentence ending in footnote 446:

And a wife of forty-five years did not condone her husband's adultery by remaining separated but married to him for thirty years after learning of his multiple affairs and nonmarital children. Both parties agreed that the wife had never forgiven him for the affairs.[446.1] In contrast, a woman who went to counseling with her husband after learning of his affair and remained with him for twelve years had condoned his adultery and was not entitled to a divorce.[446.2]

[446.1] Williams v. Williams, 303 So. 3d 824, 832 (Miss. Ct. App. 2020).

[446.2] Baughman v. Baughman, 350 So. 3d 271, 281 (Miss. Ct. App. 2022) (but granting divorce based on habitual cruelty).

[b] Of continuing offenses

Page 113. Insert in text after sentence ending in footnote 447:

A wife did not condone her husband's drinking by continuing to live with him. Condonation is conditional, based on the behavior ending. Her husband continued to drink at the time of divorce.[447.1]

[447.1] Garrison v. Courtney, 304 So. 3d 1129, 1145-46 (Miss. Ct. App. 2020).

[9] Res judicata

Page 115. Insert in text after sentence ending in footnote 465:

Similarly, a grant of separate maintenance to one spouse may be res judicata in a subsequent divorce.[465.1]

[465.1] Turner v. Turner, 385 So. 3d 827, 834 (Miss. Ct. App. 2024) (husband was barred from introducing evidence of habitual cruelty that predated separate maintenance decree, which was predicated on a finding that the wife was not materially at fault in the separation); see *supra* δ 1.13[8].

Page 115. Add to footnote 466:

Cf. Turner v. Turner, 385 So. 3d 827, 834 (Miss. Ct. App. 2024) (wife's award of separate maintenance did not bar husband from seeking divorce based on adultery of which he was unaware at the time of the separate maintenance action).

[illegible]

[8] Of Continuing Offense

[illegible]

[9] Res Judicata

[illegible]

V
DOMESTIC VIOLENCE

§ 5.01 History and overview

Page 118. Insert in text after sentence ending in footnote 4:

Survivors of violence are protected in their communications with a broad range of advocates working on their behalf. The Mississippi Advocate Confidentiality Law makes confidential a victim's communications regarding domestic violence, sexual assault, stalking, and human trafficking. The act defines an advocate as an "employee, contractor, agent or volunteer of a victim service provider whose primary purpose is to render services to victims of domestic violence, sexual assault, stalking, or human trafficking and who has completed a minimum of twenty (20) hours of training [in specified subjects]," one who supervises an advocate, or a third party whose presence is necessary for the services. An advocate may not disclose a covered communication or be compelled to testify except with the victim's consent, unless (1) state or federal law requires disclosure; (2) failure is likely to result in imminent risk of serious bodily harm or death; (3) the victim dies or is incapable of giving consent and the information is necessary for a law enforcement investigation or criminal proceeding involving death or incapacitation; or (4) based on a valid court order. A court in a civil or criminal proceeding may compel disclosure under limited circumstances if the probative value outweighs the potential harm.[4.1]

[4.1] Miss. Code Ann. § 93-21-125(1)-(2).

§ 5.02 Protection orders

[9] Appeals

Page 123. Add to footnote 52:

See Carter v. Carter, 304 So. 3d 1160, 1163 (Miss. Ct. App. 2020) (appeal of county court temporary order of protection to circuit court was properly dismissed; appeals are to chancery court).

[10] Firearms prohibitions

Page 124. Insert in text after sentence ending in footnote 55:

The Fifth Circuit held in 2023 that the prohibition is unconstitutional. The court's ruling was based on *N.Y. State Rifle & Pistol Ass'n, Inc. v. Bruen*, 142 S. Ct. 2111 (2022) which requires that a firearms restriction must be "consistent with the Nation's historical tradition of firearm regulation." Prior to *Bruen*, a restriction outside of the historical regulation of firearms could be valid nonetheless if it was part of a narrowly tailored effort to "minimize lawless violence." According to the Fifth Circuit, *Bruen* discarded the "narrowly tailored" exception.[55.1] The United States Supreme Court granted certiorari and in 2024 overruled the Fifth Circuit, upholding the Violence Against Women Act firearms provision. The Court stated, "Since the founding, our Nation's firearm laws have included provisions preventing individuals who threaten physical harm to others from misusing firearms. As applied to the facts of this case, Section 922(g)(8) fits comfortably within this tradition."

[55.1] U.S. v. Rahimi, 61 F.4th 443 (5th Cir. 2023).
[55.2] U.S. v. Rahimi, 602 U.S. 680, 690 (2024).

§ 5.03 Grounds for divorce

Page 125. Insert in text at end of introduction:

The court of appeals held in 2021 that the new ground applied in an action that was filed before the July 1, 2017 effective date of the amendment but tried after the effective date.[60.1]

[60.1] Roley v. Roley, 329 So. 3d 473, 492 n.11 (Miss. Ct. App. 2021) (divorce granted based on habitual, cruel, and inhuman treatment).

[5] Spousal domestic abuse

Page 129. Add to footnote 91:

See Williams v. Williams, 309 So. 3d 560, 565-66 (Miss. Ct. App. 2020 (corroboration not required for spousal domestic abuse ground).

Page 129. Insert in text after sentence ending in footnote 93:

In 2020, the court of appeals held that a temporary domestic abuse protection order was not res judicata with respect to a woman's tort action against her abuser for two reasons – the actions lacked identity of subject matter and res judicata applies only to final judgments, not to temporary orders. The decision suggests that at least with respect to temporary orders, res judicata will not apply to divorce actions.[93.1]

In 2022, the court of appeals emphasized the importance of focusing on the mindset of a victim of domestic violence. The court held that a chancellor erred in applying an objective, reasonable person test to judge a wife's response to her husband's threats, rather than a subjective test. In addition, the court disagreed with the chancellor's skepticism about the wife's claim of sexual assault because she did not report the assault. The court noted that only a small percentage of victims report sexual assault.[93.2]

[93.1] Griffin v. Adams, 291 So. 3d 825, 828-30 (Miss. Ct. App. 2020).
[93.2] Baughman v. Baughman, 350 So. 3d 271, 284 (Miss. Ct. App. 2022).

Page 130. Insert in text after sentence ending in footnote 94:

In cases involving non-physical violence, it is not clear whether the new ground will permit divorce on a less demanding standard than habitual, cruel, and inhuman treatment. In a 2020 case, the court of appeals denied divorce to a wife who testified that her husband took her keys and phone to prevent her from contacting her family, kept her up for hours into the night with screaming and arguments, physically forced her to bed on occasion, and made unfounded accusations of infidelity. The court held that the conduct alleged did not rise above unkindness and incompatibility.[94.1]

The court of appeals held in 2021 that the new ground applied in an action that was filed before the July 1, 2017 effective date of the amendment but tried after the effective date.[94.2]

[94.1] Wangler v. Wangler, 294 So. 3d 1138, 1144-47 (Miss. 2020) (court noted that the accusations occurred late in marriage, the physical removal to bed only happened once a month, and that in spite of husband's attempts, wife was in weekly contact with her family; also considering that she posted positive things about her husband on social media and had planned to move with him shortly before separating). *But cf.* Baughman v. Baughman, 350 So. 3d 271, 283 (Miss. Ct. App. 2022) (emphasizing subjective test for habitual cruelty; court should focus on impact on domestic violence victim).

[94.2] Roley v. Roley, 329 So. 3d 473, 492 n.11 (Miss. Ct. App. 2021).

§ 5.05 Custody of children

[1] Presumption against custody to violent parent

Page 131. Add to footnote 103:

See also Kerr v. Kerr, 323 So. 3d 462, 481 (Miss. 2021) (affirming chancellor's award of custody to a father; wife's allegations of her husband's abuse were not credible).

Page 131. Add to footnote 105:

See also Alves-Hunter v. Hunter, 351 So. 3d 468, 475 (Miss. Ct. App. 2022) (a single incident of violence between parents during separation did not constitute a history of family violence).

Page 131. Insert in text after sentence ending in footnote 105:

And the presumption was not triggered by a father's agreement to allow a court to award his wife a divorce based on habitual cruelty in order to move the lengthy divorce proceedings forward – he admitted to habitual cruelty, not to a history of family violence.[105.1]

[105.1] Lambes v. Lambes, 345 So. 3d 592, 607-08 (Miss. Ct. App. 2022) (also finding that even if the presumption was triggered, it was rebutted).

Page 131. Insert in text after sentence ending in footnote 108:

The presumption was rebutted by evidence that a father attended parenting classes, that there was no evidence of family violence during the five-year litigation, and that the mother's mental health affected her ability to care for the children.[108.1]

[108.1] Lambes v. Lambes, 345 So. 3d 592, 608 (Miss. Ct. App. 2022) (also questioning whether the conflicting evidence was sufficient to raise the presumption).

§ 5.07 Tort actions based on domestic violence

Page 135. Insert in text after section [3]:

[3a] Relationship to protection orders [NEW]

In 2020, the court of appeals rejected a man's argument that his former partner's tort action for abuse was barred by res judicata because she obtained a temporary restraining order against him. The order was not res judicata for two reasons – the two actions lacked identity of subject matter and res judicata applies only to final judgments, not to temporary orders.[136.1]

[136.1] Griffin v. Adams, 291 So. 3d 825, 830 (Miss. Ct. App. 2020).

[4] Statute of limitations

Page 135. Replace sentence ending in footnote 139 with the following:

In 2021, the supreme court overruled prior decisions applying the one-year statute, holding that intentional infliction of emotional distress actions are governed by the general three-year statute of limitations.[139]

[139] GEICO Cas. Co. v. Stapleton, 315 So. 3d 464, 468 (Miss. 2021).

VI
PROPERTY DIVISION

§ 6.01 History and overview

[5] Equitable distribution in Mississippi
[b] The Mississippi system
[ii] Presumption in favor of marital property

Page 142. Add to footnote 29:

See Cannon v. Cannon, 375 So. 3d 697, 710 (Miss. Ct. App. 2023) (husband had burden of proving that properties held by real estate business were acquired prior to marriage). See *infra* § 6.03[4][b] for discussion of burden of proof.

§ 6.02 Classification: The basic system

[1] Failure to classify or error in classification

Page 143. Insert in text after sentence ending in footnote 33:

For example, a chancellor erred in failing to classify a Mazda, a fifteen-year-old tractor, personal clothing, a four-wheeler, tools and equipment, bank accounts, and the wife's mother's wedding ring as separate or marital.[33.1]

[33.1] Brown v. Brown, 350 So. 3d 1169, 1181-82 (Miss. Ct. App. 2022); *see also* Davis v. Davis, 361 So. 3d 725, 735 (Miss. Ct. App. 2023) (failure to classify guns, various debts, and separate property portion of husband's PERS account); Johnson v. Johnson, 357 So. 3d 1168, 1175 (Miss. Ct. App. 2023) (failure to explain reason for classification of assets as marital).

[3] "During the marriage"
[a] Beginning date

Page 145. Insert in text after sentence ending in footnote 49:

In contrast, a wife was not entitled to a portion of her husband's retirement benefits accumulated in their fourteen-year cohabitation between marriages. She was a homemaker and did not contribute financially to the accumulation of assets. There was no basis for treating their cohabitation as a business partnership.[49.1] Remarriage between spouses does not convert property divided in their first marriage into marital property. A wife divorcing her husband for the second time was not entitled to division of assets accumulated by the couple during their first, three-year marriage or their brief cohabitation prior to their second marriage. The property settlement agreement from their first marriage divided property accumulated during that marriage. No marital property remained after the divorce. [49.2]

[49.1] Chambliss v. Chambliss, 385 So. 3d 1246, 1254-55 (Miss. Ct. App. 2023) (also rejecting her argument that their cohabitation revoked the divorce).
[49.2] McGee v. McGee, 399 So. 3d 163, 167-68 (Miss. 2024).

Page 145. Insert footnote at end of section [3][a]:

[49.3] See Bunyard v. Bunyard, 828 So. 2d 775, 778 (Miss. 2002).

[b] Ending date

Page 146. Add to footnote 55:

See also Wildman v. Wildman, 301 So. 3d 787, 794 (Miss. Ct. App. 2020) (chancellor has discretion to set cutoff date; affirming date of trial rather than date of separation as cutoff date).

Page 147. Add to footnote 57:

Case v. Case, 339 So. 3d 796, 811 (Miss. Ct. App. 2022) (affirming temporary order as the demarcation date even though the chancellor used some values closer to the trial date).

Page 147. Insert in text after sentence ending in footnote 59:

A chancellor properly classified a home bought after the couple's separation as a wife's separate property, even though the bank required that she put her husband's name on the deed. She obtained a loan in her name and made payments with post-separation income.[59.1] In several cases, the court has suggested that financial interdependence during separation is an important factor in setting the cutoff date. For example, a divorce-date cutoff was proper for a couple who continued to operate as an economic unit during fifteen years of separation.[59.2] In contrast, a chancellor properly set the ending date at separation based on proof that neither spouse provided support for the other after separation.[59.3]

[59.1] Coleman v. Coleman, 324 So. 3d 1204, 1212 (Miss. Ct. App. 2021); *see also* Lewis v. Lewis, 360 So. 3d 298, 301-02 (Miss. Ct. App. 2023) (rejecting husband's argument that court should have used divorce date because wife used his temporary alimony to pay the mortgage, increasing the home's equity between the temporary support order and the divorce).
[59.2] Williams v. Williams, 303 So. 3d 824, 832 (Miss. Ct. App. 2020).
[59.2] Randolph v. Randolph, 199 So. 3d 1282, 1285 (Miss. Ct. App. 2016).

Page 148. Add to footnote 68:

See also Thompson v. Thompson, 380 So. 3d 945 (Miss. Ct. App. 2024) (reversing in part because chancellor failed to explain reason for selecting January 2019 as date for couple separated from 2013 to 2022).

§ 6.03 Separate property

[1] Gifts and inheritances

[a] Joint gifts

Page 150. Insert in text after sentence ending in footnote 91:

However, a chancellor properly classified fifty-nine acres as a wife's separate property even though her grandmother deeded the property to both her and her husband. The wife testified that her grandmother intended that the property go to her; however, she was afraid of her husband's reaction if his name was not on the deed. There was sufficient evidence that the property was intended to be the wife's separate property.[91.1]

[91.1] Anderson v. Anderson, 310 So. 3d 1176, 1180-82 (Miss. Ct. App. 2020) (wife was granted a divorce based on husband's abuse).

[4] Income and appreciation from separate property

[a] The active-passive test

Page 152. Add to footnote 109:

See also In re Conservatorship of Geno, 365 So. 3d 287, 293-94 (Miss. Ct. App. 2021) (passive growth of $322,403 on premarital share of husband's defined contribution retirement plan was separate property).

Page 152. Insert in text after sentence ending in footnote 109:

In contrast, the income on a wife's separate property inheritance was marital – her husband paid the taxes on the income, converting the increase in value to marital property.[109.1]

[109.1] Osing v. Osing, 392 So. 3d 442, 449 (Miss. Ct. App. 2024) (inheritance, which was not commingled or used for family purposes, remained separate).

[b] Burden of proof

Page 153. Add to footnote 118:

See Dean v. Dean, 304 So. 3d 156, 167 (Miss. Ct. App. 2020) (wife had burden of proving that husband's premarital business appreciated during the marriage and that the appreciation was marital).

Page 153. Add to footnote 120:

Cf. Cannon v. Cannon, 375 So. 3d 697, 710 (Miss. Ct. App. 2023) (husband had burden of proving that premarital real estate business was separate; he did not present evidence to show that properties owned by the business were acquired prior to marriage).

Page 154. Insert in text after sentence ending in footnote 121:

The supreme clarified the burden of proof in a 2024 case, holding that the presumption in favor of marital property applies only to assets acquired during marriage – not to premarital property. Accordingly, the spouse seeking separate property classification has the burden of proof with regard to assets acquired during marriage. The nonowning spouse has the burden of proof with regard to assets acquired outside of marriage – the presumption does not apply to those assets.[121.1]

The court of appeals carved out a special rule for retirement accounts in a 2025 case. The court held that a chancellor erred in classifying a husband's retirement benefit (acquired before and during marriage) as all marital because he failed to prove the amount of the premarital portion. The court relied on *Arthur v. Arthur*, 691 So. 3d 997 (Miss. 1997), as holding that a chancellor must determine the premarital portion of a retirement account even if neither of the parties presented evidence – the premarital portion of a retirement account cannot be treated as marital property[121.2]

[121.1] Cassell v. Cassell, 389 So. 3d 305, 314-15 (Miss. 2024); *see also* Baird v. Baird, 2025 WL 2962388 (Miss. Ct. App. Oct. 21, 2025) (husband met the burden of proving that real estate acquired during marriage was gifted to him by his mother and therefore separate);.Smith v. Smith, 379 So. 3d 954, 965, 966 (Miss. Ct. App. 2024) (wife failed to prove that husband's premarital LLC had appreciated in value through marital efforts and become marital) (husband failed to meet his burden of proving that land acquired during marriage remained separate).

[121.2] Tauzin v. Tauzin, 2025 WL 2317673, at *8, *9 (Miss. Ct. App. Aug. 12, 2025) (quoting the concurring opinion in *Arthur* that "both parties bear responsibility" for presenting evidence on the issue).

§ 6.04 Exchanges of Property: Tracing

[2] Burden of proof

Page 156. Add to footnote 140:

See also Lageman v. Lageman, 313 So. 3d 1075, 1081-82, 1084 (Miss. Ct. App. 2021) (court properly classified husband's retirement account as marital even though it contained premarital contributions; he provided no proof of the amount of premarital value; court properly classified house as marital because no proof of separate contributions).

Page 156. Insert in text following sentence ending in footnote 140:

In contrast, a court erred in classifying a husband's premarital life insurance policies as marital. He proved that all premiums during the marriage were paid with separate funds.[140.1]

The supreme clarified the burden of proof in a 2024 case, holding that the presumption in favor of marital property applies only to assets acquired during marriage – not to premarital property. Accordingly, the spouse seeking separate property classification has the burden of proof with regard to assets acquired during marriage. The nonowning spouse has the burden of proof with regard to assets acquired outside of marriage – the presumption does not apply to those assets.[140.2] The court of appeals carved out a special rule for retirement accounts in a 2025 case. The court held that a chancellor erred in classifying a husband's retirement benefit (acquired before and during marriage) as all marital because he failed to prove the amount of the premarital portion. The court relied on *Arthur v. Arthur*, 691 So. 3d 997 (Miss. 1997), as holding that a chancellor must determine the premarital portion of a retirement account even if neither of the parties presented evidence – the premarital portion of a retirement account cannot be treated as marital property.[140.3]

[140.1] Doe v. Doe, 341 So. 3d 953, 972 (Miss. Ct. App. 2021) (husband introduced bank statements to show that his mother had paid all premiums on two premarital life insurance policies in his name).

[140.2] Cassell v. Cassell, 389 So. 3d 305, 314-15 (Miss. 2024).

[140.3] Tauzin v. Tauzin, 2025 WL 2317673, at *8, *9 (Miss. Ct. App. Aug. 12, 2025) (quoting the concurring opinion in *Arthur* that "both parties bear responsibility" for presenting evidence on the issue).

§ 6.05 Conversion of separate property to marital

[1] Conversion by implied gift or family use

[b] The Mississippi family use doctrine

Page 159. Add to footnote 162:

But cf. Warner v. Warner, 341 So. 3d 152, 160 (Miss. Ct. App. 2022) (acknowledging family use doctrine but affirming chancellor's classification of wife's golf cart and jet skis as separate in spite of grandchildren's use).

Page 159. Insert in text after sentence ending in footnote 162:

Minimal use does not convert an asset to marital. For example, sixty-five acres inherited by a wife were not converted to marital by the husband's occasional bush-hogging, recreational use, or storage of business equipment on the property. In contrast, the home purchased by the husband two years prior to marriage was marital – the family lived there together for fifteen years.[162.1]

[162.1] Gaskin v. Gaskin, 304 So. 3d 641, 649, 651 (Miss. Ct. App. 2020); *see also* Baird v. Baird, 2025 WL 2962388, at *6 (Miss. Ct. App. Oct. 21, 2025) (fact that a husband and children occasionally visited undeveloped property did not convert it to marital by family use); Dean v. Dean, 304 So. 3d 156, 168-69 (Miss. Ct. App. 2020) (fact that the family occasionally rode four-wheelers across the larger tract did not convert it to marital).

Page 159. Add to footnote 163:

Cf. Oates v. Oates, 291 So. 3d 803, 808 (Miss. Ct. App. 2020) (fact that wife mortgaged her separate property and used some of the funds for marital purposes did not convert her land to marital).

Page 159. Insert in text after sentence ending in footnote 164:

In 2021, however, the court of appeals stated, "merely using inherited property or cash for a joint purpose does not in and of itself equate into a conversion of separate property to marital property." The court rejected the husband's argument that his wife's use of mortgage proceeds from her separate land for marital purposes converted the land itself to marital.[164.1]

[164.1] Oates v. Oates, 291 So. 3d 803, 808 (Miss. Ct. App. 2020).

Page 160. Add to footnote 168:

But see McGovern v. McGovern, 372 So. 3d 138, 146 (Miss. Ct. App. 2023) (rejecting a husband's argument that he should receive a greater share of equity in their home because he used separate property to renovate it; home was marital based on family use; both spouses contributed to accumulation of assets).

Page 160. Add to footnote 170:

Cf. Warner v. Warner, 341 So. 3d 152, 160 (Miss. Ct. App. 2022) (acknowledging family use doctrine but affirming chancellor's classification of wife's golf cart and jet skis as separate in spite of grandchildren's use).

Page 160. Add to footnote 173:

See also Neely v. Neely, 305 So. 3d 164, 171-72 (Miss. Ct. App. 2020) (couple's occupancy of wife's inherited house for two years before separation, and after children left home, did not convert house to marital; wife paid all expenses of the home).

Page 161. Add to footnote 175:

See also Davidson v. Davidson, 369 So. 3d 607, 614 (Miss. Ct. App. 2023) (rejecting wife's argument that debt-free premarital home should have been separate property; it was converted by family use; husband contributed $28,000 to repairs; not error to give him a portion of equity).

Page 161. Insert in text after sentence ending in footnote 175:

However, in a 2020 case, the court of appeals affirmed a chancellor's finding that two years of marital occupancy did not convert a wife's separate property home to marital. Interestingly, the court relied in part on evidence that the couple maintained separate bank accounts and handled finances separately to support the holding.[175.1]

[175.1] Neely v. Neely, 305 So. 3d 164, 172 (Miss. Ct. App. 2020).

Page 161. Add to footnote 176:

See also Woods v. Woods, 423 So. 3d 720, 733 (Miss. Ct. App. 2025) (house purchased before marriage in joint names became marital based on commingling of funds and family use during two-year marriage).

Page 161. Insert in text after sentence ending in footnote 177:

However, a wife's use of inherited, uncommingled funds for herself and her children – but not for her husband – did not convert the funds to marital through family use.[177.1]

The scope of conversion is unrelated to the statutory homestead exemption. The court of appeals rejected a wife's argument that the marital home should have included forty acres owned by the husband prior to their marriage because they filed homestead exemption on the forty acres. The determination of homestead property for tax purposes and the test for marital property are not the same. The property used by the family included the home and three fenced acres.[177.2]

[177.1] Osing v. Osing, 392 So. 3d 442, 449 (Miss. Ct. App. 2024) (rejecting husband's argument that use for his children benefitted him indirectly and converted the funds to marital).

[177.2] Dean v. Dean, 304 So. 3d 156, 168-69 (Miss. Ct. App. 2020) (fact that the family occasionally rode four-wheelers across the larger tract did not convert it to marital).

[3] Conversion by commingling

[b] Commingling in Mississippi

Page 166. Add to footnote 210:

See also Cannon v. Cannon, 375 So. 3d 697, 712 (Miss. Ct. App. 2023) (funds from wife's premarital home were commingled into family home; both spouses contributed to home; not error to classify as marital and divide equally).

Page 166. Insert in text after sentence ending in footnote 210:

A 2024 Mississippi Supreme Court case appears to adopt the approach of most states to commingling, allowing a husband to trace separate funds that had been commingled in an account with marital funds throughout the marriage. His testimony that he used separate funds from the account to purchase land was sufficient to support classification of the property as separate. The court stated, "In *Oliver,* the Court of Appeals,...held that the transmutation of property does not automatically occur simply because they are placed in the same account. We opine that the intent of the court in *Johnson* and other cases of its kind was that a party must prove that these commingled funds were not only present in a joint marital account but were being used for the benefit of the other spouse and/or the entire family.'[210.1] In contrast, a wife's separate property funds that were commingled with marital funds and untraceable were converted to marital.[210.2]

[210.1] Cassell v. Cassell, 389 So. 3d 305, 315 (Miss. 2024) (citing the Mississippi minority line of cases). *But cf.* Woods v. Woods, 423 So. 3d 720, 733 (Miss. Ct. App. 2025) (house purchased before marriage became marital based on commingling of funds and family use during two-year marriage, even though purchased primarily with husband's separate contributions).

[210.2] Ware v. Ware, 387 So. 3d 1050 (Miss. Ct. App. 2024).

Page 166. Insert in text after sentence ending in footnote 211:

For example, a husband's retirement account was a mixed asset – the premarital value of $893,190 and passive growth of $322,403 on the premarital value was his separate property. The fact that he made additional contributions during marriage did not require marital classification of the entire account. The court stated, "The key to determining when there has been transmutation by commingling is whether the marital interest can be identified, i.e., can be traced."[211.1]

[211.1] *In re* Conservatorship of Geno, 365 So. 3d 287, 293-94 (Miss. Ct. App. 2021).

§ 6.06 Specific types of property

[7] Assets acquired with loan proceeds

Page 171. Add to footnote 255:

See also Franks v. Franks, 394 So. 3d 467, 480 (Miss. Ct. App. 2024) (husband's rental property classified as marital because wife signed promissory note for a loan on the property); Smith v. Smith, 379 So. 3d 954, 965, 966 (Miss. Ct. App. 2024) (land husband acquired during the marriage was marital; he repaid his father's loan to buy the property by taking out a credit line secured by the marital home and contributed marital funds to the business).

§ 6.07 Valuation

[1] The measure of value

Page 174. Add to footnote 287:

Cf. Dean v. Dean, 304 So. 3d 156, 165 (Miss. Ct. App. 2020) (in a case in which neither party provided reliable valuation, chancellor did not err in valuing husband's business using the amount paid to purchase the business four years earlier).

Page 174. Insert in text after sentence ending in footnote 293:

Assets held by businesses are valued as a part of the business. A chancellor did not err in in valuing 183 acres owned by the husband's business as an asset of the business. The court rejected the wife's argument that the land should have been valued separately at $818,520, the value assigned to the land in the parent company report. The report used book value, not fair market value. The chancellor properly included the land in the overall valuation of the parent company.[293.1]

[293.1] Case v. Case, 339 So. 3d 796, 812-13 (Miss. Ct. App. 2022).

[2] Findings of fact regarding value

Page 175. Add to footnote 294:

See Davis v. Davis, 361 So. 3d 725, 737-38 (Miss. Ct. App. 2023) (failure to value wife's hair styling business and husband's auto sales business, guns, and trailer); Johnson v. Johnson, 357 So. 3d 1168, 1175 (Miss. Ct. App. 2023) (failure to value marital assets); Williams v. Williams, 303 So. 3d 824, 833 (Miss. Ct. App. 2020) (failure to value marital businesses).

Page 175. Insert in text after sentence ending in footnote 297:

For example, a chancellor's failure to value lamps and pictures awarded to a wife did not require reversal – a chancellor is not required to value every item.[297.1]

[297.1] Warner v. Warner, 341 So. 3d 152, 160-61 (Miss. Ct. App. 2022).

Page 175. Add to footnote 300:

See Brown v. Brown, 350 So. 3d 1169, 1180 (Miss. Ct. App. 2022) (not error to value marital home close to the midpoint between parties' values).

Page 175. Insert in text after sentence ending in footnote 300:

When neither party provided a reliable business valuation, a chancellor properly valued the husband's business based on the amount he paid four years earlier to purchase the business.[300.1]

[300.1] Dean v. Dean, 304 So. 3d 156, 165 (Miss. Ct. App. 2020).

Page 176. Insert in text after sentence ending in footnote 307:

In recent years, the court of appeals has emphasized the importance of valuing personal property as well. The court reversed a chancellor's $30,000 lump sum valuation of personal property for failure to value individual items such as a boat, tractor, four-wheeler, golf cart, furniture, and appliances. Considering the high value, the chancellor should have required evidence of value for each item, assigned possession of each, and included the value in equitable distribution[307.1] And the court of appeals held that a chancellor erred in failing to state a value for a gun safe and contents valued by the wife at $31,000 and by the husband at $2,400. [307.2] In contrast, a chancellor did not err in awarding a wife sixty percent of assets in part because the husband had a significant retirement account, without valuing the account. The chancellor repeatedly requested that the husband provide a valuation which he failed to do.[307.3] In 2022, the court of appeals reversed a chancellor's valuation of a grandfather clock because the value was based on the chancellor's personal experience and not on evidence presented at trial. The court also reversed the chancellor's valuation of a curio cabinet and vehicle at an amount lower than the parties' stipulated values, based on the wife's statement that the actual value was lower – the chancellor did not explain the amount of the reduction.[307.4]

[307.1] Doe v. Doe, 341 So. 3d 953, 972-73 (Miss. Ct. App. 2021); *see also* Davis v. Davis, 361 So. 3d 725, 737-38 (Miss. Ct. App. 2023) (error to value items as a whole rather than individually); Brown v. Brown, 350 So. 3d 1169, 1180-82 (Miss. Ct. App. 2022) (chancellor erred in valuing personal property and equipment collectively and then assigning some assets to husband and some to wife, without valuing individual items).

[307.2] Begnaud v. Begnaud, 409 So. 3d 604, 611-12 (Miss. Ct. App. 2025).

[307.3] Denham v. Denham, 364 So. 3d 874, 892-93 (Miss. Ct. App. 2022), *reversed in part on other grounds*, 351 So. 3d 954 (Miss. 2022) (reversing custody but not reversing property division).

[307.4] Warner v. Warner, 341 So. 3d 152, 160-62 (Miss. Ct. App. 2022).

[3] Date of valuation

Page 177. Add to footnote 309:

See Bowman v. Bowman, 332 So. 3d 317, 327 (Miss. Ct. App. 2021) (chancellor properly valued automobile at the time of divorce rather than at the time of separation).

[5] Proof of value

[a] Expert testimony

Page 178. Add to footnote 323:

See also Brown v. Brown, 350 So. 3d 1169, 1184-85 (Miss. Ct. App. 2022) (rejecting husband's argument that chancellor should have secured expert to value husband's used-car business; chancellor could value based on evidence or appoint expert at his discretion).

Page 179. Add to footnote 326:

Cf. In re Conservatorship of Geno, 365 So. 3d 287, 295-96 (Miss. Ct. App. 2021) (valuing husband's law practice at $772,000, based on opinion of court-appointed expert).

[b] Testimony of the parties or other lay witnesses

Page 179. Insert in text after sentence ending in footnote 333:

And a chancellor did not err in accepting a husband's valuation of his poultry business based on his twenty-five years of experience in the business. [333.1]

[333.1] Norwood v. Norwood, 305 So. 3d 175, 179, 181 (Miss. Ct. App. 2020) (four dissenters argued it was error not to require valuation of couple's primary asset).

[c] Financial statements

Page 180. Add to footnote 338:

See also Dickinson v. Dickinson, 293 So. 3d 322, 331 (Miss. Ct. App. 2020) (chancellor did not err in accepting tax assessor's valuation of home rather than the husband's valuation for which he provided no support).

[e] Appraisals

Page 180. Insert in text after sentence ending in footnote 344:

The appellate courts have approved chancellors' use of tax appraisals to determine property value. A chancellor did not err in taking judicial notice of a tax assessor's valuation of the marital home as the measure of value when the parties presented substantially varying values.[344.1]

[344.1] Herron v. Herron, 338 So. 3d 662, 671 (Miss. Ct. App. 2022); *see also* Sullivan v. Sullivan, 942 So. 2d 305, 307 (Miss. Ct. App. 2006) (parties relied on figure).

[f] Sale of property [NEW]

In some cases, a chancellor may value property based on the amount for which it sold. A chancellor did not err in valuing a marital home based on the amount for which it sold during the proceedings, rather than the higher value included in the wife's financial statement.[344.2]

[344.2] Case v. Case, 339 So. 3d 796, 812 (Miss. Ct. App. 2022).

§6.08 DIVISION OF MARITAL PROPERTY

[1] Basic principles of division

[b] Equal division not required

Page 182. Insert in text after sentence ending in footnote 350:

For example, an award of 91% of assets and 90% of debt to a wife was not inequitable. She had limited resources and had contributed to the husband's business. The award allowed the court to avoid alimony and division of the husband's business.[350.1]

[350.1] Lacoste v. Lacoste, 313 So. 3d 1097, 1102-03 (Miss. Ct. App. 2021); *see also* Chambliss v. Chambliss, 385 So. 3d 1246, 1255-56 (Miss. Ct. App. 2023) (chancellor did not err in awarding wife 37% of marital assets – 30% of husband's $204,863 retirement plus $49,000 in personal property; wife dissipated assets and husband provided all financial support for family).

Page 182. Add to footnote 351:

See also Whitlock v. Whitlock, 421 So. 3d 638, 647-48 (Miss. Ct. App. 2025) (error to award wife assets valued at $90,000, plus a portion of the husband's FERS account, and alimony of $1,200 a month and husband only a portion of his FERS account and the value of a house burdened with equal debt) (award left him with a monthly deficit). *But cf.* Thornton v. Thornton, 2025 WL 3638400, at *12-13 (Miss. Ct. App. Dec. 16, 2025) (not error to award husband over $2 million in debt associated with his restaurant business; the business was profitable, earning over $100,000 net income a year; the debt was considered in reaching the -$123,000 value of the business).

[c] Division of each asset not required

Page 182. Insert in text after sentence ending in footnote 353:

The court of appeals also rejected a husband's argument that a chancellor erred in awarding his wife liquid assets while awarding him assets burdened with debt that he could not pay on his income. The court noted that his abuse ended the marriage and that he had the option of selling assets he could not afford.[353.1]

[353.1] Garner v. Garner, 343 So. 3d 1097, 1103-05 (Miss. Ct. App. 2022).

Page 182. Insert in text after sentence ending in footnote 354:

However, it is error to disregard a marital asset. A chancellor erred in failing to value and assign a wife's marital retirement account because the husband had not specifically requested division of the account.[354.1]

[354.1] Wooten v. Wooten, 333 So. 3d 610, 615-16 (Miss. Ct. App. 2022).

[g] Findings of fact

Page 183. Add to footnote 362:

Johnson v. Johnson, 297 So. 3d 342, 347 (Miss. Ct. App. 2020) (reversing for failure to address factors).

Page 184. Add to footnote 365:

See also Begnaud v. Begnaud, 409 So. 3d 604, 613-14 (Miss. Ct. App. 2025) (court erred in failing to consider tax consequences to wife who would have to liquidate retirement account to meet expenses).

Page 184. Insert in text after sentence ending in footnote 365:

And the court of appeals reversed and remanded a chancellor's property division for failure to consider debt as part of the *Ferguson* analysis and failure to address a wife's separate property diamond ring as part of the analysis.[365.1] A chancellor's statement that she reviewed the factors was not sufficient in the absence of specific findings regarding the parties' contributions to accumulation of assets, the husband's disposition of assets, large expenditures, marital fault, and the disparity in their incomes.[365.2]

[365.1] Warner v. Warner, 341 So. 3d 152, 162-64 (Miss. Ct. App. 2022).

[365.2] Sistrunk v. Sistrunk, 407 So. 3d 207, 216-217 (Miss. 2025) (also instructing chancellor to consider under "other factors" that wife was responsible for caring for an adult disabled daughter).

Page 184. Add to footnote 366:

Cf. Johnson v. Johnson, 376 So. 3d 362, 369-70 (Miss. Ct. App. 2023) (rejecting husband's argument that chancellor should have used *Armstrong* alimony factors.

Page 184. Add to footnote 372:

See Johnson v. Johnson, 357 So. 3d 1168, 1175 (Miss. Ct. App. 2023) (chancellor cited *Ferguson* but did not include analysis of factors).

Page 185. Add to footnote 374:

See also Bowman v. Bowman, 332 So. 3d 317, 323-25 (Miss. Ct. App. 2021) (opinion did not explicitly discuss factors but chancellor considered the parties' contributions and dissipation of assets) (several factors were irrelevant in a short marriage).

Page 185. Insert in text after sentence ending in footnote 374:

A division of assets based on clearly erroneous findings will be reversed. The court of appeals reversed equal division of marital accounts based on a chancellor's finding that it was impossible to determine the parties' contributions to joint accounts. Expert testimony clearly established that the husband contributed significantly more to the accounts.[374.1]

[374.1] Bowman v. Bowman,332 So. 3d 317, 325-26 (Miss. Ct. App. 2021).

[2] The *Ferguson* factors

[a] Contribution to accumulation of assets

[i] Homemaker contribution

Page 187. Insert in text after sentence ending in footnote 395:

A chancellor erred in awarding a wife 50% of marital assets without making findings of fact on her contributions as homemaker in a case in which the evidence conflicted sharply regarding the value of her contributions.[395.1]

[395.1] Tauzin v. Tauzin, 2025 WL 2317673, at *12 (Miss. Ct. App. Aug. 12, 2025) (there must be "credible evidence that [the homemaker] contributed to the family's needs or to the stability and harmony of the marriage").

Page 187. Add to footnote 400:

See Chambliss v. Chambliss, 385 So. 3d 1246, 1255-56 (Miss. Ct. App. 2023) (chancellor did not err in awarding homemaker wife 37% of marital assets – 30% of husband's $204,863 retirement plus $49,000 in personal property; wife dissipated assets by buying marijuana; husband made all financial contributions).

[ii] Financial contribution

Page 189. Add to footnote 411:

See also Chambliss v. Chambliss, 385 So. 3d 1246, 1255-56 (Miss. Ct. App. 2023) (chancellor did not err in awarding homemaker wife less than one half of marital assets; husband provided all financial support for family; wife dissipated assets).

Page 189. Add to footnote 413:

Cf. Bowman v. Bowman, 332 So. 3d 317, 325-26 (Miss. Ct. App. 2021) (reversing chancellor's equal division of marital accounts based on chancellor's finding that it was impossible to determine contributions; expert testimony established that husband contributed more).

[iv] Contribution to marital stability

Page 191. Add to footnote 431:

See also Pond v. Pond, 302 So. 3d 1236, 1242-43 (Miss. Ct. App. 2020) (wife awarded a greater share than husband whose addiction, financial mismanagement, and resulting periods of unemployment and treatment affected the family's finances and stability) (also considering his post-separation adultery as a lesser factor); Dean v. Dean, 304 So. 3d 156, 169-70 (Miss. Ct. App. 2020) (awarding 65% of assets to husband with larger separate estate based on contribution to family stability; wife's addiction, arrests, treatment, wrecks, and inability to provide childcare negatively impacted family).

[b] Need

Page 191. Add to footnote 434:

See also Lacoste v. Lacoste, 313 So. 3d 1097, 1102-03 (Miss. Ct. App. 2021) (award of 91% of assets and 90% of debt to wife based on need).

Page 192. Insert in text after sentence ending in footnote 437:

An unemployed wife, who had been seriously injured in a wreck, was awarded only 35% of marital assets in spite of her greater need. Her husband provided the financial and emotional support for the family while her addiction, treatment, legal problems, extramarital affairs, and arrests negatively impacted the family.[437.1]

[437.1] Dean v. Dean, 304 So. 3d 156, 169-70 (Miss. Ct. App. 2020).

[c] Spouse's separate estate

Page 192. Insert in text after sentence ending in footnote 441:

In a 2022 case, the court of appeals reversed and remanded a chancellor's property division in part for failure to consider the wife's separate property diamond ring, valued at between $14,000 and $25,000, in the *Ferguson* analysis.[441.1]

[441.1] Warner v. Warner, 341 So. 3d 152, 164 (Miss. Ct. App. 2022) (also reversing for failure to value certain items).

[d] Elimination of need for alimony

Page 193. Add to footnote 443:

See also Manor v. Manor, 404 So. 3d 1256, 1264-65 (Miss. Ct. App. 2024) (award of sixty percent of assets to wife in part to avoid need for alimony); Lacoste v. Lacoste, 313 So. 3d 1097, 1102-03 (Miss. Ct. App. 2021) (award of 91% of assets and 90% of debt to wife avoided need to award alimony).

[e] Fault as factor

Page 193. Add to footnote 446:

Cf. Garner v. Garner, 343 So. 3d 1097, 1104-04 (Miss. Ct. App. 2022) (husband awarded 48% of assets in spite of abusive behavior that led to deterioration of marriage).

Page 193. Add to footnote 447:

See Coleman v. Coleman, 324 So. 3d 1204, 1211 n.4 (Miss. Ct. App. 2021) (chancellor did not err in finding that a husband's inappropriate communication with other women was a cause of disharmony in the marriage).

Page 193. Add to footnote 448:

See also Hammond v. Hammond, 327 So. 3d 173, 179 (Miss. Ct. App. 2021) (reversing award of 55% of assets to wife because chancellor failed to consider husband's affair that ended the marriage, caused his wife's depression, and affected his children).

Page 193. Insert in text after sentence ending in footnote 448:

In contrast, a chancellor did not err in dividing marital assets roughly equally in spite of a husband's adultery. The wife presented no evidence that it impacted the marriage.[448.1]

[448.1] Alves-Hunter v. Hunter, 351 So. 3d 468, 480 (Miss. Ct. App. 2022). *See also* McKenzie v. McKenzie, 397 So. 3d 510, 518-19 (Miss. Ct. App. 2024) (equal division even though husband's alcohol use caused marriage to fail; both contributed equally to the accumulation of assets); Doe v. Doe, 341 So. 3d 953, 969 (Miss. Ct. App. 2021) (reversing division based in part on fault; chancellor erred in finding that husband transmitted an STD to his wife based on judicial notice of medical facts).

[f] Prior use or disposition of assets

[i] Dissipation of assets

Page 195. Insert in text after sentence ending in footnote 462:

A wife's cash-out of her marital retirement account and unilateral decision to use it to send children to private school, without consulting her husband, was dissipation of assets.[462.1] And a chancellor properly awarded less than half of the marital estate to a wife who dissipated assets by purchasing marijuana four to five times a week.[462.2]

[462.1] Gaskin v. Gaskin, 304 So. 3d 641, 646-47, 651 (Miss. Ct. App. 2020) (husband also dissipated assets by purchasing home during separation and while having an affair).

[462.2] Chambliss v. Chambliss, 385 So. 3d 1246, 1254-55 (Miss. Ct. App. 2023) (husband provided all financial support for family; wife's alleged inability to work was not supported by the evidence).

Page 195. Insert in text after sentence ending in footnote 463:

A husband whose post-separation mismanagement of properties substantially depleted marital assets was properly awarded a smaller share of assets despite his financial contributions during the marriage.[463.1]

[463.1] Poisso v. Poisso, 300 So. 3d 1067, 1075-78 (Miss. Ct. App. 2020) (husband closed a store, foregoing substantial income, and lost multiple properties to foreclosure).

Page 195. Insert in text after sentence ending in footnote 465:

In a 2021 decision, the court of appeals held that the factor of dissipation of assets applies only to marital property, rejecting a husband's argument that his wife dissipated his separate property. Any claim for a spouse's misuse of the other's separate funds should be pursued as a claim separate from equitable distribution.[465.1]

[465.1] Hatton v. Hatton, 323 So. 3d 1149, 1154 (Miss. Ct. App. 2021).

Page 196. Add to footnote 469:

See also Alves-Hunter v. Hunter, 351 So. 3d 468, 481 (Miss. Ct. App. 2022) (wife's share of assets included $20,000 she withdrew from an account after their separation).

Page 196. Insert in text after sentence ending in footnote 473:

In a 2021 case, the court of appeals held that a chancellor erred in finding that a wife dissipated $200,000 in marital assets without making specific findings of fact. Her husband presented evidence that she dissipated $595,269 in assets.[473.1]

[473.1] *In re* Conservatorship of Geno, 365 So. 3d 287, 298-99 (Miss. Ct. App. 2021).

Page 198. Insert in text after sentence ending in footnote 484:

And a chancellor should have considered the tax consequences to a wife who testified that she would have to liquidate the retirement account that constituted most of her share of property division to meet her expenses.[484.1]

[484.1] Begnaud v. Begnaud, 409 So. 3d 604, 613-14 (Miss. Ct. App. 2025).

Page 198. Insert in text after sentence ending in footnote 484:

[i] Any other factor "which in equity should be considered" [NEW]

In a 2025 case, the supreme court held that a chancellor should have considered, under the catch-all *Ferguson* factor, that the wife was responsible for the care of and financial support for their adult disabled daughter.[484.2]

[484.2] Sistrunk v. Sistrunk, 407 So. 3d 207, 216-17 (Miss. 2025).

[4] Assignment of debt

Page 200. Add to footnote 505:

See Davidson v. Davidson, 369 So. 3d 607, 615 (Miss. Ct. App. 2023) (credit card debt incurred before separation was for family expenditures, including gas, utility bills, and insurance, and benefited both parties).

Page 202. Insert in text after sentence ending in footnote 520:

However, in 2022, the court of appeals held that a chancellor erred in dividing assets pursuant to the *Ferguson* analysis and then assigning debt without discussing the reason for the assignment. The court stated that debt must be considered as part of the *Ferguson* analysis.[520.1]

[520.1] Warner v. Warner, 341 So. 3d 152, 163 (Miss. Ct. App. 2022).

Page 202. Insert in text after sentence ending in 523:

In another case, however, the court of appeals held that a chancellor erred in assigning an $18,000 marital debt solely to the husband, stating that nothing in the record supported allocation of the full debt to him. The chancellor divided the debt equally at trial but amended the order post-trial without explanation for the change. The court ordered that on remand, the chancellor should allocate half to each spouse or provide a reason for an uneven division. [523.1]

[523.1] Doe v. Doe, 341 So. 3d 953, 973-74 (Miss. Ct. App. 2021).

[5] Unequal division

Page 202. Add to footnote 527:

See also Chambliss v. Chambliss, 385 So. 3d 1246, 1254-55 (Miss. Ct. App. 2023) (award of one half of personal property and 30% of husband's retirement equaled 37% of estate; husband made all financial contributions and wife dissipated assets).

Page 203. Insert in text after sentence ending in footnote 535:

In a 2020 case, the court of appeals affirmed an award of 91% of assets and 90% of debt to a lower-income wife based on need, her contribution to the family, and because the division would eliminate the need for alimony and avoid having to divide the husband's business.[535.1]

[535.1] Lacoste v. Lacoste, 313 So. 3d 1097, 1102-03 (Miss. Ct. App. 2021).

§ 6.09 RIGHTS OF THIRD PARTIES

[1] Impact on third-party interests

Page 204. Add to footnote 540:

Cf. Wildman v. Wildman, 301 So. 3d 787, 800-01 (Miss. Ct. App. 2020) (chancellor erred in finding that a $19,000 joint account in the names of the wife and her father, funded by her father, was his property and not partly her separate property).

[4] Constructive trust

Page 205. Insert in text after sentence ending in footnote 552:

For example, a divorcing wife's mother was properly awarded a constructive trust for life in a home she built on the couple's property with her funds and with the understanding that she would leave the home to the couple at her death.[552.1]

[552.1] Herron v. Herron, 338 So. 3d 662, 669-670 (Miss. Ct. App. 2022) (rejecting husband's argument that a constructive trust must be based on abuse of a confidential relationship).

§ 6.12 Mechanics of division

[2] Monetary award

Page 210. Insert in text after sentence ending in footnote 585:

When lump sum alimony is awarded as part of property division, the court should use the *Ferguson* factors – not the *Armstrong* alimony factors.[585.1]

[585.1] Johnson v. Johnson, 376 So. 3d 362, 369-70 (Miss. Ct. App. 2023).

[3] Sale of assets and division of proceeds

Page 210. Add to footnote 589:

See also Pace v. Pace, 324 So. 3d 369, 379-80 (Miss. Ct. App. 2021) (affirming order that wife of husband who forfeited his medical license sell the marital home, the husband's medical practice building, and other items with a total value of approximately $1,000,000 and divide the proceeds equally after payment of expenses).

[9] Security for payment

Page 213. Insert in text after sentence ending in footnote 614:

Ordinarily, for a judgment to operate as a lien it must be enrolled in the circuit clerk's office.[614.1] In a 2023 case, however, the supreme court clarified that an equitable lien granted in a divorce action need not be enrolled to be enforceable against parties with knowledge of the interest. A wife's equitable lien, established in her property settlement agreement, was enforceable against her husband's certificates of stock or the proceeds of their sale.[614.2]

[614.1] *See* Richardson v. Estate of Richardson, 392 So. 3d 1272, 1275 (Miss. Ct. App. 2024).

[614.2] West v. West, 371 So. 3d 145, 163 (Miss. 2023) (remanding to determine priority of wife's lien and corporation's lien).

Page 213. Insert in text after sentence ending in footnote 619:

In a 2025 case, the court of appeals held that an obligation to maintain life insurance to secure property division payments is nonmodifiable as a property division provision. In contrast, life insurance securing child support is modifiable. A payor's obligation to maintain insurance for both property and child support payments, which did not separate the obligations, was nonmodifiable.[619.1]

[619.1] J.T.S. V. M.L.S., 2025 WL 12206928, at *17 (Miss. Ct. App. Dec. 16, 2025) (chancellor erred in reducing required amount from $1 million to $400,000 after four of five children were emancipated).

§ 6.13 Modification and enforcement

[3] Frustration of purpose

Page 215. Insert in text after sentence ending in footnote 633:

When a wife could not secure a loan to pay her husband's share of the marital home equity, the chancellor properly ordered the home sold and the husband paid from the proceeds.[633.1]

[633.1] Archie v. Archie, 337 So. 3d 698, 703 (Miss. Ct. App. 2022); *see also* Pace v. Pace, 387 So. 3d 1067, 1076-77 (Miss. Ct. App. 2024) (chancellor properly revised judgment ordering sale of a commercial building and division of the proceeds to allow husband to buy out wife's equity – the parties were unable to sell the building after several years of attempts).

VII
RETIREMENT BENEFITS

§ 7.02 The Equitable Distribution Process

Page 220. Insert in text after sentence ending in footnote 24:

[4] Burden of proof [NEW]

In a 2025 case, the court of appeals held that a chancellor erred in classifying a husband's retirement benefit (acquired before and during marriage) as all marital because he failed to prove the amount of the premarital portion. The court relied on *Arthur v. Arthur*, 691 So. 3d 997 (Miss. 1997), as holding that a chancellor must determine the premarital portion of a retirement account even if neither of the parties presented evidence – the premarital portion of a retirement account cannot be treated as marital property.[24.1]

[24.1] Tauzin v. Tauzin, 2025 WL 2317673, at *8, *9 (Miss. Ct. App. Aug. 12, 2025) (quoting the concurring opinion in *Arthur* that "both parties bear responsibility" for presenting evidence on the issue).

§ 7.03 Defined contribution plans

[2] Classification

Page 221. Insert in text after sentence ending in footnote 27:

For example, a husband's retirement account was a mixed asset – the premarital value of $893,190 and passive growth of $322,403 on that amount was his separate property. The fact that he made additional contributions during marriage did not require marital classification of the entire account.[27.1]

[27.1] *In re* Conservatorship of Geno, 365 So. 3d 287, 293-94 (Miss. Ct. App. 2021) ("The key to determining when there has been transmutation by commingling is whether the marital interest can be identified, i.e., can be traced.") (quoting Brock v. Brock, 906 So. 2d 879, 888 (Miss. Ct. App. 2005)).

§ 7.04 Defined benefit plans

[1] Deferred distribution

[a] Classification

Page 223. Add to footnote 48:

See also Sullivan v. Sullivan, 302 So. 3d 1280, 1282 (Miss. Ct. App. 2020) (chancellor properly calculated the marital portion of husband's PERS account as 32%, dividing the number of years worked during the marriage (12) by the total number of years in service (38.75)).

Page 223. Add to footnote 49:

See also Johnson v. Johnson, 376 So. 3d 362, 371-72 (Miss. Ct. App. 2023) (properly finding that husband's military pension was 89% marital because twenty-five of twenty-eight years of service were during marriage) (awarding wife 45% of pension and 45% of military survivors' benefits).

Page 223. Insert in text after sentence ending in footnote 49:

However, a court did not err in awarding a wife 45% of her husband's pension rather than 50%, in recognition that he contributed to the fund for six years prior to their eighteen-year marriage. The husband provided no proof to divide the separate and marital portions.[49.1]

[49.1] Lageman v. Lageman, 313 So. 3d 1075, 1081 (Miss. Ct. App. 2021) (rejecting husband's argument that court should have classified the separate portions; division was fair based on the limited information available).

[2] Immediate offset

Page 224. Replace the last sentence in the first paragraph with the following:

A court may place a present value on the future benefit, classify the separate and marital portions, and award the nonemployee spouse a share of that value, to be compensated through payment of a lump sum or by an award of other property of equal value. Or, the employee may be ordered to pay their spouse a portion of the pension as it is received. The court of appeals rejected a wife's argument that she was entitled to a lump sum for her share of her husband's PERS benefits – ordering him to pay her monthly was a form of deferred distribution that was not error.[51.1]

[51.1] Sullivan v. Sullivan, 302 So. 3d 1280, 1281 (Miss. Ct. App. 2020).

[a] Valuation

Page 224. Add to footnote 56:

Cf. Pond v. Pond, 302 So. 3d 1236, 1239-40 (Miss. Ct. App. 2020) (affirming court's valuation of husband's pension at the same amount as his wife's, based on evidence that they had similar salaries, work history, and type of employment; husband initially failed to disclose the pension and when asked, said that he did not know the value).

Page 224. Insert in text after sentence ending in footnote 57:

And a chancellor did not err in using the cash-out value of a wife's PERS account rather than the present value as calculated by her expert witness. She had left employment, cashed out the account, was disabled, and might not be able to return to work. Considering the uncertainty surrounding the future stream of payments and the fact that she had in fact cashed out the retirement, using this value was appropriate.[57.1]

[57.1] Gaskin v. Gaskin, 304 So. 3d 641, 646-47 (Miss. Ct. App. 2020).

§ 7.07 MILITARY RETIRED PAY AND DISABILITY BENEFITS

[1] Military retired pay

Page 229. Insert in text after sentence ending in footnote 101:

Courts typically apply the same formula for classifying the separate and marital portions of military retirement plans as are used for non-military pensions.[101.1] In the case of National Guard and Reserve pensions, however, some authorities argue that the better rule is to use points acquired before and during marriage, rather than years of service before and during marriage, to classify the retirement.[101.2] In one case, the Mississippi Court of Appeals rejected a husband's argument that the marital share of his retirement should be determined based on points, not on years of service. The parties were married for fifteen of the twenty years of his military service. He argued that because he accumulated more retirement points prior to the marriage (2,120) than during the marriage (1,197), the court should have based the formula on marital points rather than marital years of service. The court of appeals disagreed, holding that the chancellor did not err in relying on the number of years of the marriage.[101.3]

[101.1] *See* Gerty v. Gerty, 296 So. 3d 704, 707-09 (Miss. 2020) (chancellor properly divided military retirement by dividing the number of months the husband served during the marriage by the total number of months served, and awarding the wife one-half of the marital portion, but miscalculated the number of months during the marriage).

[101.2] Patricia Shewmaker & James R. Lewis, The Complete QDRO Handbook, § 11.15 (4th ed. 2019); Mark E. Sullivan, The Military Divorce Handbook § 8.18, at 774 (3d ed. 2019).

[101.3] Ward v. Ward, 131 So. 3d 1244, 1250-51 (Miss. Ct. App. 2014).

[b] Division

[iv] Survivor benefits

Page 231. Insert in text after sentence ending in footnote 118:

The court of appeals held that a chancellor properly awarded a wife 45% of her husband's military survivors' benefits, representing one half of the marital portion of the pension.[118.1]

[118.1] Johnson v. Johnson, 376 So. 3d 362, 371-72 (Miss. Ct. App. 2023) (awarding wife 45% of pension and 45% of military survivors' benefits).

[2] Military disability benefits

[a] Agreements to divide disability

Page 231. Insert in text after sentence ending in footnote 122:

In a 2023 case, the court of appeals interpreted a couple's property settlement agreement giving the wife a 50% interest in her husband's "military retirement" to include military disability benefits. The agreement referenced a specific amount that included disability pay.[122.1]

[122.1] Manley v. Manley, 378 So. 3d 390, 395 (Miss. Ct. App. 2023). The dissenters urged that the USFSPA bars division of military disability benefits. *Id.* at 400. The majority did not disagree with this point but held that the husband waived the issue by failing to raise it at trial or on appeal. Neither opinion cites *Mosher*, the 2016 case. It does not appear that the husband in *Mosher* argued that the couple's agreement was unenforceable under the USFSPA. See Mosher v. Mosher, 192 So. 3d 1118 (Miss. Ct. App. 2016).

Page 232. Insert in text after sentence ending in footnote 132:

A serviceperson must raise the issue at trial or on appeal. A husband was barred from arguing in a collateral proceeding that a court lacked jurisdiction to order payment of military disability benefits. The court noted that he should have appealed the ruling.[132.1]

[132.1] McFall v. Osborne, 424 So. 3d 286, 292-93 (Miss. Ct. App. 2025) (court had subject matter jurisdiction over the matter).

§ 7.11 State benefits

Page 234. Add to footnote 151:

See also Sullivan v. Sullivan, 302 So. 3d 1280, 1282, 1285 (Miss. Ct. App. 2020) (wife awarded one-half of marital share of husband's pension (32%) plus one-half of 32% of annual cost-of-living increase).

Page 234. Add to footnote 154:

See § 7.04[3] for a discussion of valuation.

Page 234. Insert in text after sentence ending in footnote 155:

The court of appeals revisited this issue in 2020, holding that a court's order that a husband pay his wife one-half of the marital share of his PERS pension was a form of deferred distribution and not alimony. The court of appeals also affirmed the chancellor's order that he pay her one-half of the marital portion of his annual cost-of-living increase.[155.1]

[155.1] Sullivan v. Sullivan, 302 So. 3d 1280, 1281, 1285 (Miss. Ct. App. 2020).

VIII
DIVISION OF CLOSELY HELD BUSINESSES

§ 8.03 Classification: Separate and marital portions

[1] Marital property interest

[b] Acquired with joint loans or loans secured by marital assets

Page 239. Insert in text after sentence ending in footnote 10:

A husband's rental property was properly classified as marital – his wife signed a promissory note for a loan on the property.[10.1]

[10.1] Franks v. Franks, 394 So. 3d 467, 480 (Miss. Ct. App. 2024).

[2] Separate property interest

Page 240. Add to footnote 20:

See also In re Conservatorship of Geno, 365 So. 3d 287, 293 (Miss. Ct. App. 2021) (a husband's premarital LLC was separate property; the fact that his law practice paid rent to the LLC did not convert it to marital).

[3] Mixed asset

[b] Appreciated value of separate property business

Page 241. Insert in text after sentence ending in footnote 26:

And a chancellor erred in classifying a husband's premarital business as all separate – he used marital funds to pay business debt during the marriage.[26.1]

[26.1] Wallace v. Wallace, 309 So. 3d 104, 109 (Miss. Ct. App. 2020).

[4] Burden of proof

Page 242. Add to footnote 34:

See Dean v. Dean, 304 So. 3d 156, 166 (Miss. Ct. App. 2020) (wife had burden of proving that husband's premarital business appreciated during the marriage and that the appreciation was marital).

Page 242. Insert in text after sentence ending in footnote 36:

The supreme clarified the burden of proof in a 2024 case, holding that the presumption in favor of marital property applies only to assets acquired during marriage – not to premarital property. Accordingly, the spouse seeking separate property classification has the burden of proof with regard to assets acquired during marriage. The nonowning spouse has the burden of proof with regard to assets acquired outside of marriage – the presumption does not apply to those assets.[36.1]

[36.1] Cassell v. Cassell, 389 So. 3d 305, 314-15 (Miss. 2024).

§ 8.04 Valuation

[1] Expert valuation

[a] Goodwill excluded

Page 244. Add to footnote 50:

See also Lacoste v. Lacoste, 313 So. 3d 1097, 1102 (Miss. Ct. App. 2021) (after remand for proper valuation, chancellor valued husband's business at $13,900, excluding goodwill, as opposed to the earlier $347,417 valuation); Descher v. Descher, 304 So. 3d 620, 623 (Miss. Ct. App. 2020) (marital estate composed of thirteen McDonald's franchises; valuation without goodwill was approximately equal to one year's profit from the businesses).

[b] Net asset method

Page 244. Add to footnote 56:

See Roberts v. Roberts, 412 So. 3d 1256, 1262-63 (Miss. Ct. App. 2025) (chancellor erred in valuing husband's business at $149,000 based on four years of income; the only business asset was a desktop computer); Smith v. Smith, 379 So. 3d 954, 967-68 (Miss. Ct. App. 2024) (use of goodwill is prohibited in business valuation in divorce).

[2] Other evidence of value

Page 245. Add to footnote 65:

See also Norwood v. Norwood, 305 So. 3d 175, 177-78 (Miss. Ct. App. 2020) (chancellor did not err in accepting a husband's valuation of his poultry business based on his twenty-five years of experience in the business).

Page 245. Insert in text after sentence ending in footnote 66:

When neither party provided a reliable business valuation, a chancellor properly valued the husband's business based on the amount he paid four years earlier to purchase the business.[66.1]

[66.1] Dean v. Dean, 304 So. 3d 156, 163-65 (Miss. Ct. App. 2020).

IX
ALIMONY

§ 9.01 History and overview

[6] General considerations
[d] Relationship to equitable distribution

Page 261. Add to footnote 88:

See also In re Conservatorship of Geno, 365 So. 3d 287, 299 (Miss. Ct. App. 2021) (permanent alimony may be reconsidered when property division is reversed).

§ 9.02 Types of alimony

[1] Permanent alimony
[g] Termination

Page 264. Add to footnote 106:

See Phang v. Phang, 350 So. 3d 1154, 1163 (Miss. Ct. App. 2022) (chancellor erred in specifying that alimony would end upon the wife's remarriage or death, without specifying that it would also end upon the husband's death).

[2] Lump sum alimony
[b] Modern lump sum alimony

Page 267. Add to footnote 130:

See also Gussio v. Gussio, 371 So. 3d 734, 749-50 (Miss. Ct. App. 2023) (awarding $125,000 in lump sum alimony to wife whose husband had substantial separate assets protected by prenuptial agreement).

[c] Factors

Page 268. Insert in text after sentence ending in footnote 135:

In 2025, the supreme court explicitly overruled *Cheatham*, holding that it was error to use the *Cheatham* factors to determine the proper amount of lump sum alimony – the *Armstrong* factors should be used for all types of alimony awards. [135.1] When lump sum alimony is awarded as part of property division, courts should use the *Ferguson* factors for property division.[135.2]

[135.1] Cassell v. Cassell, 389 So. 3d 305, 316 (Miss. 2024).

[135.2] Johnson v. Johnson, 376 So. 3d 362, 369-70 (Miss. Ct. App. 2023).

[3] Rehabilitative alimony

[a] Purpose

Page 269. Add to footnote 153:

See also Case v. Case, 339 So. 3d 796, 815-16 (Miss. Ct. App. 2022) (four years of rehabilitative alimony of $2,500 appropriate for wife of fourteen years who planned to go to college).

Page 269. Add to footnote 154:

See Case v. Case, 339 So. 3d 796, 815 (Miss. Ct. App. 2022).

Page 270. Add to footnote 158:

See also Denham v. Denham, 364 So. 3d 874, 894 (Miss. Ct. App. 2022), *reversed in part on other grounds*, 351 So. 3d 954 (Miss. 2022) (not error to award working wife rehabilitative alimony; appropriate to award short-term alimony to help lower-income spouse transition financially).

[4] Reimbursement alimony

[a] Purpose

Page 272. Insert in text after sentence ending in footnote 174:

In a 2023 case, the court of appeals affirmed a chancellor's $125,879 award to a husband to reimburse him for paying his wife's nursing degree student loan debt with his separate funds. She filed for divorce and custody four years later.[174.1]

[174.1] Whittington v. Whittington, 373 So. 3d 1060, 1064-65 (Miss. Ct. App. 2023).

§ 9.04 Test for awarding alimony

[2] Findings of fact

Page 277. Add to footnote 222:

See Warren v. Rhea, 318 So. 3d 1187, 1192 (Miss. Ct. App. 2021) (failure to address *Armstrong* factors did not require reversal; chancellor considered marriage length and income disparity).

Page 278. Insert in text after sentence ending in footnote 229:

In a 2022 case, the court of appeals reversed a chancellor's award of $3,500 in alimony to a wife for failure to consider her separate property diamond ring, piano, jet ski, and golf cart and for failure to consider $10,000 in debt assigned to the higher-income husband.[229.1]

[229.1] Warner v. Warner, 341 So. 3d 152, 165 (Miss. Ct. App. 2022).

Page 279. Add to footnote 231:

But cf. Ewing v. Ewing, 301 So. 3d 709, 714 (Miss. Ct. App. 2020) (holding on remand that award of $500 in alimony and $938 in child support, leaving father with $1,879 a month, was not excessive; mother was supporting four children); Descher v. Descher, 304 So. 3d 620, 623 (Miss. Ct. App. 2020) (rejecting husband's argument that combined awards of $856,000 lump sum alimony, $7,500 permanent alimony, and $7,500 child support were excessive; husband had $71,000 net monthly income).

Page 279. Insert in text after sentence ending in footnote 231:

Similarly, a chancellor erred in ordering a husband with net income of $10,049 a month to pay $3,000 a month in alimony, $1,800 in child support, private school tuition, and lump sum alimony – two-thirds of his net income – leaving him unable to meet his monthly expenses.[231.1] And a chancellor abused his discretion in ordering a father with a second family, whose income dropped from $218,000 to $84,000, to pay combined child support and alimony of $36,000 a year to a wife who earned $40,000.[231.2]

[231.1] Wildman v. Wildman, 301 So. 3d 787, 798 (Miss. Ct. App. 2020). *See also* Whitlock v. Whitlock, 421 So. 3d 638, 647-48 (Miss. Ct. App. 2025) (error to award wife assets valued at $90,000, plus a portion of the husband's FERS account, and alimony of $1,200 a month and husband only a portion of his FERS account and the value of a house burdened with equal debt) (award left him with a monthly deficit).

[231.2] Krohn v. Krohn, 294 So. 3d 680, 688 (Miss. Ct. App. 2020).

[4] Factors related to financial disparity

[a] Income of the parties

[i] Income included

Page 281. Insert in text after sentence ending in footnote 239:

Similarly, a chancellor did not err in considering a husband's separate property military retirement as income for purposes of alimony. In determining alimony, a court should consider all sources of income, including income from separate property.[239.1]

[239.1] Ray v. Ray, 304 So. 3d 598, 600-01 (Miss. 2020).

[iii] Imputed income

Page 281. Add to footnote 245:

See also Garner v. Garner, 343 So. 3d 1097, 1105-06 (Miss. Ct. App. 2022) (husband of eight years earning $42,000 a year awarded $508 a month in rehabilitative alimony for two years; he was trained as an engineer and could earn more by acquiring his license; his abuse ended the marriage; his wife had custody of their children).

Page 281. Add to footnote 246:

Cf. Chambliss v. Chambliss, 385 So. 3d 1246, 1256-57 (Miss. Ct. App. 2023) (wife's claimed inability to work was not supported by evidence; denying permanent or rehabilitative alimony but awarding her $1,800 a month for twelve years for health insurance).

Page 282. Add to footnote 248:

But cf. Gussio v. Gussio, 371 So. 3d 734, 737 (Miss. Ct. App. 2023) (rejecting husband's argument that income should be imputed to his wife based on her parents' assistance during divorce; they had no obligation to assist her and were strained financially by the assistance).

Page 282. Add to footnote 249:

See also Gussio v. Gussio, 371 So. 3d 734, 746 (Miss. Ct. App. 2023) (imputing income to husband based on finding that he understated his income).

Page 282. Insert in text after sentence ending in footnote 251:

However, the court of appeals reversed a chancellor's award of alimony based in part on imputed income when the basis of the imputation was not clear. The court held that the chancellor should explain the basis for imputing $6,000 a month in income to a husband based on his monthly $10,000 in charges to a credit company card, some of which were work-related.[251.1]

[251.1] Warner v. Warner, 341 So. 3d 152, 166 (Miss. Ct. App. 2022).

[b] Earning capacity

Page 282. Add to footnote 252:

See also Baird v. Baird, 2025 WL 2962388, at *7 (Miss. Ct. App. Oct. 21, 2025) (homemaker wife of twenty years, whose husband had custody of five children, properly awarded six months of rehabilitative alimony; she had a lapsed teaching certificate and could earn more than her current part-time work at a hotel).

Page 283. Add to footnote 253:

See also McKenzie v. McKenzie, 397 So. 3d 510, 522 (Miss. Ct. App. 2024) (awarding rehabilitative alimony to a thirty-six-year-old homemaker wife who had previously worked and who received marital assets of approximately $1.7 million).

Page 283. Insert in text after sentence ending in footnote 255:

In one case involving a very high income payor, the court disregarded a wife's modest earning capacity, awarding her alimony in an amount sufficient to meet her stated expenses without regard to her earning capacity of $2,000 a month.[255.1] In contrast, a chancellor erred in ordering a husband to pay his wife $3,000 in alimony to meet her $2,900 a month deficit, without considering that she could substantially increase her earnings by working full time as a nurse anesthetist.[255.2]

[255.1] Descher v. Descher, 304 So. 3d 620, 630-32 (Miss. Ct. App. 2020) (dissent argued that court should have considered her earning capacity).

[255.2] Wildman v. Wildman, 301 So. 3d 787, 796 (Miss. Ct. App. 2020).

[c] Standard of living of the marriage

Page 284. Insert in text after sentence ending in footnote 263:

A wife with low earning capacity was properly awarded $7,500 in alimony and $7,500 in child support, in addition to a lump sum alimony award of $856,794, from a husband with net monthly income of $71,000. The court of appeals held that the award was appropriate considering the standard of living of the marriage and the enormous disparity between their incomes.[263.1]

[263.1] Descher v. Descher, 304 So. 3d 620, 623 (Miss. Ct. App. 2020) (dissent argued that court should have considered her earning capacity of $2,000 a month toward meeting her expenses).

Page 284. Insert in text after sentence ending in footnote 266:

And the court of appeals rejected a wife's argument that an alimony award of $2,500, combined with a debt-free home and $1.25 million in cash, would not allow her to live at the marriage standard of living. Because of a reduction in her husband's income, neither could maintain the marriage standard of living.[266.1]

[266.1] *In re* Conservatorship of Geno, 365 So. 3d 287, 294-95 (Miss. Ct. App. 2021). *See also* McKenzie v. McKenzie, 397 So. 3d 510, 522 (Miss. Ct. App. 2024) (because of husband's drastically reduced income neither spouse would live at the standard of living of the marriage).

[f] Presence or absence of children in the home requiring childcare

Page 287. Insert in text after sentence ending in footnote 295:

Similarly, alimony of $500 was appropriate for a mother with custody of four children, even though the award left her former husband with slightly less income than her after he paid child support and alimony.[295.1]

[295.1] Ewing v. Ewing, 301 So. 3d 709, 713 (Miss. Ct. App. 2020) (wife had net monthly income of $2,991 and expenses of $3,840; husband had income of $2,120 after paying child support and alimony).

Page 287. Add to footnote 297:

Cf. Garner v. Garner, 343 So. 3d 1097, 1105 (Miss. Ct. App. 2022) (limited rehabilitative alimony awarded to lower-income husband in part because wife had custody of children and would incur additional expenses).

Page 287. Insert in text after sentence ending in footnote 297:

A chancellor properly awarded a homemaker wife of twenty years six months of rehabilitative alimony. Her husband had custody of their five boys and was responsible for private school tuition. She paid child support of $275 a month and had taken no steps to find full-time employment even though she had a lapsed teaching certificate. She received cash assets of almost $300,000 and $52,000 in temporary support.[297.1]

[297.1] Baird v. Baird, 2025 WL 2962388, at *7 (Miss. Ct. App. Oct. 21, 2025).

Page 287. Add to footnote 298:

See also Howard v. Howard, 2025 WL 1741634, at *5 (Miss. Ct. App. June 24, 2025) (wife of twenty years who committed adultery awarded $2,000 a month in permanent alimony from husband with income of $7,500 a month compared to her $2,500 a month; assets were limited and she had custody of twenty-year-old son with autism).

[g] Obligations of the parties

Page 288. Insert in text after sentence ending in footnote 300:

In 2022, the court of appeals reversed and remanded an award of alimony because the chancellor failed to consider the assignment of $10,000 in debt to the payor husband.[300.1]

[300.1] Warner v. Warner, 341 So. 3d 152, 165-66 (Miss. Ct. App. 2022).

[h] Assets of the parties

[i] Recipient's assets

Page 289. Add to footnote 311:

Cf. Pace v. Pace, 324 So. 3d 369, 380 (Miss. Ct. App. 2021) (wife of thirteen years who received $1 million in assets plus $120,000 cash denied alimony from former physician husband who relinquished license after suspension for addiction; both were unemployed but had earning capacity; she received substantial assets).

Page 289. Insert in text after sentence ending in footnote 313:

For example, a chancellor properly awarded a sixty-year-old working wife of fifteen years $250 a month in rehabilitative alimony. The husband received marital property with $8,000 in equity and was left with no surplus. She had separate property valued at $362,000, including a debt-free home and automobile and a separate IRA and no debt. She had received temporary alimony for four years during the litigation.[313.1]

[313.1] Thornhill v. Thornhill, 421 So. 3d 626, 638 (Miss. Ct. App. 2025)

Page 289. Add to footnote 314:

See also Manor v. Manor, 404 So. 3d 1256, 1264-65 (Miss. Ct. App. 2024) (award of sixty percent of assets to wife in part to avoid need for alimony).

Page 290. Insert in text after sentence ending in footnote 321:

And the court of appeals reversed and remanded an award of alimony based on failure of the chancellor to consider the wife's separate property, including a valuable diamond ring, a piano, jet skis and a golf cart.[321.1]

[321.1] Warner v. Warner, 341 So. 3d 152, 165 (Miss. Ct. App. 2022).

[ii] Payor's assets

Page 290. Insert in text after sentence ending in footnote 325:

And a court properly awarded $125,000 in lump sum alimony and $1,500 a month in rehabilitative alimony for thirty months to a homemaker wife of nine years with four children. As a result of their premarital agreement, her husband had substantial separate property assets while she received only personal property.[325.1]

[325.1] Gussio v. Gussio, 371 So. 3d 734, 749-50 (Miss. Ct. App. 2023).

[5] Factors related to reducing disparity

Page 291. Add to footnote 329:

See Neely v. Neely, 305 So. 3d 164, 173-74 (Miss. Ct. App. 2020) (all alimony denied; parties had equal earnings, neither had debt, and division of assets adequately met their needs).

[a] Length of marriage

Page 292. Insert in text after sentence ending in footnote 335:

A spouse's serious health issues may warrant permanent alimony after a shorter marriage. The court of appeals rejected a husband's argument that $2,500 in permanent alimony was excessive for a thirty-eight-year-old wife of ten years who dissipated assets – she had no income, and her mental illness and treatment needs supported the award.[335.1]

[335.1] *In re* Conservatorship of Geno, 365 So. 3d 287, 299 (Miss. Ct. App. 2021) (wife received $1.25 million in cash and a debt-free house).

Page 292. Insert in text after sentence ending in footnote 337:

For example, a chancellor's award of two years of rehabilitative alimony of $500 a month to a wife of twenty-five years, with income of $646 a month, from a husband with monthly income of $12,150, was reversed as grossly inadequate.[337.1]

[337.1] Hammond v. Hammond, 327 So. 3d 173, 179-80 (Miss. Ct. App. 2021).

Page 293. Insert in text after sentence ending in footnote 341:

Factors other than marriage length may lead to an award of short-term alimony. A wife of twenty years was properly awarded six months of rehabilitative alimony in spite of the disparity in the couple's incomes. The husband had custody of their five boys and was responsible for most of their expenses, including private school.[341.1]

[341.1] Baird v. Baird, 2025 WL 2962388, at *7 (Miss. Ct. App. Oct. 21, 2025) (wife had lapsed teaching certificate and made no efforts to renew it or to become employed full time.).

Page 293. Add to footnote 343:

But see Anderson v. Grabmiller, 394 So. 3d 493, 507 (Miss. Ct. App. 2024) (affirming award of $1,000 a month in permanent alimony from physician wife to her forty-one-year-old homemaker husband of fourteen years, noting that fourteen-year marriage was "relatively long").

[b] Health

[i] Payee's health

Page 293. Insert in text after sentence ending in footnote 345:

The court of appeals rejected a husband's argument that $2,500 in permanent alimony was excessive for a thirty-eight-year-old wife of ten years who dissipated assets – she had no income, and her mental illness and treatment needs supported the award.[345.1]

[345.1] *In re* Conservatorship of Geno, 365 So. 3d 287, 299 (Miss. Ct. App. 2021) (wife received $1.25 million in cash and a debt-free house).

Page 294. Add to footnote 347:

See also Gaskin v. Gaskin, 304 So. 3d 641, 651-52 (Miss. Ct. App. 2020) (disabled wife of seventeen years awarded $1,000 a month in permanent alimony from husband with monthly income of $12,085); Oates v. Oates, 291 So. 3d 803, 806-07 (Miss. Ct. App. 2020) (award of $504 in permanent alimony to disabled wife with expenses of $2,000 a month, from husband with annual income of $33,000 and monthly expenses of $2,300).

Page 294. Add to footnote 348:

See also Coleman v. Coleman, 324 So. 3d 1204, 1208, 1214 (Miss. Ct. App. 2021) (all alimony denied to a disabled husband of twenty years with $1,500 a month in Social Security disability from a wife with monthly income of $2,781).

[c] Age

Page 295. Add to footnote 362:

See McKenzie v. McKenzie, 397 So. 3d 510, 522 (Miss. Ct. App. 2024) (awarding rehabilitative alimony of $5,000 a month for three years to a thirty-six-year-old homemaker wife who had previously worked and who received marital assets of approximately $1.7 million).

Page 296. Insert in text after sentence ending in footnote 363:

A forty-one-year-old husband of fourteen years, who had been a homemaker and now earned less than $3,000 a month, was awarded periodic alimony of $1,000 a month from his physician wife.[363.1]

363.1 Anderson v. Grabmiller, 394 So. 3d 493, 507-08 (Miss. Ct. App. 2024).

[d] Fault

[i] Payee's fault

Page 296. Add to footnote 366:

See also Garner v. Garner, 343 So. 3d 1097, 1105 (Miss. Ct. App. 2022) (husband's abuse that ended the marriage was a factor in two-year award of alimony of $503, even though wife's income was ten times his income).

Page 296. Add to footnote 369:

See also Howard v. Howard, 2025 WL 1741634, at *5 (Miss. Ct. App. June 24, 2025) (wife of twenty years who committed adultery awarded $2,000 a month in permanent alimony from husband with income of $7,500 a month compared to her $2,500 a month; assets were limited and she had custody of twenty-year-old son with autism).

[ii] Payor's fault

Page 297. Add to footnote 371:

See also Hammond v. Hammond, 327 So. 3d 173, 176-77, 179 (Miss. Ct. App. 2021) (husband's affair ended twenty-five-year marriage; wife had monthly income of $646 while his was $12,150).

[e] Dissipation of assets

Page 298. Insert in text after sentence ending in footnote 379:

However, a wife of ten years who received substantial assets at divorce was awarded permanent alimony of $2,500 a month even though she dissipated hundreds of thousands in assets – she suffered from mental illness, was under a conservatorship, and had no ongoing income.[379.1]

[379.1] *In re* Conservatorship of Geno, 365 So. 3d 287, 299 (Miss. Ct. App. 2021) (wife received $1.25 million in cash and a debt-free house).

§ 9.06 Third-party payments as alimony

[1] Payment of medical expenses

Page 308. Add to footnote 476:

But cf. Chambliss v. Chambliss, 385 So. 3d 1246, 1256-57 (Miss. Ct. App. 2023) (denying rehabilitative or permanent alimony but awarding wife $1,800 a month for twelve years to obtain health insurance).

Page 309. Insert in text after sentence ending in footnote 478:

On the other hand, the court of appeals held that a chancellor properly limited a husband's obligation for health insurance to two years, even though the court erred in limiting her alimony to two years.[478.1]

[478.1] Hammond v. Hammond, 327 So. 3d 173, 182 (Miss. Ct. App. 2021).

§ 9.07 Mechanics of award

[1] Form of award

[b] Variation in amount

[ii] Variation tied to anticipated change

Page 311. Add to footnote 505:

But see Williamson v. Williamson, 296 So. 3d 206, 210 (Miss. Ct. App. 2020) (awarding $1,500 a month permanent alimony for one year, then $1,200 a month; not tied to specific change; reduction may have been related to wife's responsibility for short-term debt).

[4] Security for award

[c] Life insurance

Page 313. Insert in text after sentence ending in footnote 524:

And a chancellor erred in ordering a husband to provide a $91,000 life insurance policy to secure unpaid alimony in the event of the husband's death. The policy would be sufficient to cover a default in thirty-three monthly payments of the $2,700 alimony award. However, the evidence showed that the husband had regularly paid any court-ordered support. While admitting that there is no "rule of thumb" as to the amount that should be ordered, the court held that the amount was error and remanded for the chancellor to determine whether any insurance was necessary and if so to set an amount appropriate to the husband's obligations.[524.1]

[524.1] Phang v. Phang, 350 So. 3d 1154, 1163-64 (Miss. Ct. App. 2022).

§ 9.08 Modification

[2] Test for modification

[a] Material change

Page 316. Insert in text after sentence ending in footnote 546:

Modification is based on a present change in circumstances – not a change anticipated in the future. For example, the court of appeals rejected a husband's argument that an alimony award to his wife would be excessive in two years when he retired – chancellors are to focus on the parties' current financial situation, not on future events.[546.1]

[546.1] Phang v. Phang, 350 So. 3d 1154, 1161-62 (Miss. Ct. App. 2022).

[d] Comparison of financial circumstances

Page 318. Insert in text after sentence ending in footnote 561:

In contrast, a husband whose income had dropped from $218,000 a year to $84,132 without fault on his part was entitled to a reduction in alimony and child support. His wife's income remained the same.[561.1]

[561.1] Krohn v. Krohn, 294 So. 3d 680, 688 (Miss. Ct. App. 2020) (requiring husband to pay $36,000 of his income in child support and alimony while supporting a second family was an abuse of discretion).

[6] Petition to reduce alimony

[a] Payor's decreased resources

[i] Involuntary income reduction

Page 322. Add to footnote 600:

See also Krohn v. Krohn, 294 So. 3d 680, 688 (Miss. Ct. App. 2020) (chancellor erred in denying a husband's request to modify alimony after an unexpected and involuntary loss of more than half of his income).

Page 323. Insert in text after sentence ending in footnote 607:

And a payor who alleged, but did not prove, that his retirement benefits had been reduced, was denied modification.[607.1]

[607.1] Weeks v. Weeks, 401 So. 3d 195, 201 (Miss. Ct. App. 2024).

[b] Payee's increased resources

[ii] Receipt of Social Security benefits

Page 325. Insert in text at end of section [ii]:

In a 2022 case, the court of appeals relied on *Alford* to reject a husband's argument that an alimony award to his sixty-two-year-old wife should have been reduced because she could have drawn Social Security at sixty-two. The court stated, "We know of no precedent under which a party to a divorce can be required to apply for Social Security benefits." In keeping with *Alford,* the husband could petition for modification when she did begin receiving benefits. Similarly, his argument that the amount would be excessive in two years when he retired failed – chancellors are to focus on the parties' current financial situation.[616.1]

[616.1] Phang v. Phang, 350 So. 3d 1154, 1162 (Miss. Ct. App. 2022).

[8] Effective date of modification

Page 326. Insert in text after sentence ending in footnote 633:

A chancellor may require that a payor who is granted a temporary reduction in alimony but denied permanent modification, repay the alimony recipient the amount by which the alimony was temporarily reduced.[633.1]

[633.1] Weeks v. Weeks, 401 So. 3d 195, 201 (Miss. Ct. App. 2024).

§ 9.10 Termination based on cohabitation

[1] Termination based on cohabitation

Page 329. Insert in text after sentence ending in footnote 651:

The court of appeals continued this approach in 2023, affirming a chancellor's reduction of a former wife's alimony from $700 to $400 – her cohabitant paid some of the household expenses, reducing her costs. The court rejected the payor's argument that alimony should have been terminated – upon proof of cohabitation, there is a presumption of mutual support, which the alimony recipient must rebut. If it is not rebutted, the chancellor should consider the *Armstrong* factors to determine whether alimony should be modified or terminated. It was appropriate to modify rather than terminate alimony upon a finding that the alimony reduced but did not eliminate the need for financial support.[651.1]

[651.1] Gillenwater v. Redmond, 359 So. 3d 232, 235-36 (Miss. Ct. App. 2023).

[2] Termination based on de facto marriage

Page 329. Insert in text after sentence ending in footnote 653:

In 2024, the court of appeals decided the first de facto marriage case in almost twenty years. The court affirmed termination of alimony to a wife who cohabited with a man for over thirty years, based on their de facto marriage. The court agreed with the chancellor that alimony terminates automatically upon entry into a de facto marriage – the payor need not file a petition to trigger termination. The court distinguished mere cohabitation, which may or may not lead to termination of alimony, depending on its impact on the circumstances of the case.[653.1]

[653.1] Collins v. Collins, 397 So. 3d 856, 860-61 (Miss. Ct. App. 2024).

X
ATTORNEYS' FEES

§ 10.01 Fee awards based on need

[3] Determining need
[a] Inability to pay

Page 334. Add to footnote 24:

See also Alford v. Alford, 298 So. 3d 983, 993-94 (Miss. 2020) (reversing award of $11,000 in attorneys' and expert fees to a wife who received substantial marital assets and was awarded alimony).

§ 10.02 Amount of award

[1] Factors

Page 335. Insert in text after sentence ending in footnote 33:

In a 2023 case, a chancellor properly awarded a wife's attorneys $200,000 in fees. The trial spanned five years, fifteen days of hearings, 91 motions, and multiple attorney changes by the husband. The chancellor found that the case required extensive research and discovery, prevented the attorneys from taking other work, and that the fees were reasonable, necessary, and reflected the actual work done.[33.1]

[33.1] Gussio v. Gussio, 371 So. 3d 734, 754-56 (Miss. Ct. App. 2023).

[2] Evidence of fees

Page 336. Insert in text after sentence ending in footnote 37:

And the court of appeals affirmed an award of $200,000 in attorneys' fees based on a statement listing dates and amounts of fees but not describing the work performed or by whom. The court stated that an itemized statement is not necessary in all cases – a chancellor may determine reasonableness of fees based on the court's experience and observation of the litigation.37.1 In contrast, the court affirmed a chancellor's award of only $3,500 of a wife's $13,047 in attorney's fees. The case was simple, involving admitted grounds for divorce, few assets, and only one marital account to divide.[37.2]

[37.1] Gussio v. Gussio, 371 So. 3d 734, 753-55 (Miss. Ct. App. 2023). The court was split evenly. Five justices dissented, arguing that the court should remand for an itemized statement. *Id.* at 758-60.

[37.2] Chambliss v. Chambliss, 385 So. 3d 1246, 1257 (Miss. Ct. App. 2023) (award provided wife with sufficient funds to pay the remainder of her fees).

Page 336. Add to footnote 38:

Cf. Hardin v. Hardin, 335 So. 3d 1088, 1093-94 (Miss. Ct. App. 2022) (chancellor properly denied attorneys' fees when it was not possible to tell what amount of the fees remained unpaid).

[3] Findings of fact regarding amount

Page 336. Add to footnote 42:

Cf. Coleman v. Coleman, 324 So. 3d 1204, 1215 (Miss. Ct. App. 2021) (court need not address *McKee* factors if spouse fails to prove inability to pay; factors relate to proper amount of award).

[4] Reduction in fees

Page 337. Insert in text after sentence ending in footnote 46:

In a 2025 case, the court of appeals reversed a chancellor's award of only $10,000 of a wife's requested attorneys' fees of $147,121 in a two-year contempt action, holding that the chancellor should have made more detailed findings of fact to support such a drastic reduction.[46.1]

[46.1] J.T.S. V. M.L.S., 2025 WL12206928, at *28 (Miss. Ct. App. Dec. 16, 2025).

§ 10.03 Awards based on defendant behavior

[2] Contempt actions

Page 338. Add to footnote 57:

But cf. Alves-Hunter v. Hunter, 351 So. 3d 468, 481-82 (Miss. Ct. App. 2022) (chancellor had discretion to deny attorneys' fees to husband even though his wife was found in contempt for interfering with his use of a vehicle).

Page 338. Insert in text after sentence ending in footnote 63:

A husband who was in contempt for failure to pay substantial amounts of support was properly ordered to pay his wife's attorneys' fees even though she was also in contempt. Her contempt involved a minor violation of the agreement.[63.1] However, a court did not err in refusing to award a wife attorneys' fees when both she and her ex-husband were in contempt.[63.2]

[63.1] Krohn v. Krohn, 294 So. 3d 680, 689 (Miss. Ct. App. 2020) (clean hands doctrine did not bar award).
[63.2] Covin v. Covin, 405 So. 3d 160, 170 (Miss. Ct. App. 2023).

[3] Unfounded allegations of abuse

Page 339. Add to footnote 66:

See also Baird v. Baird, 2025 WL 2962388, at *10 (Miss. Ct. App. Oct. 21, 2025) wife ordered to pay husband's attorneys' fees of $10,000 and 70% of the guardian ad litems' fees connected with her unsubstantiated allegations that one of their older boys had sexually abused one of the younger boys).

Page 339. Add to footnote 69:

See also Baumann v. Baumann, 304 So. 3d 175, 183 (Miss. Ct. App. 2020) (affirming denial of father's request for fees; mother's allegations of abuse were unsubstantiated but were not "without foundation").

[4] Frivolous litigation

Page 339. Add to footnote 71:

See Hornsby v. Hornsby, 353 So. 3d 507, 515-16 (Miss. Ct. App. 2022) (affirming an award of $9,196 in attorneys' fees under Rule 11 and the Litigation Accountability Act; father's contempt petition against mother lacked substantial justification); *cf. In re* L.T., 335 So. 3d 599, 602-03 (Miss. Ct. App. 2022) (reversing chancellor's award of fees against CPS under Rule 11 for frivolous abuse petition filed against children's custodian – the petition was filed by the prosecutor, not filed or initiated by CPS, which was unaware of the petition).

Page 339. Insert in text after sentence ending in footnote 72:

And a court erred in dismissing a wife's request for attorneys' fees in her husband's tort action against her – all of his claims were dismissed, and some were clearly without foundation.[72.1]

[72.1] Herbert v. Herbert, 374 So. 3d 562, 580-81 (Miss. Ct. App. 2023).

Page 340. Insert in text after sentence ending in footnote 74:

§ 10.03A Awards based on contract

Parties may provide by contract for payment of attorneys' fees. However, a wife was not entitled to attorneys' fees in her former husband's unsuccessful attempt to modify alimony based on income loss. She argued that fees were required by their Tennessee property settlement agreement, which stated that the prevailing party would be entitled to attorneys' fees "should litigation be necessary to enforce any provision of the Agreement." The court of appeals held that the provision was inapplicable – she was not required to bring suit to enforce the agreement. Her husband was not in breach, having made all alimony payments. He was entitled to seek a modification of alimony when he lost his employment.[74.1]

[74.1] Rawlings v. Rawlings, 374 So. 3d 1261, 1263-64 (Miss. Ct. App. 2023).

XI
ESTABLISHING PARENTAGE

§ 11.02 PARENTAGE BASED ON MARRIAGE

[4] Mississippi

Page 348. Insert in text after sentence ending in footnote 22:

However, a husband who contested paternity at divorce but failed to submit to court-ordered genetic testing was properly found to be the child's father and ordered to pay child support based on the marriage presumption.[22.1]

[22.1] Greer v. Greer, 312 So. 3d 414, 416 (Miss. Ct. App. 2021).

§ 11.06 PARENTAGE BASED ON CONDUCT

[1] The presumed father

[b] Mississippi

Page 353. Add to footnote 59:

See also Horn v. Seeden, 383 So. 3d 1266, 1270-71 (Miss. Ct. App. 2024) (man who believed himself to be child's father, was listed on his birth certificate, and supported and cared for him, was entitled to be treated as a parent under the in loco parentis doctrine; mother alleged that another man was the father but he did not appear in the action or seek paternity of the child).

Page 353. Insert in text after sentence ending in footnote 59:

In 2023, the supreme court again addressed the rights of persons who have acted in loco parentis to a child, expanding the doctrine beyond presumed fathers to other nonparents, at least with respect to visitation.[59.1]

[59.1] See discussion *infra* § 11.06[2][c].

[2] Nonparents other than presumed fathers

[c] Mississippi

Page 355. Insert in text after sentence ending in footnote 74:

In 2023, the supreme court changed direction on this issue, rejecting a mother's argument that the in loco parentis doctrine is limited to presumed fathers. A woman sought visitation with her former partner's children after the couple separated. The chancellor denied her petition. On appeal, the biological mother argued that nonparent visitation in Mississippi is limited to grandparents and presumed fathers. The plaintiff cohabitant argued that in loco parentis visitation is not limited to these categories. The supreme court agreed – the plaintiff's complaint stated a claim on which she could be awarded visitation, if she could prove she that she came within certain narrow, unique circumstances that rebut the natural parent presumption. The court emphasized, however, that visitation rights under the doctrine "are inferior to those of a natural parent." It was unclear from *Brownlee* whether the test for in loco parentis visitation was the same as for custody (requiring that the biological father is "not in the picture") or whether it was a broader test based on equity and the child's best interests.[74.1]

In 2025, the court of appeals held that the *Brownlee* test for awarding a nonparent visitation is not the same as the test for awarding custody. Instead, a nonparent who has acted in loco parentis to a child, caring for the child as their own in their home, may be awarded visitation in unique, limited cases when "special circumstances exist ... in which justice so requires and the child's well-being demands a relationship with a person who has stood in loco parentis in his or her life." The test does not appear to require that the absence of the biological father or to be limited to same-sex partners of the biological mother. [74.2]

[74.1] Brownlee v. Powell, 368 So. 3d 1268, 1273-74 (Miss. 2023).
[74.2] Edwards v. Johnson, 2025 WL 2837431, at *8 (Miss. Ct. App. Oct. 7, 2025).

§ 11.10 Paternity actions

[5] Genetic tests

Page 360. Add to footnote 118:

See Friday v. Mississippi Dep't Human Servs., 325 So. 3d 1200, 1201 (Miss. Ct. App. 2021) (defendant's refusal to submit to court-ordered genetic testing raised a presumption of paternity that he did not rebut); Greer v. Greer, 312 So. 3d 414, 416 (Miss. Ct. App. 2021) (husband who contested paternity at divorce but did not submit to court-ordered genetic testing properly found to be child's father and ordered to pay support).

[8] Statute of limitations

Page 361. Add to footnote 134:

Cf. Friday v. Mississippi Dep't Human Servs., 325 So. 3d 1200, 1203 (Miss. Ct. App. 2021) (court did not lose jurisdiction when child turned twenty-one during the litigation; proceedings were begun when he was twenty).

[10] Order of paternity

[b] Child support

[i] Order for back support

Page 363. Add to footnote 151:

See also Ndicu v. Gacheri, 381 So. 3d 371, 375 (Miss. Ct. App. 2023) (rejecting father's argument that Miss. Code Ann. § 93-11-65 requires a chancellor to order support back to one year prior to trial).

XII
CHILD CUSTODY AND VISITATION

§ 12.01 History and overview

[4] Custody presumptions

[b] Presumption against custody to a violent parent

Page 372. Add to footnote 21:

See also Alves-Hunter v. Hunter, 351 So. 3d 468, 477 (Miss. Ct. App. 2022) (a single incident of violence between parents during separation did not constitute a history of family violence).

Page 372. Insert in text after sentence ending in footnote 21:

And the presumption was not triggered by a father's agreement, allowing a court to award his wife a divorce based on habitual cruelty to move the divorce proceedings forward – he admitted to habitual cruelty, not to a history of family violence.[21.1]

[21.1] Lambes v. Lambes, 345 So. 3d 592, 606-08 (Miss. Ct. App. 2022) (also finding that even if the presumption was triggered, it was rebutted).

Page 372. Insert in text after sentence ending in footnote 25:

Similarly, the presumption was rebutted by evidence that a father attended parenting classes, that there was no evidence of family violence during the five-year litigation, and that the mother's mental health affected her ability to care for the children.[25.1]

[25.1] Lambes v. Lambes, 345 So. 3d 592, 607-08 (Miss. Ct. App. 2022) (also questioning whether the conflicting evidence was sufficient to raise the presumption).

Page 372. Add to footnote 28:

But cf. Kerr v. Kerr, 323 So. 3d 462, 476 (Miss. 2021) (mother's allegations of violence were not credible; court was not required to make findings regarding rebuttal of the presumption).

[7] Jurisdiction and procedure

Page 378. Insert in text after sentence ending in footnote 84:

[a1] Age of majority [NEW]

Chancellors have authority to address custody of a child until they are twenty-one, the age of majority in Mississippi. The court of appeals affirmed a chancellor's award of joint legal and physical custody of a twenty-year-old woman who was attending college. The dissent argued that it was pointless to determine custody of a twenty-year-old who could live where she pleased. The majority held that custody is a viable issue so long as a child is not emancipated.[84.1]

[84.1] Wilbourn v. Wilbourn, 388 So. 3d 580, 592 (Miss. Ct. App. 2024).

[b] Temporary custody

Page 378. Add to footnote 87:

See Hammons v. Hammons, 289 So. 3d 1214, 1219 (Miss. 2020) (temporary order does not change the burden of proof at trial).

Page 378. Add to footnote 88:

See generally Hendrix v. Whitt, 373 So. 3d 778 (Miss. Ct. App. 2023).

Page 378. Insert in text after sentence ending in footnote 89:

Nonetheless, a temporary order may have a determinative impact on final awards of custody. The supreme court affirmed a chancellor's finding that a mother had deserted her ten-year-old son by failure to support him or visit with him consistently while he was in his grandparents' temporary custody for six years. The mother did not visit her son for eighteen months after moving to Texas and having a baby. After that period, she exercised visitation once or twice a month. The supreme court acknowledged that the temporary order impacted the final order. The court also questioned whether temporary custody in the grandparents was necessary but held that the temporary order was mooted by the final custody order and could not be challenged.[89.1]

[89.1] Summers v. Gros, 319 So. 3d 479, 483, 488-89 (Miss. 2021) (also stating that the mother did not act promptly to attack the temporary order).

Page 378. Add to footnote 91:

For an unusual set of circumstances involving a temporary order of custody on remand, *see* Gossett v. Gossett, 313 So. 3d 1063, 1072-73 (Miss. Ct. App. 2021) (rejecting mother's argument that temporary order converted to final order was based on stale evidence).

Page 378. Insert in text after sentence ending in footnote 91:

In contrast, parents' out-of-court agreement that the father would have temporary custody did not acquire permanency – it was in place for only thirteen months and was not approved by a court. The chancellor erred in treating it as permanent and applying the test for modifying custody.[91.1] And a chancellor properly denied a mother's petition to treat a temporary order as permanent. An order may become permanent when it has remained unchallenged for a long period of time – in this case, the parties actively litigated the order.[91.2]

[91.1] Hendrix v. Whitt, 373 So. 3d 778, 791-92 (Miss. Ct. App. 2023).
[91.2] Wilbourn v. Wilbourn, 388 So. 3d 580, 591 (Miss. Ct. App. 2024).

Page 378. Add to footnote 92:

See Gossett v. Gossett, 313 So. 3d 1063, 1072-73 (Miss. Ct. App. 2021) (temporary orders are not appealable; parties are not entitled to Rule 59 relief regarding temporary orders).

Page 378. Insert in text after sentence ending in footnote 92:

Appellate courts will not hear challenges to temporary custody on the appeal of a final custody judgment – the temporary order becomes moot when final judgment is entered. The court of appeals declined to address a grandfather's argument that a chancellor erred in denying him temporary visitation.[92.1] And a chancellor's award of temporary custody to grandparents, removing a mother's son from her custody, could not be attacked on appeal. It was mooted by the court's entry of a final judgment of custody to the grandparents.[92.2]

[92.1] Sims v. Sims, 337 So. 3d 1085, 1100-1102 (Miss. Ct. App. 2021).
[92.2] Summers v. Gros, 319 So. 3d 479, 483-84 (Miss. 2021) (but acknowledging that the temporary order may have been significant in the final disposition).

[c] Emergency custody

Page 379. Insert in text after sentence ending in footnote 94:

After a custodial father's death, a chancellor properly awarded temporary custody to the child's grandparents without notice to her mother. The noncustodial out-of-state mother had in the past failed to return the girl after visitation and she was in violation of the agreement at the time of his death.[94.1]

[94.1] Roberts v. Conner, 332 So. 3d 272, 284 (Miss. Ct. App. 2021).

[f] Effect of out-of-court agreement

Page 381. Insert in text after sentence ending in footnote 111:

For example, a chancellor did not err in awarding a noncustodial father one month of summer visitation rather than two as the parents agreed, based on her finding that two months away from the custodial mother was not in the child's best interest.[111.1]

[111.1] Gerty v. Gerty, 296 So. 3d 704, 709-10 (Miss. 2020).

§ 12.03 Application of the *Albright* Factors

Page 383. Insert in text after sentence ending in footnote 128:

The court of appeals affirmed an award of custody to a father in a highly contested case even though none of the *Albright* factors favored him. The court found most factors to be neutral but that the mother was favored on continuity of care and moral fitness. Nonetheless, the court awarded custody to the father based on the totality of circumstances, including the guardian ad litem's recommendation that he receive custody.[128.1] However, two years later, the court of appeals reversed a chancellor's decision awarding custody of a girl to her mother even though no factors favored her. The chancellor provided no reason for the decision, which separated a sister from her two brothers.[128.2]

[128.1] Lambes v. Lambes, 345 So. 3d 592, 606 (Miss. Ct. App. 2022). *See also id.* at 609 (McCarty, J., concurring in part and dissenting in part) (arguing that custody should not be awarded to a parent not favored on any factors).
[128.2] McLellan v. McLellan, 397 So. 3d 860, 869 (Miss. Ct. App. 2024).

[1] Findings of fact

Page 384. Insert in text after sentence ending in footnote 135:

The court of appeals rejected a mother's argument that a chancellor's failure to specify who won on several factors required reversal – the chancellor discussed the evidence under each factor and the record supported the award of custody to the father.[135.1]

[135.1] Case v. Case, 339 So. 3d 796, 807 (Miss. Ct. App. 2022) ("The chancellor must address each factor that is relevant to the case, but he does not have to decide that each factor favors one parent or the other." (citations omitted)); *see also* Stuckey v. Stuckey, 341 So. 3d 1030, 1037 (Miss. Ct. App. 2022).

Page 384. Add to footnote 137:

See also Baumann v. Baumann, 304 So. 3d 175, 180 (Miss. Ct. App. 2020) (chancellor's failure to address factors did not require reversal; he adopted the guardian ad litem's findings discussing the factors).

[2] Age, health, and sex of child

Page 385. Insert in text after sentence ending in footnote 150:

In contrast, a court properly found for a mother regarding custody of a two-year-old breastfeeding child.[150.1]

[150.1] Embrey v. Young, 337 So. 3d 247, 256-57 (Miss. Ct. App. 2021).

Page 387. Insert in text after sentence ending in footnote 162:

A father who helped his child with speech development problems was favored on the factor of the children's health.[162.1]

[162.1] Tedford v. Tedford, 312 So. 3d 420, 426 (Miss. Ct. App. 2021); *see also* Leonard v. Pate, 410 So. 3d 1078, 1084 (Miss. Ct. App. 2025) (finding against mother who took child off prescribed medication); Garrison v. Courtney, 304 So. 3d 1129, 1148-49 (Miss. Ct. App. 2020) (nurse mother favored on boys' health; she was better suited to care for their health problems).

Page 387. Add to footnote 164:

See also Leonard v. Pate, 410 So. 3d 1078, 1084 (Miss. Ct. App. 2025) (finding against mother who has smoked around child with asthma since his birth).

[3] Continuing care prior to separation

Page 388. Add to footnote 177:

See also Case v. Case, 339 So. 3d 796, 804-05 (Miss. Ct. App. 2022) (continuity of care was neutral even though the mother was a homemaker; the father testified that she relied heavily on caregivers).

Page 389. Add to footnote 180:

See also Kerr v. Kerr, 323 So. 3d 462, 478 (Miss. 2021) (court did not err in considering father's post-separation care for child in awarding custody).

Page 389. Insert in text after sentence ending in footnote 182:

In a 2021 case, a court properly found for a noncustodial father on the factor of continuity of care in a modification case. The boy slept at his mother's home but was dropped off at the father's home before school each day and returned there until after dinner. He spent most of the days in the summer with his father.[182.1] And in another case, a mother was favored on the factor even though the parents shared equal joint physical custody. She had full custody for six months while the father was deployed and was significantly involved in their care during his custodial periods.[182.2]

In a modification case involving a mother's parental alienation, the factor of continuity of care was found to be neutral. Even though the mother provided more care, her interference with the father's relationship was partly responsible for her additional time with the girls and their closer bond.[182.3]

[182.1] Jones v. Jones, 332 So. 3d 365, 373-74 (Miss. Ct. App. 2021); *see also* Garrison v. Courtney, 304 So. 3d 1129, 1147-48 (Miss. Ct. App. 2020) (continuity of care was neutral even though boys remained with their father after separation; mother came to the house every day to care for them).

[182.2] Schmidt v. Schmidt, 339 So. 3d 163, 176-77 (Miss. Ct. App. 2022).

[182.3] Stewart v. Stewart, 309 So. 3d 44, 92 (Miss. Ct. App. 2020); *see also* Leonard v. Pate, 410 So. 3d 1078, 1084 (Miss. Ct. App. 2025) (father had continuity of care; disregarding two years in which his lack of time with his son was based on the mother's unsupported accusations).

[4] Parenting skills and willingness and capacity to provide childcare

[a] Parenting skills

Page 390. Add to footnote 186:

See Schmidt v. Schmidt, 339 So. 3d 163, 177-78 (Miss. Ct. App. 2022) (mother who established routine for children was favored over father who had less structured home where children did not get sufficient sleep; father also discussed litigation with children).

Page 390. Add to footnote 189:

See also Scott v. Boudreaux, 375 So. 3d 688 (Miss. Ct. App. 2023) (father was favored on parenting skills – he and his wife were more involved in the children's activities and in one daughter's treatment for adjustment disorder).

Page 390. Add to footnote 191:

See Kerr v. Kerr, 323 So. 3d 462, 478-79, 481 (Miss. 2021) (finding for father based on parenting skills; boy had excessive absences in his mother's care).

Page 390. Add to footnote 192:

See also Alexander v. Scarbrough, 421 So. 3d 316, 330 (Miss. Ct. App. 2025) (awarding custody to mother who was child's primary caregiver and involved in education over father who engaged in damaging confrontations with the boy's school and medical providers); *In re* T.D., 324 So. 3d 1187, 1196 (Miss. Ct. App. 2021) (grandmother favored on parenting skills; father sent the children to school without supplies or books, in dirty clothes; they were often late or absent).

Page 390. Add to footnote 193:

Cf. Garrison v. Courtney, 304 So. 3d 1129, 1148-49 (Miss. Ct. App. 2020) (finding against father on parenting skills based on the condition of his home).

Page 390. Add to footnote 194:

See also Kerr v. Kerr, 323 So. 3d 462, 478-79 (Miss. 2021) (finding for father based on parenting skills; mother lacked patience with son and had high stress levels when caring for him).

Page 391. Add to footnote 201:

See also Stuckey v. Stuckey, 341 So. 3d 1030, 1039 (Miss. Ct. App. 2022) (finding against mother who kept a child from her father for a significant period of time and inappropriately discussed the custody modification case with her); Riley v. Heisinger, 302 So. 3d 1243, 1256-57 (Miss. Ct. App. 2020) (finding for father on parenting skills and moral fitness over mother who interfered with his relationship with his daughter); Stewart v. Stewart, 309 So. 3d 44, 92-93 (Miss. Ct. App. 2020) (father was favored on parenting skills over mother who subjected child to unnecessary forensic examinations connected with unfounded accusations of abuse); *cf.* Lambes v. Lambes, 345 So. 3d 592, 606 (Miss. Ct. App. 2022) (custody awarded to father based on mother's animosity and unfounded accusations, even though no *Albright* factors favored the father).

Page 392. Add to footnote 207:

See also Baird v. Baird, 2025 WL 2962388, at *4 (Miss. Ct. App. Oct. 21, 2025) (affirming award of custody of five boys to father; mother's harsh parenting style alienated older boys; she made unsubstantiated claims of sexual abuse by one of boys).

Page 392. Insert in text after sentence ending in footnote 207:

And a father's abusive language toward the mother in the children's presence counted against him on parenting skills.[207.1]

[207.1] Embrey v. Young, 337 So. 3d 247, 258 (Miss. Ct. App. 2021).

Page 392. Add to footnote 208:

See also Case v. Case, 339 So. 3d 796, 806 (Miss. Ct. App. 2022) (mother's poor relationship with older children weighed against her on parenting skills).

Page 392. Add to footnote 210:

Cf. Tedford v. Tedford, 312 So. 3d 420, 426-27 (Miss. Ct. App. 2021) (finding for father on parenting skills and moral fitness over mother who used drugs and whose older daughter used drugs and was pregnant at a young age).

[b] Willingness and capacity to provide primary childcare

Page 393. Insert in text after sentence ending in footnote 217:

And a father who remained in Mississippi near extended family was favored on ability to provide childcare over the mother who moved to Virginia. [217.1]

[217.1] Jenkins v. Jenkins, 307 So. 3d 473, 480 (Miss. Ct. App. 2020).

Page 394. Insert in text after sentence ending in footnote 223:

A father with one child and assistance from his family was rated higher on ability to provide childcare than a mother with two older children and no family assistance.[223.1]

[223.1] Cox v. Upchurch, 301 So. 3d 69, 74 (Miss. Ct. App. 2020).

[5] Employment responsibilities of the parents

Page 394. Add to footnote 224:

See also Embrey v. Young, 337 So. 3d 247, 257-58 (Miss. Ct. App. 2021) (finding for self-employed, stay-at-home mother over employed father).

Page 394. Add to footnote 225:

See Kerr v. Kerr, 323 So. 3d 462, 479 (Miss. 2021) (working father favored on ability to provide childcare over unemployed mother); Riley v. Heisinger, 302 So. 3d 1243, 1256-57 (Miss. Ct. App. 2020) (employment responsibilities found to be neutral, even though the mother stayed at home and the father was a surgeon; his schedule allowed him to take his daughter to and from school).

[6] Physical and mental health and age of parents
[b] Mental health

Page 395. Add to footnote 232:

See also Edwards v. Edwards, 421 So. 3d 1248, 1254 (Miss. Ct. App. 2025) (awarding custody to father over mother with a history of clinical depression and who had attempted suicide twice).

Page 395. Add to footnote 234:

See also Jones v. Jones, 332 So. 3d 365, 374-75 (Miss. Ct. App. 2021) (finding against a mother on moral fitness and mental health; she argued frequently with her son, locked him out of the house, and moved without telling him); Kerr v. Kerr, 323 So. 3d 462, 479-80 (Miss. 2021) (father favored on mental health based on mother's involuntary commitment and failure to seek treatment for anxiety).

Page 396. Add to footnote 236:

See also In re T.D., 324 So. 3d 1187, 1199 (Miss. Ct. App. 2021) (grandmother favored on mental and physical health, based on a father's drug use and untreated schizophrenia).

Page 396. Add to footnote 237:

See also Adams v. Adams, 400 So. 3d 517, 524 (Miss. Ct. App. 2025) (no evidence that mother's prior mental health issues affected children negatively).

Page 396. Add to footnote 239:

See also Wooten v. Wooten, 333 So. 3d 610, 617 (Miss. Ct. App. 2022) (fact that a mother had experienced one or more panic attacks did not require a finding against her on health and fitness – the panic attacks did not affect her ability to care for the children).

Page 396. Add to footnote 240:

See also Garner v. Garner, 343 So. 3d 1097, 1107 (Miss. Ct. App. 2022) (sole legal and physical custody properly awarded to a mother over a father who had violent temper outbursts and engaged in verbal abuse in front of the children, abused alcohol, and once pointed a gun at his head in front of his daughter).

[c] Alcohol and drug use

Page 397. Add to footnote 244:

See Garrison v. Courtney, 304 So. 3d 1129, 1149 (Miss. Ct. App. 2020) (finding against father on mental health based on his alcohol abuse).

Page 397. Add to footnote 249:

See also Embrey v. Young, 337 So. 3d 247, 258 (Miss. Ct. App. 2021) (court not required to consider mother's use of marijuana eight years earlier during a pregnancy; there was no evidence of current drug use).

[7] Emotional ties of the parent and child

Page 398. Insert in text after sentence ending in footnote 256:

The factor weighed against a father whose relationship with his daughter was strained and who did not continue court-recommended family counseling with her.[256.1]

[256.1] Adams v. Adams, 400 So. 3d 517, 526-27 (Miss. Ct. App. 2025).

Page 398. Add to footnote 257:

See also Stewart v. Stewart, 309 So. 3d 44, 94 (Miss. Ct. App. 2020) (factors of emotional bond and child's preference were neutral, even though the older girl wanted to live with the mother; mother's interference with the father's relationship with the girl was partly responsible for their closer bond).

[8] Moral fitness

[a] Sexual conduct

Page 399. Add to footnote 264:

See Tilley v. Gibbs, 387 So. 3d 64, 77 (Miss. Ct. App. 2024) (awarding custody of three-year-old girl to father over mother who spent 170 nights with an affair partner during the last year of the couple's marriage).

Page 399. Add to footnote 265:

See also Edwards v. Edwards, 421 So. 3d 1248, 1255 (Miss. Ct. App. 2025) (awarding custody to father over mother who had multiple post-separation affairs and allowed children to spend time with partner).

Page 399. Add to footnote 268:

See also Embrey v. Young, 337 So. 3d 247, 257-58 (Miss. Ct. App. 2021) (chancellor did not err in finding factor of moral fitness neutral even though mother was living with her fiancé).

Page 400. Add to footnote 270:

See also Latham v. Latham, 357 So. 3d 1157, 1163 (Miss. Ct. App. 2023) (father who took child to church regularly favored over mother who had three nonmarital children by different fathers).

Page 400. Add to footnote 271:

See Case v. Case, 339 So. 3d 796, 808-09 (Miss. Ct. App. 2022) (neither parent favored where both had affairs). *But cf.* Wooten v. Wooten, 333 So. 3d 610, 617-18 (Miss. Ct. App. 2022) (mother's pre-separation affair did not require a finding for the father on moral fitness; there was no evidence that her affair affected the children; he had a child with his girlfriend while the couple were still married).

Page 400. Insert in text after sentence ending in footnote 272:

In a 2022 custody matter, the supreme court held that a chancellor should not have limited a husband's cross-examination of his wife regarding marital affairs because he did not plead adultery as a ground for divorce. If a court considers adultery in the custody analysis, it must allow both parties to present evidence on the issue.[272.1]

[272.1] Denham v. Denham, 351 So. 3d 954, 965 (Miss. 2022).

[c] Other

Page 401. Add to footnote 279:

See also In re T.D., 324 So. 3d 1187, 1200 (Miss. Ct. App. 2021) (grandmother favored on moral fitness based on the father's drug use, arrests, and failure to support his children).

Page 402. Add to footnote 283:

See also Scott v. Boudreaux, 375 So. 3d 688 (Miss. Ct. App. 2023) (father favored on moral fitness over mother who kept children from their maternal grandmother after she and her mother argued); Riley v. Heisinger, 302 So. 3d 1243, 1286-87 (Miss. Ct. App. 2020) (finding for father on parenting skills and moral fitness over mother who interfered with his relationship with his daughter).

Page 402. Insert in text after sentence ending in footnote 283:

And a court found for a father on moral fitness based on the mother's dishonesty about her living arrangements and her romantic relationship.[283.1]

[283.1] Bingham v. Johnson, 322 So. 3d 948, 954-55 (Miss. Ct. App. 2021); *cf.* Tedford v. Tedford, 312 So. 3d 420, 426-27 (Miss. Ct. App. 2021) (finding for father on parenting skills and moral fitness over mother whose older daughter used drugs and was pregnant at a young age).

[9] Home, school, and community record of the child

Page 402. Add to footnote 284:

See also Latham v. Latham, 357 So. 3d 1157, 1163 (Miss. Ct. App. 2023) (father favored because he helped child with schoolwork and because child had her own room in his home); Kerr v. Kerr, 323 So. 3d 462, 480-81 (Miss. 2021) (father favored on child's home and school record based on excessive absences in mother's care).

Page 402. Add to footnote 285:

Cf. Bingham v. Johnson, 322 So. 3d 948, 955 (Miss. Ct. App. 2021) (finding for father who took his daughter to church and to family activities); Tedford v. Tedford, 312 So. 3d 420, 427 (Miss. Ct. App. 2021) (father favored on children's home, school, and community record; he enrolled the children in preschool and took them to activities in his father's church).

Page 403. Add to footnote 291:

See also Johnson v. Smith, 328 So. 3d 145, 158 (Miss. Ct. App. 2021) (father favored on stability of employment and home and child's home, school, and community record; he lived in the same home near extended family and had the same job, while the mother moved to Louisiana); Jenkins v. Jenkins, 307 So. 3d 473, 479-80 (Miss. Ct. App. 2020) (father who remained in Mississippi favored over mother who moved to Virginia; children had extended family in Mississippi and were involved in church and extracurricular activities).

Page 403. Insert in text after sentence ending in footnote 293:

And a chancellor did not err in awarding custody to a mother who moved from Clay County, where the family had lived, to Monroe County. The distance did not prevent the mother and boys from spending substantial time in Clay County with friends and family.[293.1]

[293.1] Wooten v. Wooten, 333 So. 3d 610, 618 (Miss. Ct. App. 2022).

[10] Preference of a child twelve or older

Page 403. Insert in text after sentence ending in footnote 297:

As a prerequisite to hearing a child's preference, the chancellor must find that both parents are fit persons to have custody.[297.1]

[297.1] *See* Roley v. Roley, 329 So. 3d 473, 504-05 (Miss. Ct. App. 2021) (refusing to hear father's argument that the statute denied free speech rights of children under twelve; because he was found not fit to have custody no child could testify).

Page 403. Add to footnote 299:

See also Garrison v. Courtney, 304 So. 3d 1129, 1151-52 (Miss. Ct. App. 2020) (custody awarded to mother over son's request to live with father who abused alcohol and allowed underage son to drive).

Page 403. Insert in text after sentence ending in footnote 299:

In contrast, a chancellor properly awarded custody to the mother of a thirteen-year-old who wanted to live with her – the chancellor found that she was mature, competent to testify, was not influenced by her mother, and her choice was in her best interest.[299.1]

[299.1] Morland v. Morland, 396 So. 3d 501, 507-08 (Miss. Ct. App. 2024) (schoolteacher mother was able to assist her with homework; her home was a quieter environment than the father's).

Page 404. Add to footnote 306:

See Stewart v. Stewart, 309 So. 3d 44, 94-95 (Miss. Ct. App. 2020) (factors of emotional bond and child's preference were neutral, even though the older girl wanted to live with her mother; mother's interference with the father's relationship was partly responsible for their closer bond).

[11] Stability of the home environment and employment of each parent
[a] Home environment

Page 406. Insert in text after sentence ending in footnote 319:

A father was favored on home environment because his wife was more involved in the children's activities and mental health than the children's stepfather.[319.1]

[319.1] Scott v. Boudreaux, 375 So. 3d 688, 694 (Miss. Ct. App. 2023) (also favored on home environment because his eight-year assignment in Colorado would provide the children with more stability; the mother had moved several times in Mississippi).

Page 406. Add to footnote 324:

But cf. Schmidt v. Schmidt, 339 So. 3d 163, 178 (Miss. Ct. App. 2022) (rejecting argument that mother who smoked and vaped was unfit under the moral fitness factor – she stopped smoking and did not vape in the house or car).

Page 406. Add to footnote 326:

See Bingham v. Johnson, 322 So. 3d 948, 955 (Miss. Ct. App. 2021) (finding for father who remained in the marital home and his prior job while unemployed mother did not have a permanent home).

Page 406. Insert in text after sentence ending in footnote 326:

A military father who was assigned to Colorado for eight years was favored over a mother who had moved a number of times.[326.1]

[326.1] Scott v. Boudreaux, 375 So. 3d 688, 695 (Miss. Ct. App. 2023).

Page 407. Add to footnote 328:

Cf. Tedford v. Tedford, 312 So. 3d 420, 426-27 (Miss. Ct. App. 2021) (awarding employed father with stable home environment custody of young children over a mother who was unemployed and living in substandard housing).

Page 407. Add to footnote 330:

See also Scott v. Le, 373 So. 3d 1067, 1074 (Miss. Ct. App. 2023) (favoring father who lived with his parents, where his daughter had lived most of her life and had extended family, over mother who moved to Virginia where she had no family); Johnson v. Smith, 328 So. 3d 145, 159 (Miss. Ct. App. 2021) (father favored on stability of employment and home and child's home, school, and community record; he lived in the same home near extended family and had the same job while the mother moved to Louisiana).

Page 407. Add to footnote 331:

See Culver v. Culver, 371 So. 3d 726, 731 (Miss. Ct. App. 2023) (best interest of children was to remain with noncustodial father in their lifetime community and home with their activities, friends, and extensive extended family).

[12] Other relevant factors
[a] Separation of siblings

Page 409. Add to footnote 340:

But see Hackler v. Hackler, 296 So. 3d 773, 779 (Miss. Ct. App. 2020) (court did not err in separating half-siblings by awarding mother custody of her biological daughter over the adoptive father and awarding the father custody of their biological son).

Page 409. Insert in text following sentence ending in footnote 347:

And a court did not err in modifying custody of a boy to his father upon his request, even though it separated him from his sister. He already felt divided from his mother and sister based on his mother's treatment of him.[347.1]

[347.1] Jones v. Jones, 332 So. 3d 365, 372-73 (Miss. Ct. App. 2021); *see also* Baird v. Baird, 2025 WL 2962388, at *4 (Miss. Ct. App. Oct. 21, 2025) (affirming award of custody of five boys to father; mother's harsh parenting style alienated older boys; she made unsubstantiated claims of sexual abuse by one of boys; not in the younger boys' best interest to separate them from their older siblings).

[b] Parental interference

Page 410. Add to footnote 352:

See also Lambes v. Lambes, 345 So. 3d 592, 606, 609 (Miss. Ct. App. 2022) (custody awarded to father based on mother's animosity and unfounded accusations, even though no *Albright* factors favored him).

[13] Other

Page 411. Insert in text after sentence ending in footnote 363:

A court also found against a father under "other factors" based on his limited contact with an eight-year-old daughter from a prior relationship.[363.1]

[363.1] Polk v. Polk, 332 So. 3d 348, 354-57 (Miss. Ct. App. 2021).

§ 12.04 Joint custody

[1] Forms of custody

[a] Joint legal custody

Page 412. Add to footnote 371:

See also Hills v. Manns, 391 So. 3d 822, 828 (Miss. Ct. App. 2023) (affirming chancellor's modification giving custodial mother decision-making authority based on inability to agree on schedule); Wildman v. Wildman, 301 So. 3d 787, 803-04 (Miss. Ct. App. 2020) (chancellor properly held that a custodial mother should have decision-making rights after parental disputes regarding education and medical treatment).

Page 412. Insert in text after sentence ending in footnote 371:

And in a 2022 case, the court of appeals rejected a father's argument that joint legal custody gave him the right to participate in choosing his daughter's psychiatrist. The court stated that custodial parents "may determine the child's upbringing, including his education and health and dental care. Such discretion . . . is vested in the custodial parent."[371.1]

[371.1] Nowell v. Stewart, 356 So. 3d 1217, 1223, n.4 (Miss. Ct. App. 2022).

Page 413. Insert in text after sentence ending in footnote 372:

Parents may agree that in the event of a dispute, one of two joint legal custodians will be the decision-maker.[372.1] However, the supreme court held that a chancellor may override a decision-maker's choice regarding education, without finding a material change in circumstances, if the decision is not in the child's best interests. A chancellor did not err in overriding a designated decision-maker's choice of schools for his children, finding that it was in the children's best interest to attend school where their mother lived, rather than thirty miles away where their stepmother taught.[372.2]

[372.1] *See, e.g.*, Bryant v. Bryant, 348 So. 3d 309, 314-15 (Miss. 2022); see Litton v. Litton, 384 So. 3d 542, 545-46 (Miss. Ct. App. 2023) (agreement designating father as decision-maker on extracurricular activities extended to summer camp).

[372.2] Bryant v. Bryant, 348 So. 3d 309, 316 (Miss. 2022) (emphasizing that chancellors are guardians of children of divorce with a duty to protect their best interests).

[b] Joint physical custody

Page 413. Add to footnote 377:

See also Domke v. Domke, 305 So. 3d 1233, 1239-41 (Miss. Ct. App. 2020) (rejecting mother's argument that joint custody order giving her summers, spring and Thanksgiving breaks, and half of Christmas break amounted to *de facto* sole physical custody in the father; she received significant periods of physical custody).

Page 413. Insert in text after sentence ending in footnote 377:

However, a chancellor erred in significantly reducing a joint custodial father's time from fifteen days a month to eight without finding a material change in circumstances adverse to the child. The court of appeals held that the change in schedule was the equivalent of changing from joint custody to sole physical custody in the mother.[377.1]

[377.1] Briggs v. Weary, 396 So. 3d 1246, 1256-57 (Miss. Ct. App. 2024).

Page 413. Add to footnote 378:

See Johnson v. Smith, 328 So. 3d 145, 159 (Miss. Ct. App. 2021) (affirming award of joint legal and physical custody for eleven months until child started school; father was to have physical custody after eleven months).

[c] Ambiguous custody provisions

Page 413. Insert in text after sentence ending in footnote 379:

And in 2022 the court of appeals held that an agreed provision for joint legal custody "with primary physical custody to the mother . . . with custody for the father . . . as set out herein" created joint physical custody. The parents divided time with the children equally; neither paid child support; the father's time was called "custody;" holiday time for both parents was described as "visitation," and they had equal decision-making responsibilities.[379.1]

[379.1] Lamy v. Lamy, 373 So. 3d 541, 550-51 (Miss. Ct. App. 2022), *cert. granted,* 368 So. 3d 814 (Miss. Aug. 23, 2023).

[2] When joint custody may be awarded

[b] By court order

Page 414. Add to footnote 386:

Cf. Johnson v. Smith, 328 So. 3d 145, 152-53 (Miss. Ct. App. 2021) (chancellor may grant a form of custody that was not specifically requested if that is in the child's best interest).

[3] Factors

[b] Ability to cooperate

Page 416. Add to footnote 400:

See also Morland v. Morland, 396 So. 3d 501, 508 (Miss. Ct. App. 2024) (properly declining to award joint physical custody to father who blocked mother's cellphone and was unwilling to cooperate at the level needed for joint custody); Smith v. Smith,

379 So. 3d 954, 963 (Miss. Ct. App. 2024) (permanent joint custody properly denied; couple was unable to cooperate during two years of temporary joint custody).

Page 416. Add to footnote 403:

See also Thornton v. Thornton, 2025 WL 3638400, at *8 (Miss. Ct. App. Dec. 16, 2025) (court did not err in awarding joint custody to parents in acrimonious divorce; it was in children's best interest to have time with both parents; parents had shared joint custody during the proceedings).

Page 416. Insert in text after sentence ending in footnote 405:

And a chancellor properly denied a verbally abusive father with a violent temper joint legal custody. The evidence showed that he could not work cooperatively with the children's mother.[405.1]

[405.1] Garner v. Garner, 343 So. 3d 1097, 1107 (Miss. Ct. App. 2022).

[4] Joint physical custody vs. sole custody and visitation

Page 418. Insert in text after sentence ending in footnote 416:

The interpretation of an agreement as a sole or joint custody agreement also determines the appropriate standard for modification. In a 2022 case, the court of appeals held that a chancellor applied the wrong legal standard for modification after classifying an ambiguous custody agreement as one for sole physical custody to the mother. The court held that the agreement was one for joint physical custody and reversed for the chancellor to apply the appropriate legal standards for modifying joint physical custody.[416.1]

[416.1] Lamy v. Lamy, 373 So. 3d 541, 550-51 (Miss. Ct. App. 2022), *cert. granted,* 368 So. 3d 814 (Miss. Aug. 23, 2023).

§ 12.05 Restrictions and conditions on custody

Page 419. Insert in text after sentence ending in footnote 427:

However, the supreme court affirmed a chancellor's order that parents enroll a four-year-old boy in half-day daycare, based on his finding that the boy would benefit from the socialization of daycare.[427.1]

[427.1] Kerr v. Kerr, 323 So. 3d 462, 480-81 (Miss. 2021).

§ 12.06 Custody between parents and nonparents

[4] Traditional test

[a] Unfitness or immorality

Page 421. Add to footnote 446:

See also In re T.D., 324 So. 3d 1187, 1196, 1199-2000 (Miss. Ct. App. 2021) (finding father unfit based on drug use, multiple partners in the home, and failure to take medication for schizophrenia) (also finding that father abandoned children through long absences and failure to support).

Page 422. Insert in text after sentence ending in footnote 447:

When a custodial father died, custody of his daughter was awarded to family friends based on the mother's unfitness. During the mother's custody before their divorce, she neglected the girl's medical and educational needs, failing to schedule a necessary surgery and to address the child's dyslexia. The girl repeated a grade after excessive absences and tardies in the mother's care.[447.1]

[447.1] Roberts v. Conner, 332 So. 3d 272, 279, 288-90 (Miss. Ct. App. 2021) (mother was living temporarily with six people in a two-bedroom house).

[b] Abandonment or desertion

Page 422. Add to footnote 454:

See also In re T.D., 324 So. 3d 1187, 1196, 1199-2000 (Miss. Ct. App. 2021) (father abandoned children by his long absences, failure to provide financially, and neglect when he had custody after their mother's death; custody awarded to grandmother) (also finding father unfit based on drug use, multiple partners in the home, and failure to take medication for schizophrenia).

Page 423. Insert in text after sentence ending in footnote 459:

And the supreme court affirmed a chancellor's finding that a mother had deserted her ten-year-old son by failure to support him or visit with him consistently while he was in his grandparents' custody for six years. She did not visit her son for eighteen months after moving to Texas and having a baby. After that period, she visited once or twice a month and provided sporadic financial support.[459.1]

[459.1] Summers v. Gros, 319 So. 3d 479, 483-84, 488-89 (Miss. 2021) (rejecting mother's attack on temporary order as moot, although acknowledging that it made visitation difficult; mother did not act promptly to attack the order).

§ 12.08 Visitation

[1] Noncustodial parent's rights

Page 426. Add to footnote 482:

See Alves-Hunter v. Hunter, 351 So. 3d 468, 474-75 (Miss. Ct. App. 2022) (rejecting mother's argument that father's visitation with son should be restricted because of his special needs; emphasizing importance of time with noncustodial parent) (also finding that mother was encouraging son's fear of visitation).

[2] Scope of visitation

Pagae 427. Add to footnote 491:

See also Briggs v. Jackson, 2025 WL 1691698, at *7 (Miss. Ct. App. June 17, 2025).

Page 427. Add to footnote 492:

Cf. In re T.D., 324 So. 3d 1187, 1200-01 (Miss. Ct. App. 2021) (father who was found unfit to have custody was properly awarded twice-monthly weekend visitation, a day at Christmas, and three hours on each child's birthday).

Page 427. Add to footnote 496:

Cf. Kelley v. Zitzelberger, 342 So. 3d 499, 507 (Miss. Ct. App. 2022) (not error to limit out-of-state father's current visitation to Mississippi to allow father and daughter to rebuild relationship before ordering regular visitation).

Page 427. Add to footnote 499:

See also Polk v. Polk, 332 So. 3d 348, 356-57 (Miss. Ct. App. 2021) (awarding Mississippi father visitation with his son during spring, fall, and Thanksgiving breaks, a week at Christmas, most of the summer, and monthly weekend visits in South Carolina; rejecting his argument that visitation was unduly restrictive).

Page 427. Insert in text after sentence ending in footnote 499:

And a father living in Jackson, Mississippi was properly granted five weeks in the summer, two long visits each semester, alternating spring breaks, alternating holidays, and the option to visit his daughter in Nashville one weekend a month.[499.1]

[499.1] Smith v. Smith, 318 So. 3d 484, 497 (Miss. Ct. App. 2021) (rejecting father's argument that visitation was too restrictive).

Page 428. Add to footnote 508:

See also Wildman v. Wildman, 301 So. 3d 787, 802-03 (Miss. Ct. App. 2020) (chancellor did not err in refusing father's request for daily phone calls and mid-week visitation; chancellor has discretion to establish schedule that fits the children's needs).

Page 428. Insert in text after sentence ending in footnote 508:

The typical Mississippi visitation schedule provides a noncustodial parent with less visitation than in most states. In 2019, five court of appeals judges joined in a concurrence citing a recent study showing that Mississippi ranks forty-eighth in the amount of time provided to noncustodial parents, at 23% of the time. The concurrence urged that courts consider adopting a rebuttable presumption that fit parents should be awarded joint physical custody.[508.1]

[508.1] Avants v. Hamilton, 281 So. 3d 1035, 1043 (Miss. Ct. App. 2019) (Tindall, J., concurring).

Page 428. Insert in text after sentence ending in footnote 510:

In a 2021 case, the court of appeals stated that a visitation award without a specific schedule is error and ordered that the chancellor revisit the schedule on remand.[510.1] However, a chancellor did not err in awarding a father visitation only until his children were of school age. The court of appeals noted that children entering school may be a material change in circumstances – at that point the father could request modification.[510.2]

Courts are not bound by parents' agreements regarding custody and visitation. A chancellor did not err in awarding a father one month of summer visitation rather than two as the parents had agreed. Chancellors have authority to order visitation that is in the child's best interest.[510.3]

[510.1] Warren v. Rhea, 318 So. 3d 1187, 1192 (Miss. Ct. App. 2021).

[510.2] Briggs v. Jackson, 2025 WL 1691698, at *6-7 (Miss. Ct. App. June 17, 2025) (parents lived in different states).

[510.3] Gerty v. Gerty, 296 So. 3d 704, 709-10 (Miss. 2020).

[3] Responsibility for transportation

Page 429. Add to footnote 516:

See also Jefferson v. Jefferson, 327 So. 3d 1085, 1089 (Miss. Ct. App. 2021) (not error to order noncustodial father living in Japan to bear costs of son's transportation for summer visitation; father had resources to pay for travel while the mother testified that she did not).

[4] Restrictions on visitation

[a] Abusive behavior

Page 430. Insert in text after sentence ending in footnote 524:

A chancellor properly allowed a father unsupervised visitation with his daughters after finding no evidence to support the mother's repeated allegations that he had sexually abused one of the girls. Multiple reports to CPS were unsubstantiated. Police investigators testified that they found no evidence of abuse. Repeated interviews with the girl produced no statements regarding abuse and the court-appointed counselor observed a healthy interaction between the father and child.[524.1] In a 2024 case, the court of appeals affirmed a chancellor's order that neither parent contact CPS with allegations of abuse by the other unless they first contacted local law enforcement. The father had filed ten to fifteen unsubstantiated CPS reports over the previous few years.[524.2]

[524.1] Myers v. Myers, 324 So. 3d 808, 818-20 (Miss. Ct. App. 2021).
[524.2] Fortner v. Bratcher, 394 So. 3d 452, 460-61 (Miss. Ct. App. 2024) (stating that "[s]uch orders should be rare").

[b] Family or spousal violence

Page 431. Insert in text after sentence ending in footnote 530:

The court of appeals rejected a father's argument that a chancellor should not have ordered supervised visitation because there was no evidence that he abused his child – family violence includes violence toward any family member, including the parent's spouse. His wife testified to abuse throughout the marriage.[530.1]

[530.1] Brecheen v. Brecheen, 384 So. 3d 567, 572-73 (Miss. Ct. App. 2024).

Page 431. Insert in text after sentence ending in footnote 534:

A chancellor did not err in ordering a father to resolve criminal assault proceedings against him in order to have unsupervised visitation. The statute allows a chancellor to impose "any other condition" necessary for family safety.[543.1]

[534.1] Brecheen v. Brecheen, 384 So. 3d 567, 574 (Miss. Ct. App. 2024).

[c] Dangerous conduct

Page 431. Insert in text after sentence ending in footnote 537:

In another case, a chancellor properly ordered a mother to submit to ongoing quarterly drug tests after she tested negative five times. She had a history of taking unprescribed narcotics.[537.1]

[537.1] Stuckey v. Stuckey, 341 So. 3d 1030, 1041 (Miss. Ct. App. 2022).

[g] Mental health

Page 433. Insert in text after sentence ending in footnote 550:

And a court properly limited a father's visitation with his eleven-year-old daughter to no overnights. His obsessive and controlling behavior – submitting her to lengthy rituals for dressing, bathing, and meals – caused her stress and anxiety.[550.1]

[550.1] Moreland v. Moreland, 368 So. 3d 333, 345 (Miss. Ct. App. 2023).

[h] Poor parenting or household conditions

Page 433. Insert in text after sentence ending in footnote 552:

In contrast, a chancellor properly limited an out-of-state mother's visitation to Mississippi, where she had extended family with whom she and her daughter could stay. The evidence showed that the mother had no home in Florida that was suitable for a child.[552.1]

[552.1] Roberts v. Conner, 332 So. 3d 272, 286 (Miss. Ct. App. 2021).

[l] Child's special medical or educational needs

Page 436. Insert in text after sentence ending in footnote 576:

However, the court of appeals rejected a wife's argument that a chancellor erred in awarding a father regular visitation with their special-needs son, who struggled with one visitation exchange.[576.1]

[576.1] Alves-Hunter v. Hunter, 351 So. 3d 468, 474-75 (Miss. Ct. App. 2022).

§ 12.09 NONPARENT VISITATION

[1] Grandparent visitation in Mississippi
[a] Statutory requirements

Page 437. Insert in text after sentence ending in footnote 590:

The requirements must be met with respect to each child with whom the grandparent seeks visitation. A chancellor erred in awarding a grandmother visitation with three children, including a ten-month-old with whom she did not meet the test for a viable relationship. The grandmother was entitled to visitation with the two older children but not with the younger.[590.1]

[590.1] Greer v. Akers, 364 So. 3d 662, 669-70 (Miss. Ct. App. 2021) (but rejecting parents' argument that the rule against separating siblings should prevent visitation since the younger child was not included); *see also* Sims v. Sims, 337 So. 3d 1085, 1095-97 (Miss. Ct. App. 2021) (grandfather did not establish viable relationship with two younger grandchildren; his son stopped visitation shortly after the twins were born).

[2] Additional factors

Page 438. Insert in text after sentence ending in footnote 597:

The court of appeals reversed an award of visitation even though it agreed that the grandmother had a viable relationship with her grandson and had been unreasonably denied visitation – a court must address the *Martin* factors before awarding visitation.[597.1] However, a court is not required to address a child's best interests unless it first finds that the grandparent had a viable relationship with the child and that visitation was unreasonably denied.[597.2] Nor is a court required to address the factors when a parent agrees to visitation and to the amount.[597.3]

[597.1] McDonald v. Pruwitt, 2025 WL 3212972, at *6 (Miss. Ct. App. May 27, 2025) (modified opinion on motion for rehearing).

[597.2] Sims v. Sims, 337 So. 3d 1085, 1095-97, 1100-01 (Miss. Ct. App. 2021); *see also* Hutson v. Hutson, 385 So. 3d 431, 441 (Miss. Ct. App. 2023); Keasler v. Fowler, 308 So. 3d 441, 444 (Miss. Ct. App. 2020) (court need not consider factors if grandparent does not provide the court with evidence regarding all factors).

[597.3] Poole v. Poole, 392 So. 3d 1245, 1255-56 (Miss. Ct. App. 2023).

[3] Application

[a] Type 1 visitation

Page 439. Insert in text after sentence ending in footnote 604:

In a 2023 case, the court of appeals held that a grandparent may seek visitation against their own child as the custodial parent under Type 1 visitation. Until 2009, the Type 1 subsection provided that when one parent lost custody, died, or had their rights terminated, "either parent of the parent who lost custody" could seek visitation. The statute was amended to provide that when one parent loses custody, "either parent of the child's parents" could seek visitation. Thus, when the child's mother died and the father took custody, his mother could seek visitation as "either parent" of the child's parents.[604.1]

[604.1] Poole v. Poole, 392 So. 3d 1245, 1252-53 (Miss. Ct. App. 2023) (also noting that courts need not consider Type 2 unless Type 1 is unavailable).

[b] Type 2 visitation

Page 439. Add to footnote 606:

See Hutson v. Hutson, 385 So. 3d 431, 441 (Miss. Ct. App. 2023) (parents' testimony may be given more weight than grandparents' in the absence of a showing that the parents are unfit).

Page 439. Insert in text after sentence ending in footnote 608:

A son's refusal to allow his father to visit his children was reasonable – his father had been emotionally abusive and manipulative as a parent and his son saw similar behavior with the grandchildren.[608.1] And parents acted reasonably in denying visitation to a paternal grandfather who failed to comply with their request that he treat his son's stepchildren equally with his biological grandchild.[608.2]

[608.1] Sims v. Sims, 337 So. 3d 1085, 1100 (Miss. Ct. App. 2021).

[608.2] Hutson v. Hutson, 385 So. 3d 431, 438-39 (Miss. Ct. App. 2023) (he said he did not love them or consider them family; provided financial support only for his biological grandchild; his favoritism was causing problems in their family).

Page 440. Insert in text after sentence ending in footnote 611:

Similarly, a chancellor erred in awarding a grandmother visitation with a ten-month-old child with whom she had regular visitation, including overnights. The statute, which is strictly construed, requires visitation for a year or more.[611.1]

[611.1] Greer v. Akers, 364 So. 3d 662, 669-70 (Miss. Ct. App. 2021) (substantial compliance with the statute is not sufficient); *see also* Sims v. Sims, 337 So. 3d 1085, 1095-97 (Miss. Ct. App. 2021) (grandfather did not establish viable relationship with two younger grandchildren; his son stopped visitation shortly after the twins were born).

[5] Scope of visitation

Page 440. Insert in text after sentence ending in footnote 615:

A chancellor who applied the factors did not err in awarding a grandmother one weekend a month and ten days in the summer.[615.1] However, a chancellor was not required to consider the *Martin* factors when the father's attorney did not object to the court's bench ruling granting extensive visitation and consented to the visitation by drafting the order.[615.2]

[615.1] Greer v. Akers, 364 So. 3d 662, 671-72 (Miss. Ct. App. 2021 (rejecting the parents' argument that award was excessive).

[615.2] Poole v. Poole, 392 So. 3d 1245, 1257-58 (Miss. Ct. App. 2023). The dissent argued that parties are not required to object to a bench ruling. They also disagreed that the attorney consented by drafting an order "as to form" at the court's request. *Id.* 1260-61.

[6] Procedure

[d] Attorneys' fees

Page 442. Insert in text after sentence ending in footnote 631:

However, the provision applies only in Type 2 visitation. The supreme court reversed a chancellor's award of attorneys' fees to a mother in a visitation action brought by the paternal grandmother, noting that subsection (4) of the statute, which provides for attorneys' fees, refers to "petitions for visitation rights under subsection (2)." No similar provision refers to subsection (1) visitation.[631.1]

The parents' petition may be filed before or after the hearing.[631.2]

[631.1] Battise v. Aucoin, 311 So. 3d 588, 590-92 (Miss. 2021).

[631.2] Hutson v. Hutson, 385 So. 3d 431, 442-43 (Miss. Ct. App. 2023).

§ 12.10 Appointment of guardian ad litem

[1] Mandatory appointment

Page 444. Insert in text after sentence ending in footnote 652:

The court of appeals rejected parents' argument that an aunt seeking custody waived her request for a mandatory guardian ad litem by failing to raise the issue at trial – a court is required to appoint a guardian in cases involving abuse whether or not the parties raise the issue.[652.1]

[652.1] Monk v. Fountain, 296 So. 3d 761, 765-66 (Miss. Ct. App. 2020) (but finding that a guardian was not required).

Page 444. Add to footnote 653:

See also Savell v. Manning, 325 So. 3d 1208, 1217-18 (Miss. Ct. App. 2021) (chancellor properly refused to appoint a guardian ad litem; mother's allegations of abuse were general, with no specific information, and unsubstantiated by DCPS); Riley v. Heisinger, 302 So. 3d 1243, 1260-61 (Miss. Ct. App. 2020) (counselor's statement that mother's conduct could be considered emotionally abusive did not require appointment of guardian ad litem).

Page 444. Insert in text after sentence ending in footnote 653:

For example, an aunt's unsubstantiated allegations of parental drinking, fraud, and abuse and neglect did not require appointment of a mandatory guardian ad litem. The aunt provided no evidence beyond bare allegations.[653.1] However, a chancellor who appointed a guardian ad litem to investigate allegations of abuse erred in declining to review the guardian's report at trial. After hearing the case, the chancellor determined that the allegations were unsubstantiated and granted the father's motion to exclude the guardian's testimony and report. The supreme court held that the chancellor was required to make findings regarding the report and to provide reasons for rejecting the guardian's recommendations.[653.2]

In 2020, the supreme court held that there is no statutory requirement that a guardian ad litem be appointed to investigate allegations of abuse that arise in cases involving only visitation – by its terms the statute applies to custody cases. In a mother's chancery action for a temporary order of protection from domestic abuse, she sought to restrict the father's visitation and requested appointment of a guardian ad litem. The supreme court held that the requirement for appointment of mandatory guardians ad litem does not apply where custody is not litigated.[653.3]

[653.1] Monk v. Fountain, 296 So. 3d 761, 765-66 (Miss. Ct. App. 2020) (chancellors have discretion to determine whether there is sufficient factual basis to create a legitimate issue of neglect or abuse.)

[653.2] Barber v. Barber, 288 So. 3d 325, 333-35 (Miss. 2020).

[653.3] Barton v. Barton, 306 So. 3d 682, 685-86 (Miss. 2020).

[3] Duty of the guardian ad litem

Page 445. Insert in text after sentence ending in footnote 658:

A court should describe in the order of appointment the role a guardian is intended to fulfill. The court of appeals rejected a mother's argument that a court erred in granting custody to the father without requiring the guardian ad litem to provide custody recommendations. The chancellor ordered the guardian to investigate abuse allegations but did not request a custody recommendation.[658.1] A court may expand or limit a guardian's role as the needs of the case requires.[658.2] A chancellor did not err in changing a guardian's designation from expert witness to require that she testify as a guardian ad litem.[658.3] And a chancellor was not required to appoint a new discretionary guardian ad litem when the appointed guardian ended his representation prior to the end of trial and provided an oral report but did not provide a written report.[658.4]

[658.1] Hamblin v. Allison, 305 So. 3d 1255, 1259-60 (Miss. Ct. App. 2020). *See also* Patrick v. Patrick, 391 So. 3d 1220, 1238-39 (Miss. Ct. App. 2024) (a GAL appointed for the limited purpose of determining whether abuse or neglect had occurred was not required to make a recommendation on whether custody should be modified).

[658.2] S.G. v. D.C., 13 So. 3d 269, 281 (Miss. 2009); *cf.* Gibson v. Gibson, 333 So. 3d 103, 109 (Miss. Ct. App. 2022) (not error that discretionary guardian closing law practice was allowed to testify without providing a written report).

[658.3] Summers v. Gros, 319 So. 3d 479, 485-86 (Miss. 2021).

[658.4] Gibson v. Gibson, 333 So. 3d 103, 109 (Miss. Ct. App. 2022) (chancellor had discretion to determine whether additional GAL was needed; there were no allegations of abuse or neglect).

[a] Guardian as arm of the court

Page 445. Add to footnote 663:

But see C.P. v. Lowndes County Dep't of Child Protection Services, 349 So. 3d 1209, 1224-25 (Miss. Ct. App. 2022) (guardian's report was adequate even though she did not interview the child, parents, or visit the parents' home); Bullock v. Miss. Dep't Child Protection Services, 343 So. 3d 1079, 1088 (Miss. Ct. App. 2022) (rejecting mother's argument that a report was insufficient because the guardian did not interview her; she spoke with the mother individually prior to the TPR proceedings, visited the children, attended the hearing and watched all of the forensic interviews); Chitwood v. Stone County Department of Child Protection Services, 364 So. 3d 644, 648 (Miss. Ct. App. 2020) (rejecting a father's argument that the guardian ad litem's failure to interview him required reversal; he did not respond to her attempts to contact him by phone or through social media); *In re* J.K., 304 So. 3d 184, 192-93 (Miss. Ct. App. 2020) (rejecting father's argument that guardian ad litem's report was inadequate because she never interviewed him or the child; she participated in all court hearings and heard testimony from the father).

Page 445. Add to footnote 664:

See also Gibson v. Gibson, 333 So. 3d 103, 109 (Miss. Ct. App. 2022) (discretionary guardian not required to visit father's home – child was not living with father and he failed to cooperate by providing an address); Roberts v. Conner, 332 So. 3d 272, 280-82 (Miss. Ct. App. 2021) (guardian was not required to visit mother's Florida house that was infested with black mold; there was no evidence that the visit would have provided helpful information).

Page 446. Add to footnote 667:

Cf. Stewart v. Stewart, 309 So. 3d 44, 77 (Miss. Ct. App. 2020) (a mother waived objections to a guardian's qualifications as an expert by failing to object within ten days as required by the court's order).

Page 446. Add to footnote 669:

Cf. Lamy v. Lamy, 373 So. 3d 541, 550-51 (Miss. Ct. App. 2022), *cert. granted,* 368 So. 3d 814 (Miss. Aug. 23, 2023) (rejecting father's argument that guardian's report contained documents that the mother should have provided in discovery, noting that "the majority of those documents were not referenced with any specificity at trial"; the GAL had a duty to provide all documents that she reviewed); *In re* Adoption of M.R.H., 312 So. 3d 385, 389-90 (Miss. Ct. App. 2020) (chancellor did not err in considering medical and school records in the guardian ad litem's report; the father did not object to the order of appointment stating that the guardian was to report on these records).

Page 446. Insert in text after sentence ending in footnote 669:

The fact that a court considers hearsay in a guardian's report does not require reversal if the decision was based on substantial non-hearsay testimony and evidence and was supported by the record.[669.1] In a 2023 opinion, the court of appeals rejected a mother's claim that a guardian who was not designated as an expert could not rely on hearsay in the report. The chancellor instructed the guardian to investigate and report on all matters related to the child, the instructions comported with the statutory duties of a guardian ad litem, and there was substantial non-hearsay evidence to support the court's decision.[669.2] An appellant's failure to object to hearsay at trial is a waiver of the issue on appeal.[669.3]

[669.1] *See In re* Adoption of Jane, 360 So. 3d 286, 297 (Miss. Ct. App. 2023); Denham v. Lafayette County Dep't of Child Protection Services, 356 So. 3d 173, 185 (Miss. Ct. App. 2023); Stewart v. Stewart, 309 So. 3d 44, 78-79 (Miss. Ct. App. 2020) (rejecting argument that guardian's report contained improper hearsay; most of the witnesses and documents discussed in the report were introduced at trial).

[669.2] Denham v. Lafayette County Dep't of Child Protection Services, 356 So. 3d 173, 185-86 (Miss. Ct. App. 2023).

[669.3] *See In re* Adoption of Jane, 360 So. 3d 286, 298 (Miss. Ct. App. 2023).

[4] Findings of fact

Page 447. Insert in text after sentence ending in footnote 674:

The court of appeals reversed and remanded a chancellor's award of visitation to a mother. The order did not state the chancellor's reasons for disregarding the guardian ad litem's recommendation that visitation with the mother would be damaging to the child.[674.1] Similarly, the court of appeals reversed and remanded a chancellor's termination of a father's parental rights because the chancellor did not summarize the guardian's qualifications and recommendations or explain the reasons that she did not follow the guardian's recommendations.[674.2]

[674.1] Warren v. Rhea, 318 So. 3d 1187, 1190-91 (Miss. Ct. App. 2021); *cf.* Embrey v. Young, 337 So. 3d 247, 254-55 (Miss. Ct. App. 2021) (chancellor was not required to appoint a mandatory guardian when the father made allegations of abuse by a family member for the first time at trial, presented no specifics, did not request a guardian ad litem, and the child's counselor and DCPS found the statements unsubstantiated).

[674.2] Roach v. Phillips, 361 So. 3d 174, 179 (Miss. Ct. App. 2023).

[6] Fees

Page 447. Add to footnote 678:

See also Stewart v. Stewart, 309 So. 3d 44, 80-81 (Miss. Ct. App. 2020) (non-prevailing mother ordered to pay seventy percent of guardian's fees).

§ 12.11 Modification of custody orders: Overview

[2] Procedure

[d] Evidence of pre-decree conduct

Page 451. Add to footnote 703:

See also Patrick v. Patrick, 391 So. 3d 1220, 1227 (Miss. Ct. App. 2024) (a chancellor properly considered facts predating a father's unsuccessful 2017 petition to modify custody – a court may consider circumstances arising since the last modification, which was in 2014).

Page 451. Add to footnote 705:

Cf. Roberts v. Conner, 332 So. 3d 272, 287-88 (Miss. Ct. App. 2021) (in a third-party custody action, a court did not err in considering evidence regarding the noncustodial mother's conduct prior to the divorce decree awarding custody to the father).

Page 452. Insert in text after section [4]:

[4a] Clean hands doctrine [NEW]

The court of appeals rejected a mother's argument that the father lacked clean hands to seek custody modification because he failed to take an anger management course as ordered in the divorce decree. The clean hands doctrine cannot override a chancellor's duty to ensure custody that is in the children's best interest.[715.1]

[715.1] Stewart v. Stewart, 309 So. 3d 44, 70-71 (Miss. Ct. App. 2020). *Cf.* Edwards v. Johnson, 2025 WL 2837431, at *11 (Miss. Ct. App. Oct. 7, 2025) (clean hands doctrine not applicable to woman's suit for visitation based on in loco parentis doctrine).

§ 12.12 Between parents

[1] The material change-best interests test

[a] Material change

Page 453. Insert in text after sentence ending in footnote 726:

Parents may not determine in advance that a particular event will be a material change in circumstances.[726.1] A chancellor found void and against public policy an agreement that a material change in circumstances would occur when the youngest child started school or when one of them moved more than one hundred miles away.[726.2]

[726.1] See *infra* § 12.12[3][d] (parents may not agree that relocation is a material change).

[726.2] Schmidt v. Schmidt, 339 So. 3d 163, 173 (Miss. Ct. App. 2022) (but finding that the parents' inability to work cooperatively was a material change).

Page 454. Insert in text after sentence ending in footnote 739:

And a mother's one-time use of marijuana and her discontinued relationship with a convicted sex offender did not require modification.[739.1]

[739.1] Wall v. Wall, 350 So. 3d 620, 622, 627 (Miss. Ct. App. 2022); *see also* Grantham v. Ginn, 372 So. 3d 1047, 1052-53 (Miss. Ct. App. 2023) (modification properly denied in spite of mother's prior drug use and questionable choice of boyfriends; she was sober and remarried to a stable man).

[b] Adverse effect

Page 455. Add to footnote 741:

See also Grantham v. Ginn, 372 So. 3d 1047, 1052-53 (Miss. Ct. App. 2023) (mother's discontinued drug use was material change, but child was not adversely impacted; mother was sober, remarried, and child was doing well); Wall v. Wall, 350 So. 3d 620, 626-27 (Miss. Ct. App. 2022) (even if a material change was shown, boy was not adversely impacted; he was doing well in school, engaged in sports and activities).

Page 455. Add to footnote 746:

Cf. Blagodirova v. Schrock, 368 So. 3d 1261, 1267-68 (Miss. 2023) (court of appeals erred in holding that child was not adversely affected by his stepfather's name-calling, arrest as illegal immigrant, and erratic driving; reinstating chancellor's modification of custody to father).

Page 456. Insert in text after sentence ending in footnote 752:

A chancellor's determination that a mother had engaged in behavior to alienate her son from his father did not require modification – there was no proof that the four-year-old was adversely affected by her actions.[752.1]

[752.1] Martin v. Martin, 416 So. 3d 988, 994-95 (Miss. Ct. App. 2025).

[2] Combined circumstances as material change

Page 457. Add to footnote 757:

See also Thornton v. Thornton, 322 So. 3d 485, 494-95 (Miss. Ct. App. 2021) (modifying custody based on mother's relationship with man convicted of violent crime, younger son's drop in school performance, mother's attempt to alienate boys from their father, and her failure to inform him of children's events or medical problems). *But cf.* Wall v. Wall, 350 So. 3d 620 (Miss. Ct. App. 2022) (modification denied; mother's relationship with sex offender had ended; her use of marijuana occurred on only one occasion; boy's excessive tardies were related to Covid; although eleven-year-old was left at home at night, he was supervised by family in houses next door; no showing of adverse impact).

[3] Specific changes
[b] Substance abuse

Page 457. Add to footnote 762:

See also Stuckey v. Stuckey, 341 So. 3d 1030, 1038-39 (Miss. Ct. App. 2022) (modifying custody from mother who abused prescription drugs and cohabited with a married man who abused alcohol and who had a violent temper).

[c] Custodial parent's remarriage

Page 458. Add to footnote 765:

See also Young v. Neblett, 372 So. 3d 497, 505-06 (Miss. Ct. App. 2023) (modification proper based on proof that stepfather was controlling and emotionally abusive to girls, impacting their mental health).

Page 458. Insert in text after sentence ending in footnote 767:

However, a chancellor properly refused to modify custody from a father based on evidence that his new wife was hostile to the child's mother. Although the guardian ad litem and court-appointed psychologist testified to the stepmother's rage and hostility and expressed concern that it could impact the mother-daughter relationship, the chancellor found that the child had not been adversely affected by her attitude. The court of appeals affirmed, stating that remarriage is a basis for modification only in extreme circumstances.[767.1]

[767.1] Kreppner v. Kreppner, 341 So. 3d 132, 138 (Miss. Ct. App. 2022).

[d] Relocation

Page 459. Insert in text after sentence ending in footnote 778:

In a 2021 case, the court of appeals declined to address a father's request that the court revise the relocation rule, noting that the rule was long-established and should be addressed by the supreme court, not the court of appeals.[778.1]

[778.1] Smith v. Smith, 318 So. 3d 484, 492-93, 497 (Miss. Ct. App. 2021) (mother's relocation from Memphis to Nashville was a not a material change in circumstances that warranted modification of custody to the father; chancellors have broad discretion in setting a visitation schedule that works in the child's best interests).

Page 460. Insert in text after sentence ending in footnote 782:

In a 2023 case, the court of appeals emphasized that a chancellor may consider the impact of a custodial parent's move on the child and the custody arrangement. The court affirmed the chancellor's modification to a noncustodial father with extensive visitation, when the custodial mother moved to Virginia.[782.1]

[782.1] Culver v. Culver, 371 So. 3d 726, 731 (Miss. Ct. App. 2023) (best interest of children was to remain in their lifetime community and home with their activities, friends, and extensive extended family); *see also* May v. Brown, 390 So. 3d 996, 1005 (Miss. Ct. App. 2024) (modifying custody to father when custodial mother moved to Texas without notice, prevented father from seeing his son for three months, and refused to give her Texas address); Fox v. Fox, 381 So. 3d 391, 397 (Miss. Ct. App. 2023) (court should consider impact on child and custody arrangement).

[e] Child's choice

Page 460. Add to footnote 784:

See also Spivey v. Spivey, 404 So. 3d 180, 183-84 (Miss. Ct. App. 2025) (reversing court's order modifying custody based on thirteen-year-old child's request to live with her father).

[f] Custodial parent's cohabitation or sexual behavior

Page 462. Insert in text after sentence ending in footnote 798:

In contrast, custody was properly modified from a mother who cohabited with a married man who abused alcohol and who had a violent temper.[798.1]

[798.1] Stuckey v. Stuckey, 341 So. 3d 1030, 1038 (Miss. Ct. App. 2022) (mother also abused prescription drugs).

Page 462. Insert in text after sentence ending in footnote 801:

A father's cohabitation with a woman and her two children was a material adverse change in circumstances, particularly since the divorce agreement restricted the parents' ability to have romantic partners around their children.[801.1]

[801.1] Day v. Day, 424 So. 3d 1229, 1240 (Miss. Ct. App. 2025).

[h] Interference by custodial parent

Page 463. Add to footnote 806:

See also Kreppner v. Kreppner, 341 So. 3d 132, 139 (Miss. Ct. App. 2022) (custodial father's interference with mother's knowledge of and attendance at events was not a material change in circumstances).

Page 463. Add to footnote 807:

Cf. Croney v. Solangi, 328 So. 3d 749, 753-55 (Miss. Ct. App. 2021) (applying alternative *Riley v. Doerner* test to modify custody of son suffering from anxiety and depression related to parents' decade-long litigation over custody).

Page 463. Add to footnote 808:

See also Patrick v. Patrick, 391 So. 3d 1220, 1229 (Miss. Ct. App. 2024) (affirming modification of custody to father; mother filed multiple unsubstantiated reports of abuse, subjected boys to multiple medical and psychological examinations and recruited sons to spy on father); Riley v. Heisinger, 302 So. 3d 1243, 1256 (Miss. Ct. App. 2020) (modifying custody from mother who denied visitation and disobeyed court orders, refusing to put father's name on the child's birth certificate and on school documents); Stewart v. Stewart, 309 So. 3d 44, 88-90 (Miss. Ct. App. 2020) (mother's attempts to alienate children from their father was a material change in circumstances; she refused visitation, interfered with the girls' therapy, and was complicit in unsubstantiated allegations of abuse).

Page 463. Add to footnote 809:

See also Thornton v. Thornton, 322 So. 3d 485, 498-99 (Miss. Ct. App. 2021) (modifying custody in part because mother interfered with father's relationship, including failing to list the father as an emergency contact, refusing to allow visitation if he was late, failing to inform him of his sons' events or medical issues, and changing schools without letting the father know).

Page 463. Insert in text after sentence ending in footnote 809:

However, a finding of parental alienation did not require modification in the absence of evidence that a four-year-old boy was adversely affected by his mother's conduct.[809.1]

[809.1] Martin v. Martin, 416 So. 3d 988, 994-95 (Miss. Ct. App. 2025).

[i] Friction between child and custodial parent

Page 465. Add to footnote 817:

See also Day v. Day, 424 So. 3d 1229, 1240 (Miss. Ct. App. 2025) (modifying custody from joint to sole custody in mother, based in part on tensions between father and son; son began cutting himself and his grades suffered); Young v. Neblett, 372 So. 3d 497, 505-06 (Miss. Ct. App. 2023) (mother and stepfather's punishment of child – isolation from family for a month – and anger at child for remarks to therapist made child distrust her mother and fear her stepfather; modification affirmed).

[j] Child's behavioral problems

Page 465. Add to footnote 819:

See also Wall v. Wall, 350 So. 3d 620, 625 (Miss. Ct. App. 2022) (no evidence that boy's expression related to self-harm was linked to changes in mother's home rather than to divorce; parents had addressed the issue with counseling).

[4] Alternate test: Ongoing adverse environment

Page 467. Insert in text after sentence ending in footnote 839:

A chancellor properly applied the *Riley v. Doerner* test to modify custody from a mother to a father. The chancellor found no change in the mother's home but stated that the boy's best interest was to live with his father. The son was struggling with anxiety and depression related in large part to the parents' decade of litigation over custody and the mother's attempts to alienate the boy from his father.[839.1] And a chancellor properly modified joint custody of an older boy and younger sister to sole custody in the mother. While there was no proof of an adverse impact on the girl, she had observed the conflicts between her brother and father and it was in her best interest not to be separated from her brother.[839.2]

[839.1] Croney v. Solangi, 328 So. 3d 749, 751, 753, 758-59 (Miss. Ct. App. 2021) (the boy's counselor and guardian ad litem recommended that his mental health would improve if he lived with his father).

[839.2] Day v. Day, 424 So. 3d 1229, 1241-42 (Miss. Ct. App. 2025).

Page 467. Add to footnote 841:

Cf. Kreppner v. Kreppner, 341 So. 3d 132, 138 (Miss. Ct. App. 2022) (rejecting mother's argument that child was living in adverse circumstances with father and stepmother who was hostile to the mother).

[5] Modification of joint physical custody

Page 468. Add to footnote 844:

See also Phillips v. Phillips, 303 So. 3d 835, 840 (Miss. Ct. App. 2020) (a chancellor erred in modifying joint physical custody to sole custody in the father without finding a material change in circumstances).

Page 468. Insert in text after sentence ending in footnote 845:

However, a chancellor erred in significantly reducing a joint custodial father's time from fifteen days a month to eight without finding a material change in circumstances adverse to the child. The court of appeals held that the change in schedule was the equivalent of changing from joint custody to sole physical custody in the mother.[845.1]

[845.1] Briggs v. Weary, 396 So. 3d 1246, 1256-57 (Miss. Ct. App. 2024). However, in two cases involving relocation, the court of appeals has affirmed a substantial change in the custodial time without modifying from joint physical custody to sole custody in one parent. See Scott v. Boudreaux, 375 So. 3d 688, 693-94 (Miss. Ct. App. 2023) (also discussing material change/best interests test); *see also* Domke v. Domke, 305 So. 3d 1233, 1239-41 (Miss. Ct. App. 2020) (rejecting mother's argument that chancellor's modification of joint custody schedule giving her summers and holidays amounted to *de facto* sole physical custody in the father; she received significant periods of physical custody).

[a] Relocation

Page 468. Add to footnote 848:

See Fox v. Fox, 381 So. 3d 391, 398 (Miss. Ct. App. 2023) (chancellor erred in finding that joint custodial mother's move to Florida was not a material change in circumstances; the move made alternating weeks of custody impractical).

Page 469. Add to footnote 852:

See also Smith v. Bellville, 301 So. 3d 678, 683-84 (Miss. Ct. App. 2020) (joint custodial mother's move from Hattiesburg to Tupelo was a material change in circumstances that supported modification to sole custody in father who remained in Hattiesburg).

Page 469. Insert in text after sentence ending in footnote 853:

In two cases, the court of appeals has affirmed a chancellor's modification of a joint custody schedule – rather than modifying to sole custody – when one parent relocated. A chancellor properly modified a military couple's joint custody schedule when the father was assigned to eight years in Colorado. The chancellor found that the children would have greater stability by living with the father during the school year and the mother in the summers and on holidays. The court of appeals affirmed, noting that a custody schedule is similar to a visitation schedule, which may be modified when it is not working.[853.1]

[853.1] Scott v. Boudreaux, 375 So. 3d 688, 693-94 (Miss. Ct. App. 2023) (also discussing material change/best interests test); *see also* Domke v. Domke, 305 So. 3d 1233, 1239-41 (Miss. Ct. App. 2020) (rejecting mother's argument that chancellor's modification of joint custody schedule giving her summers and holidays amounted to de facto sole physical custody in the father; she received significant periods of physical custody). *But cf.* Briggs v. Weary, 396 So. 3d 1246, 1256-57 (Miss. Ct. App. 2024) (holding that chancellor erred in modifying joint custodial father's visitation time from fifteen days a month to eight days a month without finding a material change in circumstances; change amounted to sole custody in mother) (not a relocation case).

[b] Inability to cooperate

Page 469. Insert in text after sentence ending in footnote 856:

The court of appeals also affirmed a chancellor's modification of joint physical custody based on the parents' inability to co-parent, verbal altercations in the children's presence, and failure to work together on medical treatment and education.[856.1]

[856.1] Schmidt v. Schmidt, 339 So. 3d 163, 175 (Miss. Ct. App. 2022) (finding that the children were negatively impacted by the conflict).

[c] Child reaching school age

Page 469. Add to footnote 858:

See Jones v. Curtis, 394 So. 3d 511, 517 (Miss. Ct. App. 2024) (child's reaching school age may in itself be a material change in circumstances allowing modification of joint custody).

[6] Modification of joint legal custody

Page 470. Add to footnote 862:

See also Hopkins v. Perry, 420 So. 3d 354, 366 (Miss. Ct. App. 2025) (reversing a chancellor's modification from sole legal custody in the mother to joint legal custody, based on her interference with visitation and attempts to exclude the father from decision-making; the chancellor did not find that the child was adversely impacted by her actions or that modification was in his best interest).

Page 470. Insert in text after sentence ending in footnote 863:

And a chancellor properly found that parents' inability to work cooperatively over three years of litigation required modification from joint legal custody to sole legal custody in the parent with physical custody of each child.[863.1] A chancellor properly modified joint legal custody to sole legal custody in a mother, finding that the father's obsessive and controlling behavior was a material change in circumstances that was causing his eleven-year-old daughter extreme stress and anxiety.[863.2]

In a 2022 case, the supreme court affirmed a chancellor's order overruling a father's decision regarding his children's education. The parents were joint physical and legal custodians with the father having the right to make decisions in the event of a dispute. When the father enrolled the children in a school where he lived, thirty minutes from the mother's home, the chancellor properly ordered that it was in the children's best interest to attend school where their mother lived.[863.3]

[863.1] Smith v. Smith, 318 So. 3d 484, 493 (Miss. Ct. App. 2021).

[863.2] Moreland v. Moreland, 368 So. 3d 333, 344 (Miss. Ct. App. 2023) (father insisted his daughter go through time-consuming rituals, including bathing and choice of clothing; refused to allow her to have guests; also limiting visitation).

[863.3] Bryant v. Bryant, 348 So. 3d 309, 314-15 (Miss. 2022) (chancellors may alter or modify an agreement between the parties in the children's best interests). The dissenters argued that it was error to override the father's decision without finding a material change in circumstances. *Id.* at 318-19 (Coleman, J., dissenting).

[7] Modification of visitation

Page 470. Add to footnote 866:

See Hopkins v. Perry, 420 So. 3d 354, 367 (Miss. Ct. App. 2025) (chancellor incorrectly cited material change in circumstances test to support change in visitation, but his findings also showed that the order was unworkable).

Page 471. Insert in text after sentence ending in footnote 872:

And a chancellor properly modified a father's summer visitation from one month to two months in the summer based on the mother's ongoing interference with visitation.[872.1] In a 2025 case, the court of appeals affirmed a chancellor's order denying the mother's request to limit visitation and granting the father's request for additional visitation. The court addressed the mother's concerns by including provisions for regular bedtime and that neither party drive with the child after drinking.[872.2]

[872.1] Hopkins v. Perry, 420 So. 3d 354, 368-69 (Miss. Ct. App. 2025).

[872.2] Luke v. Kirkland, 2025 WL 3456661, at *4 (Miss. Ct. App. Dec. 2, 2025).

§ 12.13 Modification in parent-nonparent custody cases

[2] Court-ordered custody to nonparent

Page 472. Insert in text after sentence ending in footnote 879:

However, in a 2025 case, the court of appeals affirmed a youth court's modification of durable legal custody from grandparents to the mother – the material change was the mother's improved circumstances.[879.1]

[879.1] Interest of A.B., 419 So. 3d 976, 983 (Miss. Ct. App. 2025) (mother completed probation, secured employment and housing, and cared for her child for two years in the grandparents' home).

Page 472. Add to footnote 881:

But cf. In re B.P., 383 So. 3d 1259, 1266 (Miss. Ct. App. 2023) (in ruling against father's petition to terminate guardianship and granting legal and physical custody to guardians, court looked to whether the natural parent presumption was overcome; finding that father was unfit to have custody).

§ 12.15 Guardianship of Minors

[2] Procedure

Page 476. Replace footnote 910 with the following:

[910] Miss. Code Ann. § 93-20-113(1).

[4] Duties and powers of the guardian

Page 478. Insert in text after sentence ending in footnote 930:

A chancellor erred in denying a guardian's petition to change his adult disabled ward's last name. She was named for her mother's husband, who was presumed to be her father until he disestablished paternity when she was a teenager. The guardian believed that the ward would have made the choice to change her surname to that of her mother if she was able to do so. A guardian acts in the ward's best interest – the court erred in denying the petition.[930.1]

[930.1] *In re* Jones by and through Taylor, 411 So. 3d 1169, 1175 (Miss. Ct. App. 2025).

[6] Termination of guardianship

Page 478. Insert in text after sentence ending in footnote 933:

A court properly declined a father's request to terminate the guardianship of his infant daughter after he attempted to abscond with her during a visitation, then drew a firearm on the guardians' family members who tried to stop him. The court found that the natural parent presumption was overcome by his actions, which showed that he was unfit to have custody. The court awarded legal and physical custody to the guardians.[933.1]

[933.1] *In re* B.P., 383 So. 3d 1259, 1266 (Miss. Ct. App. 2023).

Insert in text at end of chapter:

§ 12.16 CHILD'S NAME CHANGE [NEW]

In 2025, the supreme court held that chancellors have discretion to determine whether a name change requested by a minor is in the child's best interest. The minor, who was born female but identified as male, petitioned for the name change with the support of both parents. The chancellor entered an order dismissing the petition without prejudice and stating that the petitioner should mature before the name change would be considered. The petitioner appealed, arguing that chancellors have no discretion to deny an uncontested petition for name change. MISS. CODE ANN. ∆ 93-17-1(1) provides that chancellors have jurisdiction "upon the petition of any person to alter the names of such person." Language formerly requiring "good cause shown" for the name change was removed many years ago. The supreme court held that a chancellor may deny a minor's uncontested request for name change based on the child's best interest. The court acknowledged that, ordinarily, a person is entitled to a name change in the absence of a fraudulent purpose. However, in *Marshall v. Marshall,* 93 So. 2d 822 (Miss. 1957), the Mississippi Supreme Court distinguished name change cases involving minors, holding that a chancellor properly refused to change a boy's name to that of his stepfather over his father's objections because it was not in his best interest.[939]

---

[939] Matter of the Petition of S.M.-B., 407 So. 3d 1050 (Miss. 2025).

XIII
CHILD SUPPORT

§ 13.02 Children entitled to support

[4] Disabled adult children

Page 488. Insert in text after sentence ending in footnote 75:

In a 2025 case, the court of appeals held that a chancellor should have considered – under the *Ferguson* factors of "need" and "other factors" – that a mother was responsible for the care and support of her adult disabled daughter.[75.1] And a mother's care for a disabled son who would soon be twenty-one was one of the reasons supporting an alimony award to her.[75.2]

An adult disabled child who is not under a guardianship should be named as a party to the support action. In a 2020 case, the court of appeals affirmed a chancellor's denial of support because an adult disabled son was not joined in the action. The court distinguished *Ravenstein* – in that case, the son was under his mother's guardianship.[75.3]

[75.1] Sistrunk v. Sistrunk, 407 So. 3d 207, 216-17 (Miss. 2025).

[75.2] Howard v. Howard, 2025 WL 1741634, at *5 (Miss. Ct. App. June 24, 2025).

[75.3] Burrell v. Burrell, 289 So. 3d 749, 754, 754 n.10 (Miss. Ct. App. 2020).

§ 13.03 Persons responsible for support

[2] Adoptive parents

Page 489. Add to footnote 85:

See also Hackler v. Hackler, 296 So. 3d 773, 780 (Miss. Ct. App. 2020) (chancellor erred in failing to order adoptive father to pay child support for his wife's biological child).

§ 13.04 Calculating support under the guidelines

[1] The Mississippi guidelines

Page 491. Insert in text after sentence ending in footnote 97:

A chancellor may apply the statutory guidelines to income above $100,000 or deviate from the guidelines. A decision to apply the guidelines must be based on a finding that the statutory guidelines are appropriate under the circumstances. A chancellor did not err in applying the guidelines to a husband's monthly adjusted income of $21,386, ordering that he pay $4,000 in support for two children, based on a finding that the amount was reasonable.[97.1]

In 2022, the Mississippi Legislature amended the guidelines to address child support orders involving low-income payors. The amended statute provides that courts "shall take into account the basic subsistence needs of the obligated parent who has a limited ability to pay."[97.2]

[97.1] Lageman v. Lageman, 313 So. 3d 1075, 1082-83 (Miss. Ct. App. 2021) (court may take family standard of living into account in setting support).

[97.2] MISS. CODE ANN. § 43-19-101(4) (2022). The amendment also provides that courts should not impute a standard amount of income to unemployed or underemployed parents but should look to the parent s individual circumstances. *Id.* (5).

[b] Findings of fact

Page 491. Add to footnote 104:

See Dixon v. Olmstead, 296 So. 3d 227, 233-34 (Miss. Ct. App. 2020) (error to award support based on DHS testimony that guidelines would produce award of $491 without findings regarding payor's income).

Page 492. Add to footnote 111:

See Jones v. Jones, 332 So. 3d 365, 376-77 (Miss. Ct. App. 2021) (chancellor erred in modifying support without evidence and findings regarding the parties' incomes).

Page 492. Insert in text after sentence ending in footnote 112:

The court of appeals has stated that it will not find an abuse of discretion when the amount of child support awarded is presumptively correct under the guidelines.[112.1]

[112.1] Stuckey v. Stuckey, 341 So. 3d 1030, 1040-41 (Miss. Ct. App. 2022). *But see* Doe v. Doe, 341 So. 3d 953, 976-79 (Miss. Ct. App. 2021) (abuse of discretion for chancellor to apply guidelines when father had visitation 42% of the time).

[2] Determining gross income

Page 493. Add to footnote 117:

See also Denham v. Denham, 364 So. 3d 874, 889 (Miss. Ct. App. 2022) (rejecting father's argument that guidelines should have been applied to future anticipated income), *reversed in part on other grounds,* 351 So. 3d 954 (Miss. 2022).

Page 493. Insert in text after sentence ending in footnote 118:

A court should consider all evidence of a payor's income. A chancellor erred in basing child support on the income stated in a payor's 8.05 Financial Statement (reflecting one month of income) after his attorneys provided evidence that the amount stated substantially exceeded his actual earnings for the last six years.[118.1]

[118.1] Chapman v. Chapman, 395 So. 3d 447, 453, 454 (Miss. Ct. App. 2024) (job that lasted one month showed monthly income of $6,939; highest annual income for last six years was $3,691 a month; no evidence to support that payor could earn more) (also noting the importance of averaging income in cases in which income fluctuates).

[a] Overtime and second jobs

Page 494. Add to footnote 122:

See also Williamson v. Williamson, 296 So. 3d 206, 209 (Miss. Ct. App. 2020) (payor's overtime income properly included as part of income for calculation of child support).

[d] Federal and state benefits payable to a child

Page 496. Add to footnote 148:

See Howard v. Howard, 2025 WL 1741634, at *6 (Miss. Ct. App. June 24, 2025).

Page 496. Insert in text after sentence ending in footnote 148:

Similarly, state adoption supplemental benefits payable to children identified as having special needs should not be deducted from the payor's child support obligation. The benefits are for the child's special needs, not a replacement for the payor's obligation.[148.1]

[148.1] Begnaud v. Begnaud, 409 So. 3d 604, 615 (Miss. Ct. App. 2025).

[f] Current spouse's income

Page 496. Insert in text after sentence ending in footnote 154:

A chancellor properly denied a father's request for reduction, in part because some of his listed expenses were shared equally with his current wife. Courts may consider the extent to which a spouse assists with living expenses.[154.1]

[154.1] Hornsby v. Hornsby, 353 So. 3d 507, 512 (Miss. Ct. App. Dec. 2022).

[g] Employment benefits

Page 497. Add to footnote 157:

See also Jefferson v. Jefferson, 327 So. 3d 1085, 1088 (Miss. Ct. App. 2021) (father's gross income included military benefits such as payments for basic allowable subsistence, basic allowable housing, cost of living allowance and clothing entitlements).

Page 497. Insert in text after sentence ending in footnote 158:

However, a court erred in including in a father's income the amount of per diem payments that he received on days on which he worked out of town.[158.1]

[158.1] Chapman v. Chapman, 395 So. 3d 447, 454 (Miss. Ct. App. 2024).

[h] Fluctuating income

Page 497. Insert in text after sentence ending in footnote 161:

The court of appeals clarified the use of averaging in a 2020 case, rejecting a husband's argument that the chancellor should have averaged his income over several years – his income did not fluctuate up and down, but increased steadily for the last three years.[161.1]

[161.1] Williamson v. Williamson, 296 So. 3d 206, 209 (Miss. Ct. App. 2020).

[j] Gifts to payor

Page 498. Insert in text after sentence ending in footnote 167:

In contrast, the court of appeals rejected a custodial father's argument that a chancellor should have ordered an unemployed mother to pay support based on her parents' regular and substantial gifts, distinguishing the two previous cases as involving more regular stipends.[167.1]

[167.1] Smith v. Smith, 318 So. 3d 484, 494-95 (Miss. Ct. App. 2021).

[3] Gross income from self-employment

[a] Determining gross income

Page 498. Insert in text after sentence ending in footnote 172:

The court of appeals in a 2024 case reviewed the cases dealing with self-employed payors and emphasized that (1) chancellors must consider all evidence of income presented by the parties, including tax returns, bank deposits, withdrawals, and expenses; (2) tax returns should be scrutinized carefully for legitimate business expenses and for personal expenses paid through the business; (3) withdrawals in excess of business income should be considered in determining a payor's income. Applying these principles, the court held that a chancellor erred in determining a father's income consisted of his $400 a week salary plus an annual business income of $24,000 shown on his taxes. His bank statements reflected higher income and substantial unexplained withdrawals. He also paid all of his personal expenses through the business, which should have been added to his income.[172.1]

172.1 Myles v. Lewis, 388 So. 3d 598, 609-10 (Miss. Ct. App. 2024).

[b] Business v. personal expenses

Page 499. Add to footnote 178:

See also Briggs v. Jackson, 2025 WL 1691698, at *8 (Miss. Ct. App. June 17, 2025); Myles v. Lewis, 388 So. 3d 598, 610 (Miss. Ct. App. 2024).

[4] Imputing earning capacity

Page 500. Insert in text after sentence ending in footnote 192:

In 2022, the Mississippi Legislature amended the child support guidelines to address imputation of income to unemployed or underemployed parents. The amended statute provides: "Imputation of income shall not be based upon a standard amount in lieu of fact-gathering." If there is insufficient evidence of the parent's past earnings to use as a basis for support, the court should look to the parent's specific circumstances, including, but not limited to the "assets, residence, job skills, educational attainment, literacy, age, health, criminal record and other employment barriers, and record of seeking work, as well as the local job market, the availability of employers willing to hire the obligated parent, prevailing earnings level in the local community, and other relevant factors in the case."[192.1]

[192.1] MISS. CODE ANN. § 43-19-101(5) (2022).

[b] Good faith/voluntariness test

[i] Voluntary unemployment or income reduction

Page 501. Insert in text after sentence ending in footnote 203:

A chancellor properly based an award of $1,200 a month support for one child on an unemployed father's earning capacity of over $100,000. The father relinquished his medical license rather than pay the annual cost of monitoring required by the Physician's Health Program after he underwent treatment for addiction.[203.1]

[203.1] Pace v. Pace, 324 So. 3d 369, 377-78 (Miss. Ct. App. 2021).

[ii] Discharge from employment

Page 502. Insert in text after sentence ending in footnote 212:

However, in 2022, the court of appeals affirmed a chancellor's denial of a father's request to reduce support after he was fired for violating company policy, holding that his job loss was in bad faith. The court stated that bad faith is a voluntary act that reduces income and does not require an intent to harm the child's interests.[212.1]

[212.1] Tolliver v. Tolliver, 334 So. 3d 1228, 1231-32 (Miss. Ct. App. 2022) (father violated company policy by working other jobs while on health leave for Covid).

[iii] Income reduction due to illness

Page 503. Add to footnote 215:

See also Pace v. Pace, 324 So. 3d 369, 378 (Miss. Ct. App. 2021) (finding no evidence that father's stroke years earlier prevented him from working).

Page 503. Insert in text after sentence ending in footnote 217:

In a 2021 case the court of appeals held that a chancellor erred in denying modification to an ophthalmologist father whose income dropped from $280,000 to $54,283. He lost income due to licensure-board mandated in-patient treatment for alcohol abuse, followed by five years of limited days of practice each week. He also lost income due to COVID-19 shutdowns. The court disagreed with the chancellor's determination that his income loss was voluntary, stating that otherwise, "no modification could be granted to a person whose reckless behavior leads to a loss of income."[217.1]

[217.1] Braswell v. Braswell, 336 So. 3d 1121, 1131-32 (Miss. Ct. App. 2021) (also finding that income loss due to COVID shutdown was a material change in circumstances).

[vi] Imprisonment

Page 504. Insert in text after sentence ending in footnote 229:

In 2023, the Mississippi Legislature enacted a new statute addressing child support payments by incarcerated payors. The statute provides, "The court may not consider incarceration as intentional or voluntary unemployment or underemployment when establishing or modifying a child-support order."[229.1]

[229.1] Miss. Code Ann. § 43-19-105.

[5] Imputing hidden income

[c] Based on inconsistent lifestyle or other evidence

Page 505. Add to footnote 237:

See also Gussio v. Gussio, 371 So. 3d 734, 746-47 (Miss. Ct. App. 2023) (not error to award support based on net income of $9,091 even though father's stated income was $4,347; his income was inconsistent with his spending and there was no evidence he incurred debt to support his lifestyle).

[6] Adjustments to gross income

[b] Voluntary deductions

Page 505. Add to footnote 242:

See Bird v. Ladner, 2025 WL 2450057, at *11-12 (Miss. Ct. App. Aug. 26, 2025).

Page 505. Insert in text after sentence ending in footnote 242:

The deduction for taxes does not include payments that exceed the amount of tax due.[242.1]

[242.1] Bird v. Ladner, 2025 WL 2450057, at *11 (Miss. Ct. App. Aug. 26, 2025) (error to deduct all tax payments made by father who received federal tax refund of over $8,000).

[c] Support for other children

[ii] Earlier-born children living in payor's home

Page 506. Insert in text after sentence ending in footnote 248:

However, a chancellor properly reduced a payor's income $130 below the guidelines to reflect that he supported two children in his home.[248.1]

248.1 Morland v. Morland, 396 So. 3d 501, 509 (Miss. Ct. App. 2024).

§ 13.05 Deviation from the guidelines

Page 507. Add to footnote 260:

See also Capocaccia v. Capocaccia, 372 So. 3d 1106, 1117 (Miss. Ct. App. 2023) (reversing child support award for findings of fact; award far exceeded statutory guidelines, without explanation for the deviation).

[2] Extraordinary medical or educational expenses

[b] Educational expenses

Page 508. Add to footnote 265:

See also McGovern v. McGovern, 372 So. 3d 138, 144-145 (Miss. Ct. App. 2023) (award of basic support plus tuition, books, after school care, and activity and sports fees substantially exceeded statutory guidelines; reversing for chancellor to consider educational costs and order support in light of those expenses).

Page 509. Insert in text after sentence ending in footnote 266:

Ordinarily, a parent who did not agree to send a child to private school should not be ordered to pay for private school tuition or expenses. The court of appeals noted however, that a payor has been ordered to pay over their objection if the child has special needs that can be addressed by private schooling.[266.1] A parent's agreement that a child should attend private school is not, in itself, sufficient to support a deviation. The court must also find that the award is reasonable in light of the payor's financial circumstances.[266.2]

[266.1] Myles v. Lewis, 388 So. 3d 598, 611-12 (Miss. Ct. App. 2024) (mother unilaterally enrolled girl in private school because of sports opportunities).

[266.2] Chapman v. Chapman, 395 So. 3d 447, 454-55 (Miss. Ct. App. 2024) (stating that a deviation occurs if basic support plus private school tuition and expenses exceed statutory guidelines).

Page 509. Insert in text after sentence ending in footnote 268:

A parent may agree to private school support beyond what a court may order. A father's agreement to pay the costs of any future private schools that his children might attend obligated him to pay the higher tuition of a school chosen by the mother.[268.1]

A parent's obligation for payment of basic child support is not automatically suspended when a child attends boarding school. The court of appeals rejected a noncustodial father's argument that he should not be required to pay support for the months that his son attended a boarding school in Chattanooga. A parent may not suspend support simply because a child is away at school.[268.2]

[268.1] Smith v. Smith, 318 So. 3d 484, 491-92 (Miss. Ct. App. 2021) (mother provided evidence that the more expensive school offered benefits for child with special educational needs; also noting that their agreement did not limit the costs of private school).

[268.2] Smith v. Smith, 318 So. 3d 484, 496 (Miss. Ct. App. 2021) (father also argued that because the son lived with him for several months before attending boarding school, he was the de facto custodial parent).

[3] Shared custody or extensive visitation

Page 511. Add to footnote 280:

But see Franks v. Franks, 394 So. 3d 467, 483 (Miss. Ct. App. 2024) (rejecting father's argument that court awarding joint physical custody was required to follow *Rayner* calculation; chancellor determined 14% of each spouse's income and calculated the difference, but did not reduce the difference to 50% of that amount as in *Rayner*).

Page 511. Insert in text after sentence ending in footnote 283:

However, in a 2021 case, the court of appeals held that a chancellor abused her discretion by failing to deviate downward in a support order for a father who had visitation forty-two percent of the time. The court remanded for the chancellor to set a reasonably lower amount, noting that the reduction would not harm the children since the wife's income was double that of her husband's.[283.1]

[283.1] Doe v. Doe, 341 So. 3d 953, 977-79 (Miss. Ct. App. 2021). *But see* Wooten v. Wooten, 333 So. 3d 610, 618-19 (Miss. Ct. App. 2022) (chancellor did not err in applying guidelines even though father had approximately 40% of the time in visitation); Stuckey v. Stuckey, 341 So. 3d 1030, 1040-41 (Miss. Ct. App. 2022) (citing *Wooten*, 333 So. 3d at 618-19) (stating that appellate court will not find an abuse of discretion when the amount awarded is presumptively correct under the guidelines).

[12] No order of support

Page 514. Add to footnote 310:

See Scott v. Boudreaux, 375 So. 3d 688, 696 (Miss. Ct. App. 2023) (chancellor properly ordered noncustodial mother to pay support even though father stated he did not seek support); Hackler v. Hackler, 296 So. 3d 773, 780 (Miss. Ct. App. 2020) (chancellor erred in failing to order adoptive stepfather to pay child support for his wife's biological child at divorce).

Page 514. Add to footnote 311:

But cf. Smith v. Smith, 318 So. 3d 484, 494-95 (Miss. Ct. App. 2021) (chancellor did not err in declining to order basic child support from unemployed mother with custody of one of two children; she paid some support in the form of private school tuition for her son).

§ 13.06 Support awards outside the statutory presumption

[1] Yearly adjusted income above $100,000

Page 514. Add to footnote 317:

See also McKenzie v. McKenzie, 397 So. 3d 510, 520 (Miss. Ct. App. 2024) (applying percentages for three children to father's annual income of $163,850).

Page 514. Insert in text after sentence ending in footnote 318:

Similarly, a chancellor properly ordered a husband earning $21,386 a month to pay $4,000 a month for two children. The court found that application of the guidelines was reasonable considering the family's standard of living and that the children were older and had increasing expenses. The court rejected his argument that the award was error because the amount exceeded the total of the children's listed expenses. The mother's financial statement did not list amounts for housing, utilities, transportation, and other household costs.[318.1]

[318.1] Lageman v. Lageman, 313 So. 3d 1075, 1082-83 (Miss. Ct. App. 2021) (court may take family standard of living into account in setting support).

Page 515. Add to footnote 320:

See also Wildman v. Wildman, 301 So. 3d 787, 798-99, 802 (Miss. Ct. App. 2020) (ordering $1,800 a month support for two children from payor with net income of over $10,000 a month; but reversed because combined awards of alimony and child support were excessive).

Page 515. Insert in text after sentence ending in footnote 321:

The court of appeals affirmed a chancellor's child support award of $7,500 a month for two children from a father with adjusted monthly income of $71,000. The father argued that the award should not exceed the children's listed expenses of $2,194 a month. The court held that child support is not capped at the amount of expenses stated in an 8.05 financial statement – a chancellor may consider the family standard of living in determining what is a reasonable amount of child support. A child need not live at a minimal level of comfort while the parent "lives a life of luxury."[321.1]

[321.1] Descher v. Descher, 304 So. 3d 620, 626-27, 635 (Miss. Ct. App. 2020) (Wilson, P.J., dissenting) (dissenting judges argued court erred in ordering child support at three times the amount of the children's actual expenses).

§ 13.07 ADD-ONS TO BASE SUPPORT

[1] Health insurance and medical expenses

Page 516. Insert in text after sentence ending in footnote 335:

In 2021, the court of appeals emphasized the mandatory nature of this requirement, reversing a chancellor's order for failure to address health insurance and uncovered medical expenses. The father's attorney stated in trial that the child was covered by Medicaid and CHIP; however, the chancellor's order did not address the issue. The court reversed and remanded, noting that findings regarding health insurance and provision for payment of uncovered expenses are mandatory.[335.1]

[335.1] Savell v. Manning, 325 So. 3d 1208, 1224 (Miss. Ct. App. 2021) (noting that if the child was covered by Medicaid or CHIP, the chancellor could order the parties to maintain coverage for so long as the child was eligible). *See also* Osing v. Osing, 392 So. 3d 442, 451 (Miss. Ct. App. 2024) (reversing for failure to address medical support); Myles v. Lewis, 388 So. 3d 598, 612-13 (Miss. Ct. App. 2024) (reversing; judgment addressed out-of-pocket medical expenses but not payment of health insurance premiums).

Page 517. Insert in text after sentence ending in footnote 345:

The court of appeals rejected a mother's argument that a provision limiting reimbursement for medical expenses to those presented within one year of receipt was an impermissible private statute of limitations.[345.1]

[345.1] J.T.S. V. M.L.S., 2025 WL12206928, at *18 (Miss. Ct. App. Dec. 16, 2025) (parties can agree to limit damages).

[2] Life insurance

Page 518. Insert in text after sentence ending in footnote 347:

The court of appeals rejected a husband's argument that requiring him to maintain a $900,000 life insurance policy was excessive for his child support obligations, which he calculated would be $357,115. Parents may be ordered to pay amounts in addition to support, including health insurance, out-of-pocket medical expenses, life insurance, and college education.[347.1] Similarly, a $1 million life insurance policy was reasonable to secure an award contemplating $765,000 in child support plus college support, health insurance, and medical expenses.[347.2] A parent's agreement to provide life insurance for children beyond majority is enforceable. [347.3]

[347.1] Gaskin v. Gaskin, 304 So. 3d 641, 647-48 (Miss. Ct. App. 2020).

[347.2] Descher v. Descher, 304 So. 3d 620, 630 (Miss. Ct. App. 2020).

[347.3] Talley v. Talley, 366 So. 3d 901, 905-06 (Miss. Ct. App. 2023) (enforcing a father's obligation to provide life insurance until his children were twenty-five).

[3] College expenses

Page 518. Insert in text after sentence ending in footnote 350:

The award must be based on findings of fact. The court of appeals reversed and remanded an order that a father of three pay one half of his children's college expenses without making findings of fact that the children had the aptitude for college, the father could afford the expense, and based on the children's behavior toward and relationship with him.[350.1]

[350.1] Capocaccia v. Capocaccia, 372 So. 3d 1106, 1118 (Miss. Ct. App. 2023). *Cf.* Sharp v. Sharp, 422 So.3d 472 (Miss. Ct. App. 2025) (findings under these factors are not required when the parent agreed to pay college support).

[c] Child's relationship with parents

Page 519. Add to footnote 358:

Capocaccia v. Capocaccia, 372 So. 3d 1106, 1118 (Miss. Ct. App. 2023) (reversing for failure to make findings of fact on children's relationship with father who was ordered to pay college support).

[e] Scope of college support

Page 519. Insert in text after sentence ending in footnote 362:

Similarly, the court of appeals affirmed a chancellor's order that a father pay "tuition, room and board, meals, laboratory fees, books, sorority or fraternity dues and expenses, automobile expenses, and any other cost generally associated with attendance at a four-year public or private college or university either in-state or -out-of-state."[362.1]

[362.1] Descher v. Descher, 304 So. 3d 620, 627-29 (Miss. Ct. App. 2020) (child is entitled to attend college in keeping with the family standard of living) (also declining to require in advance that basic support of $7,500 a month would be modified during college attendance).

Page 520. Add to footnote 363:

See also J.T.S. v. M.L.S., 2025 WL 12206928, at *23-25 (Miss. Ct. App. Dec. 16, 2025) (costs of college did not include mother's voluntary allowance to children nor was she entitled to reimbursement for allowing them to live rent-free in her condominium).

Page 520. Insert in text after sentence ending in footnote 363:

A chancellor's order need not provide a specific dollar amount. The court of appeals rejected a father's argument that a college support order for tuition, room and board, and "any other cost generally associated with attendance" at a four-year college subjected him to unforeseeable expenses.[363.1]

[363.1] Descher v. Descher, 304 So. 3d 620, 628-29 (Miss. Ct. App. 2020).

[g] Reduction of basic support during college

Page 521. Add to footnote 374:

See also Descher v. Descher, 304 So. 3d 620, 628-29 (Miss. Ct. App. 2020) (chancellor properly refused to provide in advance that basic support of $7,500 a month would be reduced when the children attended college; impossible to know whether they would continue to live with their mother during holidays and summers).

[i] College support after majority

Page 522. Add to footnote 377:

See Capocaccia v. Capocaccia, 372 So. 3d 1106, 1119 (Miss. Ct. App. 2023) (chancellor erred in ordering father to pay support for children "attending and completing" college without limiting support to the age of majority).

[4] Other forms of support

Page 524. Add to footnote 400:

Cf. Savell v. Manning, 325 So. 3d 1208, 1224 (Miss. Ct. App. 2021) (remanding an unclear order that parents provide support for extracurricular activities in proportion to their incomes, but with no finding regarding the mother's income).

Page 524. Insert in text after sentence ending in footnote 400:

A chancellor properly ordered a father to pay $250 a month for extracurricular activities based on the wife's testimony that the parents had always shared these costs.[400.1]

[400.1] Denham v. Denham, 364 So. 3d 874, 890 (Miss. Ct. App. 2022), *reversed in part on other grounds,* 351 So. 3d 954 (Miss. 2022) (reversing custody but not child support).

Page 524. Add to footnote 401:

See also Myles v. Lewis, 388 So. 3d 598, 613 (Miss. Ct. App. 2024) (traveling team did not qualify as an extracurricular activity; mother did not present evidence of circumstances to qualify the activity for a deviation).

Page 524. Insert in text after sentence ending in footnote 401:

A provision for payment of extracurricular activities may be modified. In a 2021 case, the court of appeals affirmed a chancellor's modification of a provision that he found was "unworkable." The father agreed at divorce to pay 100% of the activities "mutually agreed upon by the parties in advance." After the parents disputed the father's obligation for certain activities, the chancellor modified his obligation to a maximum of $6,000 a year per child. The court of appeals affirmed, based on the chancellor's finding that the provision was unworkable because the parties could not agree on activities.[401.1]

[401.1] Smith v. Smith, 318 So. 3d 484, 496-97 (Miss. Ct. App. 2021).

[5] Reasonableness of custodial parent choice

Page 525. Insert in text after sentence ending in footnote 405:

The court of appeals acknowledged the duty of reasonableness in a 2021 case involving a custodial mother's choice of private schools for a daughter with special educational needs. The father agreed at divorce to pay one-half of the costs of any private school that his children "may later attend." He objected to the mother's decision to enroll their daughter in a more expensive and more distant private school with tuition that far exceeded what he was paying at the time of the divorce. The court of appeals acknowledged the reasonableness requirement but found no abuse of discretion in the chancellor's approval of the mother's choice. The court noted that the agreement did not limit the costs of private education and that the mother presented evidence that the school provided advantages over the girl's current school.[405.1]

[405.1] Smith v. Smith, 318 So. 3d 484, 491-92 (Miss. Ct. App. 2021).

§ 13.08 Award of the dependency exemption

[1] Court-ordered transfer

Page 526. Add to footnote 416:

See also Thornton v. Thornton, 322 So. 3d 485, 497 (Miss. Ct. App. 2021) (tax exemption for one child to father; exemption was more valuable to him; no findings required).

Page 526. Add to footnote 417:

See also Wallace v. Wallace, 336 So. 3d 1151, 1158-59 (Miss. Ct. App. 2022).

§ 13.09 Termination of the support obligation

[1] At majority

Page 526. Add to footnote 420:

But cf. Miss. Code Ann. § 93-19-13 (persons eighteen years and older may enter binding contracts for personal property, mortgages, and real property; may enter residential leases and contract for utilities related to leases; and may enter contracts regarding mutual funds, stocks, bonds, and publicly traded equities).

Page 526. Add to footnote 421:

See also Bird v. Ladner, 2025 WL 2450057, at *7 (Miss. Ct. App. Aug. 26, 2025) (error to terminate child support for eighteen-year-old who chose to live temporarily with her father).

Page 527. Insert in text after sentence ending in footnote 424:

A parent may agree to provide support that extends beyond majority.[424.1] The court of appeals held that a father was bound by his agreement to pay college support for six years and to pay basic monthly child support during the six years of college.[424.2]

[424.1] See Talley v. Talley, 366 So. 3d 901, 905-06 (Miss. Ct. App. 2023) (enforcing father's agreement to provide life insurance until children were twenty-five).

[424.2] Stewart v. Stewart, 382 So. 3d 531, 540 (Miss. Ct. App. 2024) (rejecting his argument that basic support ended at twenty-one because their agreement did not specifically state that it would extend past majority).

[2] Upon emancipation

Page 527. Insert in text after sentence ending in footnote 427:

A court is not required to emancipate a child even though one of the discretionary grounds is met. A chancellor did not err in finding that a nineteen-year-old girl was not emancipated even if she cohabited with her boyfriend without her father's permission. She was not working and going to college full time.[427.1]

[427.1] Stewart v. Stewart, 382 So. 3d 531, 541 (Miss. Ct. App. 2024) (disputed whether she was cohabiting).

[3] Based on parental agreement

Page 528. Insert in text after sentence ending in footnote 435:

The court of appeals affirmed a chancellor's order finding that a father was in contempt for nonpayment of child support and orthodontic expenses in the amount of $53,825. The court rejected the father's argument that his obligation was set by the couple's property settlement agreement, incorporated into the judgment of divorce, which ended support when the youngest child turned eighteen. The fact that an agreement was judicially approved is given "great weight;" however, an agreement ending support prior to twenty-one is against public policy and unenforceable.[435.1]

[435.1] White v. White, 357 So. 3d 1165, 1167 (Miss. Ct. App. 2023).

[5] Based on a child's hostility

Page 529. Add to footnote 445:

See also Ivory v. Aubert, 309 So. 3d 1083, 1086, 1089 (Miss. Ct. App. 2020) (reversing a chancellor's order terminating a father's support obligation for a sixteen-year-old child who refused to respond to his calls and texts; her conduct did not meet the clear and extreme standard required to terminate support for a child still in high school).

Page 530. Insert in text after sentence ending in footnote 450:

Applying this test, the supreme court reversed a court of appeals decision, reinstating a chancellor's order terminating a father's child support obligation for a seventeen-year-old son who refused to visit or talk with him for over three years. The chancellor found that the son was at fault in the estrangement. The court of appeals disagreed, holding that the father's conduct was the primary reason. The supreme court reversed, holding that the court of appeals failed to apply the abuse of discretion standard to review the chancellor's finding that the son's conduct caused the estrangement.[450.1]

[450.1] Davis v. Henderson, 332 So. 3d 837, 839-840, 842 (Miss. 2022). *But see id.* at 849-51 (Kitchens, P.J., dissenting) (Coleman, J., dissenting) (two justices dissented, arguing that the facts here fell far short of earlier cases allowing termination of support).

§ 13.10 Mechanics of the award

[2] Escalation clauses

Page 533. Insert in text after sentence ending in footnote 477:

In contrast, a provision stating that a husband would provide yearly tax returns and that his child support "will be increased if appropriate based upon statutory guidelines" lacked sufficient clarity to be enforceable. The phrase "if appropriate" was ambiguous – it was not clear what percentage was to be applied.[477.1]

[477.1] Cole v. Fish, 2025 WL 2450130, at *4-5 (Miss. Ct. App., Aug. 26, 2025).

Page 536. Insert in text after sentence ending in footnote 509:

[9] Retroactivity [NEW]

The court of appeals rejected a custodial father's argument that Miss. Code Ann. § 93-11-65 requires that a court order support back to a year prior to filing the action. Chancellors have discretion to make an initial award of support retroactive up to one year prior to the action but are not required to do so. Furthermore, the court did not err in refusing to award support during the five years the action was pending – the father did not seek temporary support; he took the children to another country without permission; he did not provide evidence of his expenses for the children; and he was responsible for much of the delay in the action. [509.1]

[509.1] Ndicu v. Gacheri, 381 So. 3d 371, 376-77 (Miss. Ct. App. 2023).

§ 13.11 Modification

[1] Role of child support guidelines
[b] Mississippi presumptions

Page 537. Add to footnote 511:

See Dixon v. Olmstead, 296 So. 3d 227, 234 (Miss. Ct. App. 2020) (DHS may apply guidelines to modify support in three-year review without proving a material change in circumstances).

[2] Aspects of order subject to modification

Page 538. Insert in text after sentence ending in footnote 522:

In contrast, a father was obligated to pay the costs of higher tuition at a school chosen by the custodial mother for a child with special educational needs – he had agreed at divorce to pay the costs of any private school that his children "may later attend." The court acknowledged that the mother's choice must be reasonable but also noted that his agreement did not limit the costs of private education.[522.1]

[522.1] Smith v. Smith, 318 So. 3d 484, 492-92 (Miss. Ct. App. 2021) (mother presented evidence that the school provided advantages over the girl's current school).

[4] The material change in circumstances test

Page 538. Add to footnote 526:

Cf. Dixon v. Olmstead, 296 So. 3d 227, 234 (Miss. Ct. App. 2020) (DHS may apply guidelines to modify support in three-year review without proving a material change in circumstances).

[c] Foreseeability

Page 540. Insert in text after sentence ending in footnote 539:

The court of appeals held that a chancellor properly increased support to cover expenses related to a child's autism even though she was diagnosed prior to her parents' divorce – the extent of the costs for her treatment and support were not foreseeable at the time of the divorce.[539.1]

[539.1] Nowell v. Stewart, 356 So. 3d 1217, 1223-24 (Miss. Ct. App. 2022) (mother provided specific proof of the costs and importance of medical and psychiatric care, appropriate activities, and other expenses).

[d] Circumstances that are not a material change

Page 541. Add to footnote 547:

See also Stephens v. Stephens, 328 So. 3d 760, 768-69 (Miss. Ct. App. 2021) (fact that the father agreed to pay higher support because he expected a pay increase that did not materialize is not a material change in circumstances).

[5] Limits on modification

[b] Modification by private agreement

Page 542. Insert in text after sentence ending in footnote 554:

And a father was required to pay $8,750 in arrearages even though he and the mother agreed out of court that he could reduce his $800 a month support obligation to $550 in return for paying his daughter's cheerleading expenses and one half of her orthodontic bills.[554.1]

[554.1] Kelley v. Zitzelberger, 342 So. 3d 499, 506-07 (Miss. Ct. App. 2022) (also denying father a credit for payments for cheerleading, holding that the payments were a voluntary undertaking).

[6] Petitions to increase child support

Page 543. Insert in text after sentence ending in footnote 567:

And the court of appeals held that a chancellor properly increased support to cover expenses related to a child's autism even though she was diagnosed prior to her parents' divorce – the extent of the costs for her treatment and support were not foreseeable at the time of the divorce.[567.1]

[567.1] Nowell v. Stewart, 356 So. 3d 1217, 1223-24 (Miss. Ct. App. 2022) (mother provided specific proof of the costs of medical and psychiatric care, appropriate activities, and other expenses and the importance of them for the girl's well-being).

[b] Increase in costs for older children

Page 545. Insert in text after sentence ending in footnote 579:

However, a chancellor properly increased support based on proof that the children wore contacts and needed braces, as well as having generally increased expenses because they were older.[579.1]

[579.1] Bennett v. Bennett, 316 So. 3d 651, 656 (Miss. Ct. App. 2021) (also noting that the mother's expenses increased because the father had not exercised visitation for several months); *see also* Nowell v. Stewart, 356 So. 3d 1217, 1223-24 (Miss. Ct. App. 2022) (mother provided specific information regarding the costs and importance of psychiatric treatment for a girl with autism, special services such as a driver, expenses for the girl's pets, which were considered therapeutic, and the costs of private school); Best v. Oliver, 296 So. 3d 140, 143 (Miss. Ct. App. 2020) (mother presented sufficient proof of a teenage child's increased expenses to justify a $170 a month increase in child support).

[7] Petitions to reduce support

[a] Reduction in income

Page 546. Insert in text after sentence ending in footnote 587:

A father's income loss caused by mandated COVID-19 shutdowns combined with loss of income resulting from in-patient treatment for substance abuse was an involuntary loss of income that supported a reduction in alimony and child support.[587.1]

[587.1] Braswell v. Braswell, 336 So. 3d 1121, 1132 (Miss. Ct. App. 2021) (father was in bankruptcy, his medical building was foreclosed, and he had no assets).

Page 546. Add to footnote 591:

See also Kelley v. Zitzelberger, 342 So. 3d 499, 505 (Miss. Ct. App. 2022) (denying reduction to forty-year-old father whose military retirement led to income loss; he could work or go to school on the GI Bill but chose to remain unemployed).

Page 547. Insert in text after sentence ending in footnote 594:

Similarly, a father who failed to pay support but who continued to enjoy luxuries such as vacations, international travel, football games, and hosting guests at restaurants was not entitled to a reduction in support.[594.1]

[594.1] Stephens v. Stephens, 328 So. 3d 760, 768-69 (Miss. Ct. App. 2021) (also finding no material change; father's income dropped only slightly from $3,900 a month to $3,686 a month). *See also* Kelley v. Zitzelberger, 342 So. 3d 499, 505 (Miss. Ct. App. 2022) (father's standard of living increased, rather than decreased, after his retirement from the military); Hornsby v. Hornsby, 353 So. 3d 507, 512-13 (Miss. Ct. App. 2022) (denying reduction to father who built a new home, purchased a new BMW, and enjoyed an "upscale lifestyle").

Page 547. Insert in text after sentence ending in footnote 595:

A chancellor erred in denying modification to a father whose income dropped by 75% as a result of his mandated in-patient treatment for substance abuse and time limitations on his practice. He filed for bankruptcy, his medical office was foreclosed, he used available funds to pay arrearages, had no assets, and lived simply.[595.1]

[595.1] Braswell v. Braswell, 336 So. 3d 1121, 1132 (Miss. Ct. App. 2021) (also finding that income loss due to COVID shutdown was a material change in circumstances).

[b] Custodial parent's remarriage

Page 547. Add to footnote 596:

See Best v. Oliver, 296 So. 3d 140, 143 (Miss. Ct. App. 2020) (court properly declined to consider mother's new husband's income in setting father's support obligation).

[c] Emancipation

Page 547. Add to footnote 602:

See also Pumroy v. Sisco, 292 So. 3d 290, 293 (Miss. Ct. App. 2020) (chancellor properly modified a father's child support obligation based on the emancipation of his oldest child, reducing support to the guidelines for two children).

[d] Based on a change in custody

Page 548. Add to footnote 609:

See also Braswell v. Braswell, 336 So. 3d 1121, 1132 (Miss. Ct. App. 2021) (chancellor erred in failing to suspend a father's child support obligation for a period of months in which his son lived with him).

Page 548. Insert in text after section [d]:

[e] Based on change in controlling state guidelines [NEW]

A mother was entitled to a reduction of support without proof of a material change in circumstances when Mississippi gained jurisdiction to modify a Florida order. While the modification action was pending, the chancellor reduced her support from $428 a month to $224 a month. The court of appeals rejected the father's argument that modification was error because she failed to show a material change in circumstances. Her petition for modification was not based on her income reduction but was a request to conform the support award to the Mississippi guidelines.[615.1]

[615.1] Cadigan v. Sullivan, 301 So. 3d 779, 783-85 (Miss. Ct. App. 2020). *But cf.* Kelley v. Zitzelberger, 342 So. 3d 499, 504-06 (Miss. Ct. App. 2022) (rejecting out-of-state father's argument on appeal that chancellor should have applied Mississippi guidelines to his support order regardless of whether he proved a material change in circumstances; father sought reduction based on income loss, not on conforming to the Mississippi guidelines).

[10] Effective date of modification

Page 551. Add to footnote 637:

See also Lacoste v. Lacoste, 313 So. 3d 1097, 1101 (Miss. Ct. App. 2021) (rejecting father's unsupported argument that the rule is an unconstitutional taking of property; also noting that he requested four continuances which extended the time).

Page 551. Add to footnote 639:

See Nowell v. Stewart, 356 So. 3d 1217, 1224, 1230 (Miss. Ct. App. 2022) (chancellor properly made increase retroactive for three years after finding that the four-year litigation dragged out in part due to claims advanced by the father that delayed the proceedings). *See also* Ponder v. Ponder, 349 So. 3d 212, 216-17 (Miss. Ct. App. 2022) (award of increased support made retroactive to a date eighteen months prior to the custodial mother's filing of a modification petition).

Page 551. Insert in text after sentence ending in footnote 641:

In 2024 the legislature amended the provision dealing with the effective date of modification to comply with federal law that limits retroactivity for DHS cases. In doing so, the legislature removed the provision allowing retroactivity to the date of the event justifying modification, thus limiting retroactivity for all child support modifications, not just DHS cases. The statute now provides, "Any order for the support of minor children, whether entered through the judicial system or through an expedited process, shall not be subject to a retroactive modification except from the date that notice of such petition to modify has been given, either directly or through the appropriate agent, to the obligee or to the obligor where the obligee is the petitioner."[641.1]

[641.1] Miss. Code Ann. § 43-19-34(4).

XIV
ENFORCEMENT

§ 14.02 Establishing default in support payments

[3] Credit against arrearages

Page 555. Insert in text after sentence ending in footnote 17:

In an action for arrearages, a chancellor erred in denying credit to a payor's estate for partial payments made by the payor during his lifetime.[17.1]

[17.1] *In re* Estate of Brent, 417 So. 3d 114, 122 (Miss. 2025) (also allowing credit for $75,000 in life insurance cash-out paid to her estate).

[4] Credit against child support

[a] Based on a change in custody

Page 555. Add to footnote 18:

See also Krohn v. Krohn, 294 So. 3d 680, 686, 690 n.6 (Miss. Ct. App. 2020) (father entitled to credit against arrearages for ten months in which his daughter lived with him pursuant to an out-of-court agreement); *cf.* Cadigan v. Sullivan, 301 So. 3d 779, 784 (Miss. Ct. App. 2020) (mother did not owe arrearages for period in which parents agreed to share joint physical custody and suspend child support). *But cf.* Williamson v. Williamson, 296 So. 3d 206, 209-10 (Miss. Ct. App. 2020) (father whose emancipated child lived with him not entitled to offset of support for younger children).

Page 556. Add to footnote 24:

But cf. Wallace v. Wallace, 336 So. 3d 1151, 1156-57 (Miss. Ct. App. 2022) (refusing to credit father with custody of one of two children under an out-of-court agreement; the parties' divorce agreement stated that "no action by the parties will be effective to reduce the amount of child support, . . . and court approval must be obtained before child support can be reduced.").

[b] For direct expenditures

Page 556. Add to footnote 26:

See also Manley v. Manley, 378 So. 3d 390, 398 (Miss. Ct. App. 2023) (father not entitled to credit for payments made for items not included in child support agreement, such as car expenses and rent for son in college).

Page 556. Insert in text after sentence ending in footnote 27:

A father was not entitled to a credit on arrearages for payment of his daughter's cheerleading expenses – he voluntarily undertook to pay them in an out-of-court agreement in return for his wife's agreement to reduce his support by $250 a month.[27.1]

[27.1] Kelley v. Zitzelberger, 342 So. 3d 499, 507 (Miss. Ct. App. 2022) (but refusing to enforce the wife's out-of-court agreement to reduce support; ordering payment of $8,750 in arrearages).

[c] Credit for third-party payments

Page 557. Insert in text after sentence ending in footnote 36:

A father was not entitled to a reduction in support arrearages based on his parents' gifts to his children prior to the couple's separation – the payments were not in lieu of his support obligation.[36.1]

[36.1] Williamson v. Williamson, 296 So. 3d 206, 209-10 (Miss. Ct. App. 2020).

[d] Credit for payments after emancipation
[ii] Undivided order

Page 558. Add to footnote 41:

See also Davis v. Henderson, 332 So. 3d 837, 842 (Miss. 2022) (court should look to the child support guidelines to determine the proper amount of support for one child, rather than dividing the existing support award in half).

§ 14.03 Establishing default: Other obligations

[1] Property division and alimony
[a] Compliance with judgment of divorce

Page 560. Add to footnote 52:

See also Siders v. Zickler, 312 So. 3d 1224, 1228-29 (Miss. Ct. App. 2021) (rejecting husband's argument that obligation to maintain "the existing policy" did not apply because he allowed the policy to lapse before the agreement was signed; parties' intent to provide coverage comparable to the lapsed policy was clear).

Page 560. Insert in text after sentence ending in footnote 52:

A wife was in contempt for failure to execute a quitclaim deed to the marital home within thirty days of the judgment as required. The husband tendered a check for her equity in the home on March 6, the day of the judgment, and provided her with a quitclaim deed.[52.1]

[52.1] Wallace v. Wallace, 309 So. 3d 104, 111 (Miss. Ct. App. 2020). *But cf.* Bozant v. Nguyen, 296 So. 3d 254, 260-62 (Miss. Ct. App. 2020) (husband not in contempt for failure to pay two prior years income tax; wife had agreed to pay taxes and he to reimburse her; she had not yet paid 2013 and 2014 taxes) (husband was liable for 2015 taxes that she had paid).

[2] Child custody and visitation

[a] Interference with visitation

Page 561. Add to footnote 59:

See also Kay v. Kay, 352 So. 3d 198, 204 (Miss. Ct. App. 2022) (father was in contempt for failure to provide visitation to the noncustodial mother, failure to encourage their daughters to visit with her, and for failing to inform her of medical procedures and school events).

Page 561. Insert in text after sentence ending in footnote 62:

In a 2022 case, the court of appeals held that a chancellor did not err in refusing to find a mother in contempt for keeping the children during the father's weekly time for two months during Covid, even though the parents alternated weeks with the children and shared decision-making authority. The chancellor's ruling was based in part on the GAL's report that the children agreed that the altered schedule worked better. The court of appeals stated that the chancellor did not abuse her discretion to deny a contempt judgment "especially during this time of a global pandemic."[62.1]

[62.1] Lamy v. Lamy, 373 So. 3d 541, 552 (Miss. Ct. App. 2022), *cert. granted,* 368 So. 3d 814 (Miss. 2023).

[d] Other child-related provisions

Page 563. Add to footnote 77:

See also Stewart v. Stewart, 309 So. 3d 44, 97-99 (Miss. Ct. App. 2020) (mother who was ordered not to interfere with children's therapy was in contempt for surreptitious taping of her daughter's sessions) (rejecting her argument that she was not ordered *not* to secretly tape the sessions).

§ 14.04 DEFENSES TO JUDGMENT FOR DEFAULT

[1] Out-of-court modification

Page 563. Add to footnote 82:

See also Cadigan v. Sullivan, 301 So. 3d 779, 784 (Miss. Ct. App. 2020) (mother did not owe arrearages for period in which parents agreed to share joint physical custody and suspend child support); Krohn v. Krohn, 294 So. 3d 680, 686, 690 n.6 (Miss. Ct. App. 2020) (father entitled to credit against arrearages for ten months in which his daughter lived with him pursuant to an out-of-court agreement). *But cf.* Wallace v. Wallace, 336 So. 3d 1151, 1156-57 (Miss. Ct. App. 2022) (refusing to credit father with custody of one of two children under an out-of-court agreement; the parties divorce agreement stated that "no action by the parties will be effective to reduce the amount of child support, . . . and court approval must be obtained before child support can be reduced.").

[2] Laches and estoppel

Page 564. Insert in text after sentence ending in footnote 91:

And the court of appeals rejected a mother's argument that a provision limiting reimbursement for medical expenses to those presented within one year of receipt was an impermissible private statute of limitations.[91.1]

[91.1] J.T.S. v. M.L.S., 2025 WL 12206928, at *18 (Miss. Ct. App. Dec. 16, 2025) (parties can agree to limit damages).

Page 564. Insert in text after sentence ending in footnote 92:

However, a father was properly ordered to pay his share of his children's daycare expenses, even though the mother did not provide him with receipts for daycare expenses for eight years. It was undisputed that the father had agreed to pay one-half of daycare expenses and that he was aware the children were in daycare. The chancellor held that the mother's failure to provide receipts for many years, while unreasonable, did not excuse the father from paying his share of daycare costs.[92.1]

[92.1] Wallace v. Wallace, 336 So. 3d 1151, 1157 n. 8 (Miss. Ct. App. 2022) (father was not in contempt because of ambiguity).

[3] Clean hands doctrine

Page 565. Insert in text following sentence ending in footnote 96:

For example, a husband was excused from property settlement provisions related to personal property transfers based on the clean hands doctrine. The couple agreed to divide assets through a coin-toss procedure. However, the wife then refused to go through the process unless she received a set of blue dishes. When her husband insisted on following the coin toss process, she left the meeting. She failed to meet a subsequent court-ordered deadline to complete the process. Later, she sought to require her husband to submit to the process. The court of appeals agreed with the chancellor that the clean hands doctrine barred her from enforcing the agreement that she breached.[96.1]

[96.1] Brown v. Brown, 329 So. 3d 544, 551, 553-54, 559 (Miss. Ct. App. 2021).

[5] Statute of limitations

Page 565. Add to footnote 101:

See Siders v. Zickler, 312 So. 3d 1224, 1231 (Miss. Ct. App. 2021) (rejecting husband's argument that the three-year contracts statute of limitations barred recovery).

Page 566. Insert in text after sentence ending in footnote 105:

The statute of limitations is tolled when a spouse/creditor files suit to enforce a judgment. The supreme court rejected a husband's argument that his wife's judgment lien expired when the seven-year period ran while her action to enforce the judgment was pending.[105.1] However, a chancellor erred in denying a payor credit for partial payments of alimony because the statute of limitations had run on twelve years of arrearages. The fact that there was a substantial uncollectable arrearage did not justify denying him credit for actual payments during the period of enforceable arrearages.[105.2]

[105.1] West v. West, 371 So. 3d 145, 170-71 (Miss. 2023).
[105.2] *In re* Estate of Brent, 417 So. 3d 114, 122-23 (Miss. 2025).

[a] Alimony

Page 566. Insert in text after sentence ending in footnote 106:

A chancellor properly held that a deceased wife's estate's suit for alimony arrearages was limited to payments due within seven years prior to the filing of the suit. The supreme court also held that an alimony receipient's estate has standing to file suit for arrearages outstanding at the recipient's death without regard to whether she filed a contempt petition during her lifetime.[106.1]

[106.1] *In re* Estate of Brent, 417 So. 3d 114, 120-21 (Miss. 2025).

[c] Property division

Page 567. Insert in text after sentence ending in footnote 115:

A wife's lien on Mississippi property, granted in a 2010 Tennessee divorce, was barred by the seven-year statute of limitations. The court rejected the wife's argument that the statute began to run when she enrolled the judgment in 2012, rather than from the rendition of the judgment in 2010.[115.1]

[115.1] Coleman v. WGST, LLC, 328 So 3d. 698, 702-04 (Miss. Ct. App. 2021).

§ 14.05 Contempt

[1] Types of contempt

[a] Civil contempt

Page 568. Insert in text after sentence ending in footnote 126:

A judgment for damages, included in a divorce judgment, is enforceable by contempt. The court of appeals rejected a wife's argument that her husband's judgment against her for damages to his property, consolidated with their divorce, was not subject to contempt.[126.1]

[126.1] Martin v. Martin, 2025 WL 1741578, at *5 (Miss. Ct. App. June 24, 2025).

[b] Criminal contempt

Page 569. Insert in text after sentence ending in footnote 139:

In 2022, the court of appeals discussed whether a finding of contempt by attorneys who failed to appear for a hearing was direct or constructive. The court noted that failure to appear is ordinarily constructive; however, when an attorney informs the court in person that they will not appear, the contempt is direct. The court held that two of three attorneys were in direct contempt because they informed the court by email that they would not appear. The other was in constructive contempt and was entitled to the required due process safeguards.[139.1]

[139.1] Seals v. Stanton, 350 So. 3d 1051, 1059-62 (Miss. 2022) (four judges dissenting, arguing that in most states, only an oral statement to the judge is considered direct contempt; the exception should not include emails and letters).

[2] Defenses to contempt
[a] Inability to pay

Page 570. Insert in text after sentence ending in footnote 147:

A father who attempted to find other work, paid only those bills necessary to keep his practice open, depleted his assets, and lived frugally, should not have been held in contempt for failure to pay $7,000 a month in support orders.[147.1]

[147.1] Braswell v. Braswell, 336 So. 3d 1121, 1132-34 (Miss. Ct. App. 2021).

Page 570. Add to footnote 150:

See also Braswell v. Braswell, 336 So. 3d 1121, 1132-34 (Miss. Ct. App. 2021) (reversing contempt order; father was unable to pay $7,000 a month in support; he promptly petitioned for modification).

[i] Evidence sufficient

Page 570. Add to footnote 154:

See also Archie v. Archie, 337 So. 3d 698, 701, 704 (Miss. Ct. App. 2022) (wife who was unable to obtain home equity loan to pay husband his share of the marital home equity was not in contempt for nonpayment; chancellor properly ordered house sold to satisfy the judgment).

[ii] Evidence insufficient

Page 571. Insert in text after sentence ending in footnote 159:

A payor was properly found in contempt even though he was unemployed. He voluntarily left his job when he faced incarceration for nonpayment of child support, so that he would not be fired. However, at that point he had two months to satisfy the arrearages.[159.1]

[159.1] Stephens v. Stephens, 328 So 3d. 760, 769-70 (Miss. Ct. App. 2021); *see also* Martin v. Martin, 2025 WL 1741578, at *6-7 (Miss. Ct. App. June 24, 2025) (wife who refused to work after divorce properly held in contempt for failure to make payments).

[b] Lack of willfulness

Page 572. Add to footnote 164:

See also Domke v. Domke, 305 So. 3d 1233, 1243 (Miss. Ct. App. 2020) (husband not in contempt for being late on several mortgage payments; no indication the failure was willful and no evidence of negative impact on wife).

Page 572. Add to footnote 167:

See also Bird v. Ladner, 2025 WL 2450057, at *10 (Miss. Ct. App. Aug. 26, 2025) (husband who made payments consistent with his understanding of out-of-court agreement owed the mother but was not in contempt).

Page 572. Add to footnote 171:

Cf. Savell v. Manning, 325 So. 3d 1208, 1219 (Miss. Ct. App. 2021) (father ordered to exercise weekend visitation at home of supervising relative was not in contempt for occasionally being alone with a child for five minutes).

[c] Ambiguity

Page 573. Add to footnote 176:

See also Lindsay v. Lindsay, 303 So. 3d 770, 779-80 (Miss. Ct. App. 2020) (reversing order holding husband in contempt of temporary support order requiring him to "maintain the status quo" by paying all expenses paid prior to June 13, 2014; order did not specify expenses to be paid or the amount of any expense).

Page 573. Add to footnote 177:

See also Warner v. Warner, 341 So. 3d 152, 166-67 (Miss. Ct. App. 2022) (order to pay household bills and wife's medical expenses ambiguous as to whether it included payment for lawn maintenance and wife's glasses); Wallace v. Wallace, 336 So. 3d 1151, 1159 (Miss. Ct. App. 2022) (chancellor did not err in refusing to hold a mother in contempt for failure to provide a noncustodial father with receipts for daycare expenses – their agreement was ambiguous as to whether she had to provide receipts within thirty days).

[h] Acting on advice of counsel or other authority

Page 576. Add to footnote 198:

See also Bird v. Ladner, 2025 WL 2450057, at *5-6 (Miss. Ct. App. Aug. 26, 2025) (father who reduced support based on the emancipation of one child and when another decided to live with him was not in contempt). *Cf.* Moreland v. Moreland, 368 So. 3d 333, 346 (Miss. Ct. App. 2023) (mother who withheld visitation during Covid based on child's fear of father not in contempt where attorney advised mother not to file petition for modification for several months based on court backlog).

Page 576. Add to footnote 199:

See also Savell v. Manning, 325 So. 3d 1208, 1219-20 (Miss. Ct. App. 2021) (mother's disagreement with court's order did not justify repeatedly keeping her child from court-ordered visitation).

§ 14.06 ENTRY OF JUDGMENT

[1] Judgment for arrearages
[a] Interest on arrearages

Page 577. Add to footnote 202:

See *In re* Estate of Brent, 417 So. 3d 114, 124 (Miss. 2025).

Page 577. Add to footnote 208:

See also J.T.S. v. M.L.S., 2025 WL 12206928, at *20 (Miss. Ct. App. Dec. 16, 2025) (chancellor had discretion to set interest rate for child support at 4%).

Page 577. Insert in text after sentence ending in footnote 208:

The court of appeals rejected a former wife's argument that – unlike child support arrearages – property arrearages must include interest at the legal rate. Chancellors have discretion to set the interest rate for arrearages of property division payments.[208.1]

[208.1] J.T.S. v. M.L.S., 2025 WL 12206928, at *22 (Miss. Ct. App. Dec. 16, 2025).

[6] Sanctions for contempt

[a] Incarceration

Page 580. Insert in text after sentence ending in footnote 244:

In a 2023 case, the supreme court affirmed a father's incarceration for five years for failure to comply with an order to complete court-ordered psychological testing and for nonpayment of child support. The court emphasized that contempt is a necessary tool for the operation of courts and that the defendant "held the key" to his release. A defendant may be incarcerated indefinitely until he complies with a court's order. Four justices dissented, arguing that contempt should be enforced by the least onerous method. [244.1]

[244.1] McPhail v. McPhail, 357 So. 3d 602, 615 (Miss. 2023).

Page 581. Insert in text after sentence ending in footnote 248:

A wife argued that suspending a thirty-day incarceration order contingent on her complying with visitation violated the statutory five-year limit on probation. Probation, which requires monitoring and reporting to an officer, is not the same thing as a suspended sentence. A chancellor has authority to suspend a jail sentence conditioned on compliance with an order.[248.1]

[248.1] Savell v. Manning, 325 So. 3d 1208, 1221-22 (Miss. Ct. App. 2021).

§ 14.07 Collection of Judgment

Page 583. Insert in text after sentence ending in footnote 276:

[7] Seizure of unclaimed property [NEW]

In 2022, the Mississippi Legislature amended Miss. Code Ann. § 43-19-31 to authorize the Department of Human Services to cooperate with the Office of the State Treasurer to seize unclaimed property belonging to payors in arrears to satisfy their unpaid child support.[276.1]

[276.1] Laws 2022, Chp. 486 (S.B. 2310), § 1, eff. July 1, 2022.

§ 14.08 Other Enforcement Tools

[3] Criminal prosecution

Page 584. Add to footnote 282:

The statute, formerly applicable to failure to support a child under the age of eighteen, was amended in 2023 to extend to refusals to support children under the age of twenty-one who are not emancipated. *Id.*

XV
ASSISTED REPRODUCTION TECHNOLOGY

§ 15.05 Use of embryos after death: The posthumously conceived child

[1] Inheritance

Page 591. Replace the sentence after footnote 35 with the following:

In 2024, the Mississippi legislature recognized limited inheritance rights for posthumously conceived children. A child conceived using the genetic material of one who is deceased is entitled to a child's share of the decedent's personal property if (1) the decedent consented in writing to use of his or her genetic material; (2) the person intending to use the genetic material for conception notified the decedent's representative and the court within six months of death; (3) the child was in utero within thirty-six months of death; (4) the child was born within forty-five months of death; and (5) the child lived for 120 hours after birth. If more than one child is born, they share a child's share of personalty.[35.1]

[35.1] Miss. Code Ann. § 91-1-33 (also providing that the legislature intended by enacting the statute that a child meeting these requirements will be entitled to the decedent's Social Security benefits).

[3] Social Security benefits

Page 593. Insert in text after sentence ending in footnote 45:

In 2024, the Mississippi legislature recognized inheritance rights for posthumously conceived children. Children who meet the requirements of the statute are entitled to inherit a child's share of the decedent's personal property. The statute also states, "It is the intent of the Legislature that a person who is deemed to be living at the decedent's death under this statute shall be eligible for a child's benefits under [Social Security]."[45.1]

[45.1] Miss. Code Ann. δ 91-1-33.

XVI
TERMINATION OF PARENTAL RIGHTS

Introduction

Page 603. Add to footnote 5:

But cf. In re Adoption of M.R.H., 312 So. 3d 385, 388 (Miss. Ct. App. 2020) (applicable statute in termination hearing is the statute in effect at the time of termination) (applying 2017 amendment to action filed in 2016 but in which rights were terminated in 2017).

Page 603. Insert in text after sentence ending in footnote 5:

The Youth Court Act governs abuse and neglect proceedings, which typically, but not always, precede an action to terminate parental rights. The Youth Court Act was substantially revised in 2023 and 2024 to provide additional rights and protections for children, parents, and foster parents in youth court proceedings.[5.1]

[5.1] See discussion at § 16.01[A], *infra.*

§ 16.01 Jurisdiction and venue

[1] Jurisdiction

Page 604. Insert in text after sentence ending in footnote 11:

However, a youth court is not prohibited from transferring jurisdiction to chancery court to terminate parental rights in connection with an adoption action.[11.1]

Youth court jurisdiction to terminate parental rights is limited to county courts sitting as youth courts. A chancery court had jurisdiction over termination of parental rights even though proceedings were pending in a youth court presided over by a youth court referee.[11.2]

The Mississippi Legislature amended the jurisdictional statute in 2023 to clarify that youth courts' exclusive jurisdiction extends to both voluntary and involuntary termination of parental rights actions. This amendment presumably overrides the supreme court's 2020 decision, *In re Adoption of C.C.B. and S.R.B.,* 306 So. 3d 674, 679 (Miss. 2020). The court there held that a chancery court may hear an adoption action if the parents have executed voluntary releases of their parental rights following a youth court action for abuse and neglect.[11.3]

In an issue of first impression, the supreme court rejected an eighteen-year-old child's argument that a court lacked jurisdiction to terminate her mother's parental rights. The court noted a conflict between Miss. Code Ann. §§ 43-21-15 and 43-15-151(1). The court reconciled the conflict by holding that a court may terminate the parental rights of a child under the age of twenty-one so long as the court acquired jurisdiction before the child was eighteen.[11.4]

[11.1] K.S. v. M.D, 416 So. 3d 72, 77-78 (Miss. 2025).

[11.2] *In re* Adoption of Jane, 360 So. 3d 286, 291 (Miss. Ct. App. 2023); *see also* Hattie T. v. Matthew R., 387 So. 3d 90, 96 (Miss. Ct. App. 2024).

[11.3] Miss. Code Ann. § 93–15–105(1).

[11.4] S.F. v. Lamar County Dep't of Child Protection Services, 373 So. 3d 985, 987-88 (Miss. 2023).

[2] Venue

Page 604. Insert in text after sentence ending in footnote 13:

The court of appeals noted that residence for purposes of this statute is the same as residence under the divorce statutes – residence means physical presence with an intent to remain indefinitely. An Adams County mother's temporary residence at a drug treatment facility in Hinds County, where her child was born, did not constitute "residence" under the statute. She was there involuntarily, returned to Adams County, and did not have the intent to remain indefinitely.[13.1]

[13.1] Doe v. Adams County Dep't of Child Protection Services, 361 So. 3d 1282, 1288-89 (Miss. 2023).

[3] Service of process

Page 604. Insert in text after sentence ending in footnote 15:

The court of appeals rejected a father's argument that the summons in a termination of parental rights case did not properly inform him of his right to be represented by counsel or to obtain a continuance. The summons stated, "you must be represented by an attorney in this cause unless the right to legal representation is waived." The court held that the summons substantially complied with the statute, noting that there is no requirement that a summons use the exact language of the statute. And, the father did not show any prejudice – the court appointed an attorney to represent him.[15.1]

[15.1] *In re* J.K., 304 So. 3d 184, 190 (Miss. Ct. App. 2020).

Page 605. Insert in text after sentence ending in footnote 18:

§ 16.01[A] Abuse and neglect proceedings [NEW]

The Youth Court Act governs abuse and neglect proceedings, which typically, but not always, precede a petition to terminate parental rights. In 2023 and 2024, the act was substantially revised, expanding the rights and protections for children involved in abuse and neglect proceedings. Importantly, the amendments provide that a child in an abuse and neglect proceeding is a party to the proceedings and is entitled to an attorney at all stages of the proceedings, including termination of parental rights.[18.1] The 2024 amendments provide that indigent parents are entitled to representation in termination actions.[18.2]

Also in 2023, the legislature passed a Foster Parents' Bill of Rights that provides significant rights for foster parents of children under the supervision of DCPS. These rights include notice of meetings, appointments, and court hearings; attendance at youth court hearings and communication with the GAL; summons to youth court hearings; and communication with birth and prospective adoptive parents.[18.3]

[18.1] Miss. Code Ann. § 43-21-201.
[18.2] Miss. Code Ann. § 43-21-201(2)(a).
[18.3] Miss. Code Ann. § 43-15-13(11).

§ 16.02 Parties

[2] Necessary parties

Page 605. Insert in text after sentence ending in footnote 24:

DCPS is a necessary party at all stages of abuse and neglect proceedings involving a child for whom the department has custody, including, but not limited to, detention, shelter, adjudicatory, disposition, permanency, termination of parental rights and adoption hearings.[24.1]

In 2024, the statute was amended to provide that a summons must be issued and served on a child who is twelve or older at the time of the hearing.[24.2]

A nonparent custodian does not have standing to object to a court's termination of the parents' rights – a grandmother was a necessary party but lacked standing to appeal the court's termination of parental rights.[24.3]

[24.1] Miss. Code Ann. §§ 43-21-201(7), -501.
[24.2] Miss. Code Ann. § 93-15-107(1)(c). If the child is fourteen years or older at the time of the hearing, the child's preferences regarding termination of parental rights shall be considered by the court. *Id.*
[24.3] *In re* Adoption of Jane, 360 So. 3d 286, 295 (Miss. Ct. App. 2023).

§ 16.03 Termination based on voluntary relinquishment of rights

[2] Revoking a relinquishment of rights

Page 608. Insert in text after sentence ending in footnote 50:

Under the 2016 TPR Law, however, a parent could revoke their consent until the court accepted the consent. The supreme court affirmed a chancellor's order withdrawing her acceptance of a mother's voluntary consent to adoption and allowing the mother to revoke her consent. The court rejected the adopting mother's argument that the consent could not be withdrawn without proof of coercion, duress, or fraud, holding that the new statute altered prior law on revocation.[50.1] Amendments in 2024 appear to remove the right to revoke prior to acceptance. The amendment provides that a parent's release of parental rights "shall serve as a waiver of the parent's right to have a hearing on acceptance of the release."[50.2]

[50.1] Adoption of A.M., 323 So. 3d 509, 513-17 (Miss. 2021).
[50.2] MISS. CODE ANN. § 93-15-111(2).

§ 16.04 INVOLUNTARY TERMINATION WHEN CHILD IS IN DCPS CARE

[1] Cases in which reunification efforts are required

Page 609. Add to footnote 57:

The supreme court rejected DCPS' argument that when termination is based on grounds set out in § 93-15-119 (abandonment, desertion, or unfitness), the court is not required to make the findings under § 93-15-115 related to reunification attempts. X.G.C. v. Jackson County Dep't of Child Prot. Servs, 400 So. 3d 451, 459-460 (Miss. 2025) (but finding that court made proper findings).

Page 609. Insert in text after sentence ending in footnote 59:

The court of appeals affirmed a chancellor's finding that CPS had made reasonable efforts and that the mother had failed to substantially comply with the plan – she did not show up for drug screens, failed those she did show up for, allowed CPS in her home only once over three years; and was arrested repeatedly.[59.1] In contrast, the court held that there was not substantial evidence to support a youth court's finding that CPS exercised reasonable efforts to assist a mother to comply with her reunification plan. For almost two years, CPS told the court and the mother that she was in compliance with the plan and on track to regain custody of her children. CPS then reversed its position stating that there had been no drug screening for the last year and that CPS had incorrectly reported that the mother had stable housing and employment. The court of appeals reversed – if more drug tests were needed, or better documentation of employment, that was CPS's obligation, not the mother's. CPS should have informed her of the issues rather than telling her that she was in compliance.[59.2]

[59.1] Denham v. Lafayette County Dep't of Child Protection Services, 356 So. 3d 173, 182 (Miss. Ct. App. 2023); *see also* S.Z.O. v. Harrison County Dep't of Child Protection Services, 396 So. 3d 1225, 1239 (Miss. Ct. App. 2024) (mother failed drug tests, did not secure stable housing or employment or reliable transportation, and did not visit with child for the three months prior to the termination hearing).
[59.2] *In re* Matter of L.C., 394 So. 3d 517, 532 (Miss. Ct. App. 2024).

[2] Cases in which reunification efforts are not required

Page 610. Insert in text after sentence ending in footnote 62:

The court of appeals rejected a mother's argument that DCPS was required to file a written motion to request bypass of reunification efforts based on aggravated circumstances. The statute does not require notice or a written motion requesting that the court bypass reunification.[62.1]

A mother's parental rights were properly terminated after the youth court found that reunification was not appropriate because the mother had subjected her daughter to aggravating circumstances, including chronic abuse.[62.2] A court properly bypassed reunification efforts for parents whose rights with regard to other children had been terminated.[62.3] And in 2022, the court of appeals held that parental rights were properly terminated after a youth court found that reunification efforts were not required because of a parent's mental disabilities. A psychologist testified that the mother had a severe mental disability with an IQ of 46. The father testified that he had a brain injury as a child.[62.4] The court of appeals held that a father's "extensive violent criminal history" including domestic abuse, aggravated assault, disorderly conduct and involuntary manslaughter, subjected the child to aggravating circumstances, permitting bypass of reunification efforts. The court held that the types of aggravating circumstances listed in the statute are not exclusive, focusing on the phrase "including but not limited to" and that the paramount concern is the best interest of the child, not family reunification.[62.5] However, in 2025, the court of appeals reversed a youth court's decision that DCPS had made reasonable efforts to reunite an incarcerated father with his children. The court noted that DCPS policy requires that staff work with an incarcerated parent's social worker to identify programs available at the prison and make efforts to arrange visitation. In addition, DCPS may extend the service plan for an incarcerated parent.[62.6]

[62.1] *In re* K.M., 365 So. 3d 268, 271 (Miss. Ct. App. 2020).

[62.2] Bullock v. Miss. Dep't of Child Protective Servs, 343 So. 3d 1079, 1086 (Miss. Ct. App. 2022).

[62.3] R.W. v. Mississippi Dep't of Child Prot. Servs., 395 So. 3d 63, 71 (Miss. Ct. App. 2024).

[62.4] C.P. v. Lowndes County Dep't of Child Protection Services, 349 So. 3d 1209, 1221-22 (Miss. Ct. App. 2022). Miss. Code Ann. § 43-21-603(7)(c) states that no reunification is necessary if i(i) The parent has subjected the child to aggravated circumstances, including, but not limited to, abandonment, torture, chronic abuse and sexual abuse. The court of appeals stated that, ordinarily, mental limitations should not be lumped together with physical and sexual abuse as an aggravating circumstance. However, the court held that severe intellectual disability could be an aggravated circumstance under this provision, which states that it is not limited to the listed circumstances. *Id.* at 1222.

[62.5] *In re* Interest of A.R.H., 412 So. 3d 326, 333 (Miss. Ct. App. 2024) (dissenters argued that bypass requires that parent endangered child, which was not the case).

[62.6] Interest of J.S., 422 So. 3d 1055, 1060-61 (Miss. Ct. App. 2025) (DCPS held one meeting with the father; it was not clear that he received a service plan).

[3] Termination factors

[a] Mental illness

Page 610. Insert in text after sentence ending in footnote 63:

The court of appeals held that termination of a mother's rights was appropriate based on her mental disability that made her unable to care for the child. She had an IQ of 46 and functioned on the level of an eleven-year-old child. She could not read, cook, dress, or care for herself and could not be left alone.[63.1]

[63.1] C.P. v. Lowndes County Dep't of Child Protection Services, 349 So. 3d 1209, 1222 (Miss. Ct. App. 2022).

Page 610. Insert in text after sentence ending in footnote 67:

This ground was amended in 2024. Under the amendment, termination may be based on a diagnosis by a qualified mental health professional that the parent has a severe mental illness or deficiency that is unlikely to change in a reasonable period of time and which, based upon expert testimony or an established pattern of behavior, prevents the parent, despite reasonable accommodations, from providing minimally acceptable care for the child."[67.1] Previously, the statute allowed termination if the mental illness made the parent unable "to provide an adequate permanent home" for the child and did not mention accommodation.

[67.1] MISS. CODE ANN. § 93-15-21(A).

[c] Addiction

Page 611. Insert in text after sentence ending in footnote 70:

Applying this test, the court of appeals affirmed termination of a mother's parental rights. After her children were taken into DCPS custody, she failed multiple drug tests, attempted to falsify drug samples, did not exercise visitation with her children, and failed to attend family counseling.[70.1] The court of appeals affirmed termination of an incarcerated father's rights based on his drug addiction and failure to complete drug treatment, even though he completed the only drug program offered in the facility in which he was incarcerated.[70.2]

[70.1] M.A.S. v. Lamar County Dep't of Child Protection Services, 353 So. 3d 460, 480-81 (Miss. Ct. App. 2021); *see also* Chitwood v. Stone County Dep't of Child Protection Services, 364 So. 3d 644, 649 (Miss. Ct. App. 2020) (father failed to attend drug treatment, tested positive for methamphetamine on four of his five drug tests, and failed to meet DCPS requirements for employment, housing, parenting classes, and visitation); *cf.* E.H. v. Lee County Dep't of Child Prot. Servs, 420 So. 3d 341, 351 (Miss. Ct. App. 2025) (terminating parents' rights based on ongoing drug use that prevented home placement, even though parents maintained a relationship with their children, were employed and had suitable housing).

[70.2] *In re* J.K., 304 So. 3d 184, 193-94, 199-200 (Miss. Ct. App. 2020) (termination also based on failure to visit his child and unwillingness to provide care).

[d] Unwillingness to provide care

Page 611. Add to footnote 76:

See also C.P. v. Lowndes County Dep't of Child Protection Services, 349 So. 3d 1209, 1223 (Miss. Ct. App. 2022) (father's rights terminated because he exhibited an ongoing pattern of behavior that showed that he was unwilling to provide for his child).

Page 611. Insert in text after sentence ending in footnote 76:

The Youth Court Act definition of neglect based on failure to provide was amended in 2024 to state that a neglected child is one whose parents fail to provide food, clothing or shelter necessary to sustain life or health, excluding "failure caused primarily by financial inability unless relief services have been offered and refused and the child is in imminent risk of harm."[76.1]

[76.1] Miss. Code Ann. § 43-21-105(l)(iv).

[e] Failure to exercise visitation

Page 611. Add to footnote 78:

See also J.J.B. v. Monroe County Dep't of Child Prot. Servs., 400 So. 3d 403, 409-10 (Miss. 2025) (affirming termination of rights of mother who stopped using drugs but who failed to exercise visitation with her children and who did not obtain employment, suitable housing, or transportation; rejecting her argument that failure to comply with requirements was based on poverty); S.Z.O. v. Harrison County Dep't of Child Protection Services, 396 So. 3d 1225, 1244 (Miss. Ct. App. 2024) (mother failed to exercise visitation with two-year-old child except through FaceTime for seven months, resulting in erosion of relationship).

Page 611. Insert in text after sentence ending in footnote 78:

And a chancellor properly terminated an incarcerated father's rights in part based on failure to visit his infant son. The court rejected his argument that he was unable to provide for or visit his son because he was incarcerated. As the youth court recognized, incarceration cannot be the sole reason for terminating a parent's rights, but it can be considered as a significant factor.[78.1]

[78.1] *In re* J.K., 304 So. 3d 184, 194-95 (Miss. Ct. App. 2020).

[f] Erosion of the parent-child relationship

Page 612. Add to footnote 82:

See also S.Z.O. v. Harrison County Dep't of Child Protection Services, 396 So. 3d 1225, 1244 (Miss. Ct. App. 2024) (mother failed to exercise visitation with two-year-old child except through FaceTime for seven months, resulting in erosion of relationship).

Page 612. Insert in text after sentence ending in footnote 82:

And a mother's rights were properly terminated under this section – her chronic torture and abuse of her daughter caused an erosion of the parent-child relationship.[82.1]

[82.1] Bullock v. Miss. Dep't of Child Protective Services, 343 So. 3d 1079, 1086-88 (Miss. Ct. App. 2022).

[g] Abuse

Page 613. Add to footnote 96:

Cf. Bullock v. Miss. Dep't of Child Protective Services, 343 So. 3d 1079, 1088 (Miss. Ct. App. 2022) (court of appeals affirmed termination of mother's rights to three younger children based on chronic torture and abuse of oldest child).

Page 614. Insert in text after sentence ending in footnote 96:

In several cases, newborns or infants have been removed from parents for anticipatory neglect, based on abuse of older children.[96.1]

[96.1] *See In re* K.M., 365 So. 3d 268, 271 (Miss. Ct. App. 2020); *In re* N.M., 215 So. 3d 1007, 1013-14 (Miss. Ct. App. 2017) (holding that youth court may remove newborn from home based on a recent finding of neglect of other siblings); *In re* T.T., 90 So. 3d 1283, 1285-86 (Miss. Ct. App. 2012) (infant found to be neglected based on death of one sibling and injuries to another) (finding aggravated circumstances that negated attempting reunification with parents).

[h] Offenses against a child

Page 614. Add to footnote 103:

See In re Adoption of M.R.H., 312 So. 3d 385, 389 (Miss. Ct. App. 2020) (rejecting father's argument that he was not convicted of exploitation of a child because the conviction was based on a police officer posing as a child).

§ 16.05 Involuntary termination in private cases

Page 615. Insert in text after last sentence in introduction:

For example, in a 2020 case, a chancellor held that a mother had abandoned her daughter but also looked to the termination grounds in Miss. Code Ann. § 93-15-121 as providing alternative grounds for finding reunification undesirable.[107.1]

[107.1] *In re* Z.M.J., 365 So. 3d 273, 284 (Miss. Ct. App. 2020).

[1] Abandonment

Page 615. Insert in text after sentence ending in footnote 112:

And a father who had not seen his son for four years because of his ongoing drug use and reincarceration had abandoned and deserted his son.[112.1] In a 2023 case, the supreme court affirmed termination of a mother's parental rights for "mental abandonment" of her daughters by failing to protect them from sexual assault by their adoptive father. She continued to live with him after learning he had fathered the child of her fifteen-year-old.112.2 The court of appeals affirmed a chancellor's finding that a mother who continued to abuse alcohol and drugs, rather than complying with the DCPS reunification plan, had abandoned her children. The fact that she completed a drug program after the youth court proceedings were concluded but before the termination hearing, was "too little too late."[112.3]

[112.1] *In re H.S.*, 396 So. 3d 1193, 1199 (Miss. Ct. App. 2024).
[112.2] S.F. v. Lamar County Dep't of Child Protection Services, 373 So. 3d 985, 989-990 (Miss. 2023). A mother's rights have also been terminated for failure to protect under the ground of abuse. *See* § 16.04[3][g] *supra*.
[112.3] Hattie T. v. Matthew R., 387 So. 3d 90, 98 (Miss. Ct. App. 2024).

Page 616. Insert in text after sentence ending in footnote 117:

Similarly, under the new TPR statute, a chancellor properly terminated the rights of a father who did not see his son for five years, even though he paid child support.[117.1]

[117.1] Smith v. Doe, 314 So. 3d 154, 165 (Miss. Ct. App. 2021) (allowing adoption by stepfather, who the boy regarded as his father); *see also* Rogers v. Kresse, 365 So. 3d 1047, 1054-55 (Miss. Ct. App. 2023) (court properly terminated rights of mother who had not seen children for five years; father suspended visitation based on her positive drug tests; she proved only one attempt to visit and went two years with no contact); *In re* Z.M.J., 365 So. 3d 273, 284-86 (Miss. Ct. App. 2020) (affirming termination of rights for mother who gave child to couple to raise, did not support her financially, and did not see her for two and a half years).

[2] Desertion

Page 616. Insert in text after sentence ending in footnote 121:

The court of appeals affirmed a chancellor's finding that a mother who continued to abuse alcohol and drugs, rather than complying with the DCPS reunification plan, deserted her children – she failed to make a commitment to the responsibilities of parenthood within a reasonable time after their birth. The fact that she completed a drug program after the youth court proceedings were concluded but before the termination hearing, was "too little too late."[121.1]

[121.1] Hattie T. v. Matthew R., 387 So. 3d 90, 98 (Miss. Ct. App. 2024).

[3] Unfitness

Page 617. Add to footnote 134:

See also S.Z.O. v. Harrison County Dep't of Child Protection Services, 396 So. 3d 1225, 1238 (Miss. Ct. App. 2024) (terminating mother's rights based on unfitness; she allowed four-month-old child to live in a home with known drug users, leading to the child's ingestion of cocaine rocks, and then attempted to prevent the child's medical treatment).

Page 617. Insert in text after sentence ending in footnote 134:

The supreme court affirmed a chancellors' termination of a mother's parental rights based on unfitness under the new statute. Her infant suffered multiple severe injuries that, according to expert testimony, could only have been caused by abuse, including rib fractures, hip fracture, fractures above and below both knees, and ankle fractures. The chancellor inferred that the mother bore responsibility for the injuries – she was the only person with custody of the child during the period in which the injuries occurred.[134.1] The supreme court affirmed termination of parents' rights based on their inability to care for their medically fragile child after two and a half years of preparation. At eight months of age, he suffered a catastrophic brain injury that left him quadriplegic, blind, deaf, and with multiple medical issues that required constant care characterized by the court as "a matter of life or death."[134.2] And the court of appeals affirmed termination of a father's rights under this section based on evidence that he maintained an "open house" for persons using drugs, supplied the twenty-year-old mother with drugs in return for sex with him and other men, and sent drug users to Walmart to steal for him.[134.3]

[134.1] Coulter v. Dunn, 312 So. 3d 713, 716-17, 719 (Miss. 2021). *See also* X.G.C. v. Jackson County Dep't of Child Prot. Servs, 400 So. 3d 451, 460-61 (Miss. 2025) (affirming termination of father's rights; child was injured three times in his care; expert testified the injuries were unlikely to be accidental).

[134.2] S.D.P. v. Harrison County Dep't of Child Protection Services, 397 So. 3d 466, 474-75 (Miss. 2024) (rejected parents' argument that termination was based on lack of resources; parents were not able to provide critical care for their child).

[134.3] Middlebrook v. Fuller, 349 So. 3d 816, 819-21 (Miss. Ct. App. 2022).

[4] Unlawful sexual conduct [NEW]

A parent's rights may be terminated if they committed a sexual act against the other parent that is unlawful under Miss. Code Ann. §§ 97-3-65 or 97-3-95 and which resulted in conception of the child in question.[134.4] The Mississippi Court of Appeals held that a chancellor properly terminated a father's rights to a three-year-old girl. The child was born as a result of her twenty-year-old mother's relationship with the father in which he and other men had sex with her in return for supplying her with drugs.[134.5]

[134.4] Miss. Code Ann. § 93-15-119. *See* Miss. Code Ann. § 97-3-65 (statutory rape, sex with a child under the age of fourteen, sex without consent by administering a substance that prevents effectual resistance); Miss. Code Ann. § 97-3-95 (sexual battery).

[134.5] Middlebrook v. Fuller, 349 So. 3d 816, 820 (Miss. Ct. App. 2022).

[5] Reunification is not desirable [NEW]

In addition to finding that one of the listed grounds has been proved, a court must find that reunification of the parent and child is not desirable.[134.6] For example, a mother's rights were properly terminated based on proof that she abandoned her children, and that reunification was not in the children's best interest. The younger child did not know her mother at all. The older boy did not want a relationship with his mother, wanted to be adopted by his stepmother, who he considered his mother, and feared for his little sister if they were required to visit with his mother.[134.7]

[134.6] Miss. Code Ann. § 93-15-119.

[134.7] Rogers v. Kresse, 365 So. 3d 1047, 1055 (Miss. Ct. App. 2023) (no contact for five years).

§ 16.06 Procedure

[1] Time of trial

Page 617. Insert in text after sentence ending in footnote 136:

The legislature amended Miss. Code Ann. § 93-17-3 in 2024 to require that a court hold a hearing in TPR cases within ninety days from the date of perfected service on the parents, unless the court makes specific findings that the best interest of the child is served by delaying past the ninety-day period.[136.1]

[136.1] Miss. Code Ann. § 93-15-107(6)(a).

[3] Hearing and preliminary findings

Page 618. Insert in text after sentence ending in footnote 141:

The court of appeals rejected a mother's argument that a youth court failed to advise her of her rights at the beginning of a TPR hearing at which she appeared pro se. The court substantially complied with the statutory requirements by providing the remaining notices later in the proceedings.[141.1] A court's failure to advise parents of their rights at the beginning of a termination hearing did not require reversal. They were represented by counsel and exercised the rights of which they should have been advised.[141.2]

Until 2024, a parent's failure to appeal judgments of adjudication and disposition in youth court was a waiver of alleged errors in those proceedings. A mother who appealed termination of her parental rights, but not the adjudication or disposition order, was procedurally barred from arguing that she was not given the required statutory notice or that the court failed to hold a separate disposition hearing.[141.3] In 2024, the Mississippi legislature amended the youth court statute to provide that all orders prior to the order of termination or durable legal custody, or other order ending the court's jurisdiction, are interlocutory.[141.4]

[141.1] M.A.S. v. Lamar County Dep't of Child Protection Services, 353 So. 3d 460, 477-78 (Miss. Ct. App. 2021) (noting that the mother showed no prejudice as a result of the delay).

[141.2] C.P. v. Lowndes County Dep't of Child Protection Services, 349 So. 3d 1209, 1225 (Miss. Ct. App. 2022). *See also* Interest of K.B., 424 So. 3d 908, 911 (Miss. Ct. App. 2025).

[141.3] M.A.S. v. Lamar County Dep't of Child Protection Services, 353 So. 3d 460, 476 (Miss. Ct. App. 2021) (also finding that she was present, represented by counsel, and did not object).

[141.4] Miss. Code Ann. § 43–21–651(1)(a).

[4] Right to counsel

Page 619. Replace the text from footnote 145 to 147 with the following:

In 2024, the legislature provided that indigent parents have a right to counsel in termination of parental rights proceedings. The amendment states that "All parents have the right to be appointed counsel in termination of parental rights hearings, and the court shall appoint counsel if the court makes a finding that the parent is indigent and counsel is requested by the parent." In addition, indigent custodial parents and noncustodial parents who can demonstrate a significant custodial relationship with the child are entitled to representation at all stages of youth court abuse and neglect proceedings.[146]

---

[146] Miss. Code Ann. § 43-21-201(2)(a) (indigency is to be determined pursuant to Miss. Code Ann. § 25-32-9 and Rule 7.3 of the Mississippi Rules of Criminal Procedure).

Page 619. Add to text after sentence ending in footnote 148:

Applying this statute, the supreme court affirmed a chancellor's order that DCPS pay $3,750 in attorneys' fees for an indigent father in a termination of parental rights proceeding. The court rejected DCPS's argument that the county was responsible for the fees – the statutory authorization for county payment of indigent fees is limited to criminal cases. The chancellor did not abuse his discretion in ordering DCPS, the plaintiff in the action and the agency charged with general expenses for children in its care, to pay the fees.[148.1]

Based on 2023 and 2024 amendments to the Youth Court Act and Termination of Parental Rights Law, children are now entitled to representation at all stages of abuse and neglect proceedings[148.2] and in termination of parental rights proceedings.[148.3] The amendment to the youth court statutes also provides that a guardian ad litem may act in a dual role as guardian and as the child's attorney; however, if a conflict arises, the guardian must report the conflict to the youth court. The guardian should then continue to serve in that role and the court should appoint a new attorney to represent the child.[148.4]

[148.1] Mississippi Dep't of Child Protection Services v. Bynum, 305 So. 3d 1158, 1160, 1163 (Miss. 2020) (but emphasizing that the holding did not impose responsibility on DCPS to pay indigent parents' fees in all cases).

[148.2] Miss. Code Ann. § 43-21-201(1)(c). *See also* Miss. Code Ann. § 43-21-201(4) (attorneys for all parties, including the child's attorney, owe their client "the duties of undivided loyalty, confidentiality and competent representation").

[148.3] Miss. Code Ann. § 93-15-107(1)(c) ("The court shall appoint an attorney for any minor child who is unrepresented, so the court has the benefit of knowing the child's stated interest.").

[148.4] Miss. Code Ann. § 43-21-201(1)(c). Some attorneys have expressed concern that a dual-role guardian ad litem who has obtained confidential information as a child's attorney would be ethically prohibited from continuing as guardian if a conflict arises.

[5] Alternatives to termination

Page 620. Add to footnote 150:

Miss. Code Ann. § 93-15-123 lists factors that may be considered as compelling circumstances not to terminate parental rights.

Page 620. Insert in text after sentence ending in footnote 150:

If a court does not terminate parental rights, custody of the child remains with the person or agency that has custody at that time. If the child is in CPS custody, the court must hold a permanency hearing under the youth court rules.[150.1]

The Youth Court Act provides that in neglect and abuse cases, a court may grant durable legal custody to "any person" if the court finds that temporary relative placement, adoption, or foster care placement is not available, appropriate, or not in the child's best interest, to take effect after the child has been in the person's custody for six months under DCPS supervision. The youth court retains exclusive jurisdiction over durable legal custody orders, including exclusive jurisdiction to modify the order.[150.2] The act also provides for durable legal relative guardianship for relatives or fictive kin who have had physical custody of a child for six months prior to the guardianship and if DCPS has had legal custody or exercised supervision for six months.150.3 A parent whose rights were not terminated may petition to modify an order of durable legal custody.[150.4]

A youth court judge properly modified custody from durable legal custody in the maternal grandparents to the mother. Her release from incarceration, completing probation, securing employment and housing, and caring for her son, were material changes in circumstances. It was in the boy's best interest to be with his mother.[150.5]

Durable legal custody is not an appropriate placement after parents' rights have been terminated.[150.6]

[150.1] Miss. Code Ann. § 93-15-131(1).

[150.2] Miss. Code Ann. § 43-21-609(b).

[150.3] Miss. Code Ann. § 43-21-609(c).

[150.4] *In re* Interest of A.B., 389 So. 3d 1083, 1086 (Miss. Ct. App. 2024) (mother's appeal was a request to modify durable legal custody which should have been filed in the youth court).

[150.5] Interest of A.B., 419 So.3d 976, 983 (Miss. Ct. App. 2025). *But cf.* Adams v. Johnson, 33 So. 3d, 551, 555 (Miss. Ct. App. 2010) (material change must be an adverse change in the custodial nonparent's home, not improvement in the parent's circumstances).

[150.6] Hines v. Caldwell, 384 So. 3d 1238, 1242 (Miss. 2024).

§ 16.07 Order of termination

[3] Rights after termination

Page 621. Insert in text after sentence ending in footnote 157:

A parent whose rights have been terminated is not entitled to recover as a wrongful death beneficiary of their child.[157.1]

[157.1] *In re* Estate of Provenza, 383 So. 3d 1200, 1206-07 (Miss. 2024).

§ 16.08 Appeals

Page 621. Add to text after sentence ending in footnote 161:

Prior to 2024, each disposition order and permanency order was considered a final and appealable judgment. By failing to appeal an order a party waived errors in the judgment, which were not preserved by appealing the final order of termination. For example, a mother waived the argument that an adjudication hearing summons was defective because she did not seek to set aside the order or appeal it and did not raise the issue at the termination proceeding.[161.1]

In 2024, the legislature amended the act to make these orders interlocutory. The provision states that final orders in youth court include grants of durable legal custody or durable legal relative guardianship, orders that transfer jurisdiction to another court (such as for an adoption) or otherwise terminate youth court jurisdiction over the child. "All factual findings, legal determination, and adjudication of issues" prior to the time the final order is entered "are preserved for appellate review and any common law to the contrary is expressly abrogated."[161.2]

The supreme court rejected a mother's argument that a stay of proceedings should be required any time a parent appeals an order terminating their parental rights.[161.3]

[161.1] Clark v. Tippah County Dep't of Child Protection Services, 369 So. 3d 76, 82 (Miss. Ct. App. 2023).

[161.2] Miss. Code Ann. § 43-21-651(1)(a).

[161.3] K.S. v. M.D, 416 So. 3d 72, 80 (Miss. 2025) (decision to stay proceedings is within discretion of the trial judge).

XVII
ADOPTION

§ 17.01 JURISDICTION AND VENUE

[1] Jurisdiction over adoption

Page 623. Insert in text after sentence ending in footnote 2:

The section providing for jurisdiction based on child abandonment or an emergency related to the child was amended in 2020 to require that nonresident adopting parents provide the court with the forms and home study required by the Interstate Compact on the Placement of Children.[2.1]

[2.1] MISS. CODE ANN. § 93-17-3(1)(d).

Page 624. Insert in text after sentence ending in footnote 5:

Youth court jurisdiction to terminate parental rights is limited to county courts sitting as youth courts. A chancery court had jurisdiction over termination of parental rights even though proceedings were pending in a youth court presided over by a youth court referee.[5.1] The Mississippi Legislature amended the jurisdictional statute in 2023 to clarify that youth courts' exclusive jurisdiction extends to both voluntary and involuntary termination of parental rights actions. [5.2]

[5.1] *In re* Adoption of Jane, 360 So. 3d 286, 291 (Miss. Ct. App. 2023).
[5.2] MISS. CODE ANN. § 93–15–105(1).

[4] Indian Child Welfare Act

Page 625. Insert in text after sentence ending in footnote 14:

The ICWA provides preferences for placing children in foster care and adoption – first with extended family, then with other members of the tribe, then with members of other tribes. In 2023, the United States Supreme Court upheld the adoption provisions in an action by adopting parents who challenged the law as violative of the Equal Protection Clause. The Court held that federal law did not impermissibly intrude on the traditionally state-regulated area of family law. Congress has broad authority to legislate matters related to tribes, including family law matters.[14.1]

[14.1] Haaland v. Brackeen, 599 U. S. 255 (2023).

§ 17.02 PARTIES

[1] Petitioner

Page 625. Insert in text after sentence ending in footnote 20:

The requirement that a spouse of an adopting parent join in the petition was amended in 2020 to remove the requirement for joinder (1) of a spouse who does not cohabit or reside with the adopting spouse; and (2) "in any circumstances determined by the court that the adoption is in the best interest of the child."[20.1]

[20.1] MISS. CODE ANN. § 93-17-3(4).

Page 625. Replace the sentence ending in footnote 21 with the following:

Until 2022, the statute prohibited adoption by same-sex couples.

Page 626. Replace the sentence following footnote 23 with the following:

In 2022, the legislature amended the statute to remove the prohibition against adoption by couples of the same gender.[23.1]

[23.1] Laws 2022, Chp. 425 (S.B. 2263), 1, eff. July 1, 2022 (amending MISS. CODE ANN. § 93-17-3).

[3] Grandparents

Page 627. Add to footnote 40:

See also J.B v. M.M., 396 So. 3d 1142, 1146 (Miss. Ct. App. 2024).

§ 17.04 PROCEDURE

[1] Petition

Page 628. Insert in text after sentence ending in footnote 54:

In 2022, the Mississippi Legislature amended the adoption statutes to authorize chancellors to dispense with procedural requirements of the adoption statutes, such as a doctor's certificate and home study, for adult adoptees who consent to the adoption.[54.1]

[54.1] Laws 2022, Chp. 425 (S.B. 2263), 1, eff. July 1, 2022 (amending MISS. CODE ANN. § 93-17-3).

[3] Investigation

Page 629. Insert in text after sentence ending in footnote 64:

The statute was amended in 2020 to provide that home studies may be performed by guardians ad litem who are trained to perform investigations.[64.1] And in 2023, the legislature provided that judges have discretion to dispense with home studies in cases involving foster-to-adopt placements.[64.2]

[64.1] MISS. CODE ANN. § 93-17-3(6).
[64.2] MISS. CODE ANN. § 93-17-11(4).

Page 629. Add to footnote 65:

See In re Adoption of C.C.B. and S.R.B., 306 So. 3d 674, 680-82 (Miss. 2020) (rejecting argument that adoption was invalid because no home study was performed; the requirement is not jurisdictional and may not be raised for the first time on appeal).

§ 17.07 DECREE OF ADOPTION

[2] Effect of decree

[e] Grandparent visitation rights

Page 634. Insert in text after sentence ending in footnote 110:

Visitation awarded to a maternal grandmother was not terminated when the child was adopted by her paternal grandfather and his wife.[110.1]

[110.1] J.B v. M.M., 396 So. 3d 1142, 1147-48 (Miss. Ct. App. 2024).

[3] Nontraditional adoptions

[a] Natural parent visitation

Page 634. Insert in text after sentence ending in footnote 114:

Unfulfilled promises by adoptive parents that a mother would have visitation with her daughter, not mentioned in pleadings or included in the order of adoption, were not a basis to set aside the adoption.[114.1]

[114.1] *In re* Adoption of D.A.S., 391 So. 3d 1181, 1186-87 (Miss. Ct. App. 2024) (denying mother's petition to set aside adoption based on fraud).

[4] Records and confidentiality

Page 635. Insert in text after sentence ending in footnote 118:

Confidentiality applies to all "pleadings, reports, files, testimony, exhibits and records" pertaining to the adoption.[118.1]

[118.1] MISS. CODE ANN. § 93-17-25.

§ 17.08 Actions to set aside adoption

[1] Six-month statute of limitations

Page 635. Add to footnote 125:

See also In re Adoption of D.A.S., 391 So. 3d 1181, 1187 (Miss. Ct. App. 2024) (denying mother's petition to set aside five-year-old adoption for misrepresentations about an "open" adoption).

[4] Challenge based on fraud

Page 637. Insert in text after sentence ending in footnote 133:

And in 2020, the supreme court held that a child's biological father could petition to set aside an adoption for fraud on the court after the six-month statute of limitations had passed. The deceased mother's husband and the adopting parents told the court that the husband was the child's father, knowing that he was not and with knowledge of the biological father's identity.[133.1] The court of appeals held in 2024 that a mother's petition to set aside a five-year-old adoption was not timely even if she could prove fraud on the court, in light of the policy favoring finality in adoptions.[133.2]

[133.1] Stacks v. Smith, 291 So. 3d 809, 816-18 (Miss. 2020) (also holding that failure to join the child's known father, as a necessary party, was a jurisdictional defect allowing him to set aside the adoption after the six-month statute of limitations had passed). *But cf. In re* Adoption of D.A.S., 391 So. 3d 1181, 1186-87 (Miss. Ct. App. 2024) (mother's petition to set aside five-year-old adoption for misrepresentations about an "open" adoption did not amount to fraud on the court).

[133.2] *In re* Adoption of D.A.S., 391 So. 3d 1181, 1187 (Miss. Ct. App. 2024).

[5] Challenge to jurisdiction

Page 637. Insert in text after sentence ending in footnote 138:

In a 2020 case, the supreme court held that a known biological father could set aside an adoption after the six-month statute of limitations had passed. Failure to join him as a necessary party was a jurisdictional defect that could be raised after the running of the six-month statute of limitations. A biological father who has not established his paternity "has a constitutional right to notice of an adoption proceeding if he 'has attempted to establish a substantial relationship with the child.'" The court reversed and remanded for the chancellor to make findings regarding whether the father had established a substantial relationship with the child. If he had, he was a necessary party, and the adoption must be set aside.[138.1]

[138.1] Stacks v. Smith, 291 So. 3d 809, 816-18 (Miss. 2020) (also holding that an adoption can be set aside after the six-month period for fraud on the court).

XVIII
JURISDICTION

§ 18.01 Courts with jurisdiction

[3] Family law exception to federal court jurisdiction

Page 645. Insert in text following sentence ending in footnote 21:

The exception does not apply to cases involving federal questions. In a 2020 case, a federal court retained jurisdiction in a divorce action in which the husband argued that the Mississippi divorce statute is unconstitutional. After he was denied divorce based on constructive desertion, he sued for divorce based on irreconcilable differences. When his wife refused to consent to divorce, he argued that the Mississippi divorce scheme is unconstitutional. His wife removed the case to federal court. The court rejected his argument that the family law exception to federal jurisdiction required abstention. The exception applies only to diversity jurisdiction, not to federal question jurisdiction.[21.1]

[21.1] Watson v. Watson, 2021 WL 1254354, at *3-4 (S.D. Miss. April 5, 2021).

§ 18.02 Overview of jurisdiction

[3] Service of process

Page 650. Add to footnote 79:

See Mississippi Dep't of Human Servs. v. Johnson, 396 So. 3d 1151, 1156 (Miss. 2024) (paternity judgment based on less than thirty days service was void; however, defendant waived the objection by later entering into a stipulated agreement for payments under the judgment without raising the issue).

§ 18.03 Jurisdiction in specific types of actions

[7] Cases alleging abuse or neglect of a child

[a] Jurisdiction within the state

Page 660. Insert in text after sentence ending in footnote 178:

In 2024, the legislature clarified that chancery courts hearing custody matters in which allegations of neglect first arise (and of which the court had no notice prior to the proceedings) may make a determination regarding neglect.[178.1] A chancery court is not required to take jurisdiction – a chancellor did not err in refusing to hear the emergency custody petition of a wife in a dormant divorce action. The case was properly in youth court, which had jurisdiction to modify its order of durable legal custody.[178.2]

[178.1] MISS. CODE ANN. § 43-21-151(1)(C).
[178.2] TAYLOR V. FAIR, 2025 WL 2601027, AT *5 (MISS. CT. APP. SEPT. 9, 2025).

[8] Termination of parental rights

Page 661. Insert in text after sentence ending in footnote 192:

In contrast, a chancery court may proceed with termination proceedings even though an action is pending in a youth court presided over by a youth court referee – the exclusive jurisdiction applies only to county courts sitting as youth courts.[192.1]

[192.1] *In re* Adoption of Jane, 360 So. 3d 286, 291 (Miss. Ct. App. 2023); *see also* Hattie T. v. Matthew R., 387 So. 3d 90, 96 (Miss. Ct. App. 2024).

Page 661. Add to footnote 193:

See Doe v. Adams County Dep't of Child Protection Services, 361 So. 3d 1282, 1288-89 (Miss. 2023) (Adams County mother's temporary, involuntary residence in Hinds County drug treatment facility was not residence; she did not intend to remain indefinitely).

Page 662. Insert in text after sentence ending in footnote 196:

The Mississippi Legislature amended the jurisdictional statute in 2023 to clarify that youth courts' exclusive jurisdiction extends to both voluntary and involuntary termination of parental rights actions. [196.1]

[196.1] MISS. CODE ANN. § 93–15–105(1).

[9] Adoption

Page 662. Insert in text after sentence ending in footnote 201:

When parental rights must be terminated prior to an adoption, a county court sitting as a youth court has exclusive jurisdiction over the termination of rights if an action regarding the child is pending in youth court.[201.1]

[201.1] See discussion § 18.03[8] *infra.*

[11] Proceedings under the Indian Child Welfare Act

Page 664. Insert in text following sentence ending in footnote 225:

The *en banc* court split 8-8 on whether the Act's placement preference is constitutional, leaving the district court decision in place. A majority of the court held that Congress had authority to enact the ICWA and that certain provisions are constitutional, including the right to appointed counsel and the right to intervene in state proceedings.[225.1] However, a majority also ruled that certain provisions unconstitutionally commandeer states, particularly a provision requiring proof of active efforts to prevent the breakup of Native American families and another requiring expert witness testimony in state actions to remove children from homes based on abuse.[225.2] The United States Supreme Court granted *certiorari* to hear the case and upheld the adoption provisions.[225.3] The Court held that federal law did not impermissibly intrude on the traditionally state-regulated area of family law. Congress has broad authority to legislate matters related to tribes, including family law matters. The Court did not, however, address the plaintiff's equal protection challenges.[225.4]

[225.1] Brackeen v. Haaland, 994 F.3d 249, 414 (5th Cir. 2021) (en banc).
[225.2] Brackeen v. Haaland, 994 F.3d 249, 404-06 (5th Cir. 2021) (en banc).
[225.3] Brackeen v. Haaland, 142 S.Ct. 1205 (2022) (mem.).
[225.4] Haaland v. Brackeen, 599 U. S. 255 (2023).

§ 18.05 Interstate conflicts over divorce

[1] Concurrent divorce actions

Page 668. Add to footnote 256:

See also McGrew v. McGrew, 319 So. 3d 1147, 1150-51 (Miss. Ct. App. 2020) (chancellor properly found that Mississippi was an inconvenient forum for hearing a divorce action after both spouses moved to California; wife and children established residence there and action had proceeded to discovery in California).

[2] Full faith and credit

Page 669. Insert in text after sentence ending in footnote 268:

A foreign state's judgment of property division pursuant to divorce, based on proper jurisdiction over the Mississippi resident, may be enforced in Mississippi. However, a foreign decree must be registered for property division to be enforced. In a 2022 opinion, the supreme court held that a Mississippi court had no jurisdiction to divide a couple's marital assets. The husband had obtained a Texas divorce and property division judgment but failed to register the Texas judgment as required for enforcement in Mississippi.[268.1]

[268.1] Ellis v. Ellis, 334 So. 3d 1148, 1153 n. 7 (Miss. 2022) (the court lacked independent jurisdiction to address marital assets because the parties' divorce petitions were dismissed with prejudice).

§ 18.06 Interstate conflicts over support: UIFSA

[4] Modification under UIFSA

[a] Modification of child support

[iii] After all parties have moved

Page 675. Add to footnote 317:

Cf. Cadigan v. Sullivan, 301 So. 3d 779, 785 (Miss. Ct. App. 2020) (payor who moved from Florida to Mississippi entitled to have support reduced to Mississippi guidelines during pendency of modification action).

§ 18.07 Interstate conflicts over custody and parentage: The UCCJEA

[4] Subject matter jurisdiction

[a] Child's home state

Page 679. Add to footnote 357:

See also Smith v. Banks, 350 So. 3d 1191, 1194-95 (Miss. Ct. App. 2022) (Mississippi court lacked jurisdiction over custody dispute involving child whose mother brought him from Louisiana to Mississippi shortly before the hearing).

[9] Jurisdiction to modify custody

[b] Modification in second state

Page 684. Insert in text after sentence ending in footnote 404:

Similarly, a Mississippi court retained jurisdiction to hear a modification petition even though both parents had moved from the state. At the time of filing, the child was living with her grandparents in Mississippi.[404.1]

[404.1] Daly v. Raines, 394 So. 3d 924, 928-29 (Miss. Ct. App. 2023).

XIX
PROCEDURE

§ 19.01 Parties to the action

[7] Pro se parties

Page 693. Add to footnote 47:

See also Guinn v. Claiborne, 352 So. 3d 646, 651 (Miss. Ct. App. 2022) (chancellor properly denied divorce to pro se litigant whose complaint failed to list children born during the marriage or mention property acquired during the marriage).

§ 19.03 Sufficiency of complaint

[1] Request for divorce

Page 696. Add to footnote 72:

See Guinn v. Claiborne, 352 So. 3d 646, 651 (Miss. Ct. App. 2022) (chancellor properly denied divorce to pro se litigant whose complaint failed to list children born during the marriage or mention property acquired during the marriage; complaint failed to meet statutory requirements).

[a] Grounds for fault-based divorce

Page 697. Add to text after sentence ending in footnote 76:

However, a complaint for divorce based on habitual, cruel, and inhuman treatment includes the spousal domestic abuse ground, which is a subset of habitual cruelty. The ground need not be pled separately.[76.1]

[76.1] Wangler v. Wangler, 294 So. 3d 1138, 1141-42 (Miss. 2020) (chancellor erred in refusing to consider ground; wife sought to amend pleadings day before trial to add spousal domestic abuse to request divorce based on cruelty; no amendment was necessary).

[2] Request for financial awards

[b] Child support

Page 698. Add to footnote 93:

See Wallace v. Wallace, 336 So. 3d 1151, 1160 (Miss. Ct. App. 2022) (mother's request for increase in child support sufficient to support award of health insurance).

[c] Request for relief

Page 699. Add to footnote 99:

See also Archie v. Archie, 337 So. 3d 698, 703-04 (Miss. Ct. App. 2022) (request for court to address payment of husband's equity in marital home supported court's order for sale of home, even though not specifically requested).

[3] Custody

Page 699. Insert in text after sentence ending in footnote 101:

And a court did not err in awarding sole custody to a father even though his pleadings requested joint custody. A chancellor may grant a form of custody that was not specifically requested if that is in the child's best interest.[101.1]

[101.1] Johnson v. Smith, 328 So. 3d 145, 153-55 (Miss. Ct. App. 2021) (granting parents joint physical custody for eleven months until child started school, then shifting to physical custody in the father).

[4] Attorney's fees

Page 699. Insert in text after sentence ending in footnote 102:

However, in a 2025 case the supreme court disagreed with a chancellor's ruling that a wife was not entitled to attorney's fees because she did not request them in her pleadings. An award of attorneys' fees is within the broad equitable powers of a chancellor hearing a divorce matter. The court stated that a general prayer for relief is sufficient notice of a request for fees "in certain cases." Because the case was remanded on other matters, the court could consider attorneys' fees on remand.[102.1]

[102.1] Sistrunk v. Sistrunk, 407 So. 3d 207, 218 (Miss. 2025).

§ 19.04 Summons and Service of Process

[1] Summons

[b] In Rule 81 matters

Page 701. Add to footnote 116:

Cf. Clark v. Tippah County Department of Child Protection Services, 369 So. 3d 76, 82 (Miss. Ct. App. 2023) (summons for adjudication hearing was ineffective because it named the wrong county; however, mother waived argument by failing to appeal the adjudication order or raise the issue in the termination proceeding).

Page 701. Add to footnote 117:

Cf. Matter of Conservatorship of Bennett, 418 So. 3d 1256, 1277 n.13 (Miss. Ct. App. 2025) (absence of attached petition was rectified by attachment of transfer order including charges and docket numbers of petitions).

Page 701. Insert in text after sentence ending in footnote 120:

And service was ineffective when it was made twenty-nine days prior to a hearing, rather than thirty days prior as required by Rule 81(d).[120.1]

[120.1] Mississippi Dep't of Human Servs. v. Johnson, 396 So. 3d 1151, 1156 (Miss. 2024) (but waived by failure to raise issue in stipulated agreement).

Page 701. Add to footnote 122:

Cf. Wallace v. Wallace, 309 So. 3d 104, 113-14 (Miss. Ct. App. 2020) (wife waived objections to service of a Rule 81 summons on her attorney rather than on her; she responded on the merits without raising the issue).

[c] Service in contempt proceedings

Page 702. Insert in text after sentence ending in footnote 125:

The court of appeals clarified in 2024 that all petitions for contempt – even those filed in a pending action in which all parties have been joined – must be noticed through service of a Rule 81(d) summons.[125.1]

[125.1] Bolivar v. Bolivar, 378 So. 3d 433, 439 (Miss. Ct. App. 2024); *see also* Pace v. Pace, 387 So. 3d 1067, 1074 (Miss. Ct. App. 2024) (chancery court lacked jurisdiction to hear contempt action not noticed through Rule 81(d) summons).

[2] Manner of service

[a] On resident defendant

Page 702. Insert in text after sentence ending in footnote 130:

However, a resident who is out of state may be served by certified mail.[130.1]

[130.1] Roach v. Roach, 419 So. 3d 446, 451 (Miss. Ct. App. 2025).

[3] Inadequate service of process

Page 704. Insert in text after sentence ending in footnote 148:

A judgment of divorce was void based on the defendant's proof that personal service of process included only a complaint and not the summons.[148.1] And a Rule 81(d) summons for a paternity action was void because it required attendance at a hearing in twenty-nine days, rather than thirty days.[148.2]

[148.1] Wells v. Wells, 394 So. 3d 1011, 1024 (Miss. Ct. App. 2024) (husband, sister, and nephew testified that the service did not include a summons).

[148.2] Mississippi Dep't of Human Servs. v. Johnson, 396 So. 3d 1151, 1156 (Miss. 2024) (void judgment may be set aside at any time) (but finding that issue was waived).

Page 704. Insert in text after sentence ending in footnote 151:

The fact that a father's arrearages in support were listed as one of several issues to be heard at trial did not cure the failure to serve him with a Rule 81(d) summons for the mother's contempt petition. His attorney made a timely objection to lack of jurisdiction. [151.1]

151.1 May v. May, 410 So. 3d 1087, 1093 (Miss. Ct. App. 2025).

§ 19.05 Responsive pleadings

[1] In divorce actions

[b] Affirmative defenses

Page 705. Add to footnote 160:

See also West v. West, 371 So. 3d 145, 171 (Miss. 2023) (husband waived statute of limitations defense by failing to raise it in pleadings).

Page 705. Insert in text after sentence ending in footnote 160:

An argument that a claim is barred by a prenuptial agreement must be raised as an affirmative defense.[160.1]

In an action in which an answer is not required, affirmative defenses must be raised in the first pleading. A wife who failed to file an answer in her husband's divorce action was not barred from raising the defense six months later in her first pleading in the matter – parties are not required to answer in suits for divorce. [160.2]

[160.1] Herbert v. Herbert, 374 So. 3d 562, 569-70 (Miss. Ct. App. 2023) (wife's argument that her husband's tort claim was barred by their prenuptial agreement was waived because she failed to include it as an affirmative defense).

[160.2] Turner v. Turner, 385 So. 3d 827 (Miss. Ct. App. 2024).

[2] Rule 81 matters

[a] Preserving objections to jurisdiction

Page 706. Add to footnote 167:

See also Garrison v. Courtney, 304 So. 3d 1129, 1153 (Miss. Ct. App. 2020) (husband waived argument that Rule 81 hearing was noticed for six instead of seven days by appearing and participating without objection).

Page 706. Insert in text after sentence ending in footnote 168:

However, a defendant waived his right to set aside a void paternity judgment by later entering two stipulated agreements regarding support imposed by the judgment, without arguing improper service of process.[168.1]

[168.1] Mississippi Dep't of Human Servs. v. Johnson, 396 So. 3d 1151, 1156 (Miss. 2024).

[c] Counterclaims

Page 706. Insert in text after sentence ending in footnote 173:

However, in a 2024 case, the court of appeals held that a court did not have jurisdiction over a father's counterclaim for custody because he did not serve the child's mother with a Rule 81(d) summons.[173.1]

[173.1] Jones v. Curtis, 394 So. 3d 511, 515 (Miss. Ct. App. 2024) (mother waived the objection by participating in the hearing).

§ 19.06 PRE-TRIAL PROCEEDINGS

[2] Discovery

Page 708. Insert in text after sentence ending in footnote 189:

And a mother in a custody action was entitled to discover documents relied on by a guardian ad litem, including the child's records and the GAL's correspondence with the child's doctors, therapists, and teachers, in the absence of a showing that the documents fell under an exception listed in Rule 45.[189.1]

[189.1] Daly v. Raines, 394 So. 3d 924, 929-30 (Miss. Ct. App. 2023).

Page 709. Add to footnote 192:

See also Lindsay v. Lindsay, 303 So. 3d 770, 782-83 (Miss. Ct. App. 2020) (noting, in denying wife divorce on habitual cruelty, that she failed to respond to requests for admission on the issue and did not request a withdrawal for two years).

[3] Continuances

Page 709. Insert in text after sentence ending in footnote 197:

The court of appeals held that a wife should have been granted a continuance in her divorce action when her attorney informed the court that he had been diagnosed with dementia and was no longer licensed to practice law. As a result, she was not able to testify directly, to present her evidence, or to offer evidence to rebut her husband's case.[197.1] And a chancellor erred in denying a continuance requested by both attorneys in a custody matter. They agreed that neither acted in bad faith and that a continuance was necessary to adequately present their cases.[197.2]

[197.1] Brim-Wright v. Wright, 297 So. 3d 1134, 1138-39 (Miss. Ct. App. 2020).
[197.2] Eaglin v. Burse, 425 So. 3d 1007, 1010 (Miss. Ct. App. 2025).

Page 710. Add to footnote 199:

Cf. Garrison v. Courtney, 304 So. 3d 1129, 1154-55 (Miss. Ct. App. 2020) (no new process required when Rule 81 hearing scheduled for January 3, during the trial of a divorce, was held the following day; husband appeared and defended).

Page 710. Insert in text after sentence ending in footnote 200:

In 2022, the court of appeals held that no new Rule 81(d)(5) summons is required when a matter is continued indefinitely and a date later set by agreement of counsel. The parties and attorneys had actual notice of the hearing and could not complain of the lack of a summons.[200.1]

[200.1] Seals v. Stanton, 350 So. 3d 1051, 1061 (Miss. 2022) (finding party and attorney in contempt for failure to appear).

[5] Motions

[a] Motion to recuse

Page 711. Add to footnote 211:

See also Thornton v. Thornton, 322 So. 3d 485, 493-94 (Miss. Ct. App. 2021) (a chancellor was not required to recuse himself after a litigant posted on social media that she "was being treated unfairly by a biased judge" – she produced no evidence that he was biased by the post); Lockhart v. Lockhart, 324 So. 3d 777, 794-96 (Miss. 2021) (fact that wife's lawyer's law firm hosted a fundraiser for the judge and that the judge worked for his firm fifteen years earlier did not require recusal); Watson v. Watson, 306 So. 3d 800, 805-08 (Miss. Ct. App. 2020) (recusal not required even though wife filed complaint against judge's former law partners; judge severed the claim to be heard by another judge).

Page 711. Add to footnote 214:

Cf. Hammons v. Hammons, 289 So. 3d 1214, 1220-21 (Miss. 2020) (chancellor had discretion to recuse himself to avoid appearance of impropriety after he was visited in chambers by litigant's sister, a former court reporter).

§ 19.07 Trial

[1] Proceedings

Page 713. Insert in text after sentence ending in footnote 225:

A court may not award permanent relief without holding a hearing and making findings. The supreme court reversed a chancellor's order removing a child from CPS custody and dismissing CPS without holding a hearing and making findings. The court erred in ordering relief after holding an in-chambers, off-the-record discussion with the attorneys.[225.1]

[225.1] Hines v. Caldwell, 384 So. 3d 1238, 1241 (Miss. 2024).

Page 713. Insert in text after section [b]:

[c] Right to trial [NEW]

The court of appeals held that a mother's due process rights were denied when a court refused to delay a custody trial after she was arrested during the trial for driving with a suspended license. The court noted parents' liberty interest in the care and custody of their children and the importance of hearing from both parents in a custody dispute.[229.1] And a chancellor erred in awarding custody to a child's older sister without hearing from the father's witnesses or allowing him to conduct an examination on redirect.[229.2]

[229.1] Kreps v. Hyland, 331 So. 3d 590, 594-96 (Miss. Ct. App. 2021).
[229.2] D.R. v. Bradford, 292 So. 3d 604, 605-06 (Miss. Ct. App. 2020).

[2] No default; requirement of proof

Page 713. Add to footnote 235:

See also Schaubhut v. Schaubhut, 373 So. 3d 802, 807 (Miss. Ct. App. 2023).

[3] Limits on testimony

Page 714. Insert in text after sentence ending in footnote 242:

Similarly, a court erred in awarding custody to a nonparent without allowing the father to present his witnesses.[242.1] And in a 2022 case, the supreme court held that a chancellor should not have limited a husband's right to present evidence of marital affairs for the purposes of custody, even though he did not plead adultery as a ground for divorce.[242.2]

[242.1] D.R. v. Bradford, 292 So. 3d 604, 605-06 (Miss. Ct. App. 2020).
[242.2] Denham v. Denham, 351 So. 3d 954, 963 (Miss. 2022).

[4] Stipulations

Page 714. Insert in text after sentence ending in footnote 243:

The court of appeals rejected a husband's argument that his oral stipulation during trial to pay $20,000 in college support was unenforceable because the irreconcilable differences divorce statute requires a writing. The court distinguished an earlier case, *Cook v. Cook,* 725 So. 2d 205 (Miss. 1998), in which a couple submitted issues to the court and then orally submitted an agreement resolving all of the issues but one.[243.1]

[243.1] Johnson v. Johnson, 297 So. 3d 342, 347-49 (Miss. Ct. App. 2020).

Page 715. Insert in text after sentence ending in footnote 246:

[7] Sealed records [NEW]

A chancellor may seal the record of a family law matter after conducting a balancing test to determine whether the public interest in access to the records is outweighed by the need for confidentiality. In addition, Rule 48 of the Mississippi Rules of Appellate Procedure allows an appellate court to seal a record if disclosure will cause substantial harm to a child or the record contains sensitive information so that disclosure will cause substantial harm. The court of appeals held that the record of a custody modification proceeding should remain sealed because it contained the child's sensitive medical records and public disclosure could cause her substantial harm.[246.1]

[246.1] Nowell v. Stewart, 356 So. 3d 1217, 1231 (Miss. Ct. App. 2022); *cf.* Colbert v. Colbert, 403 So. 3d 729, 737 (Miss. Ct. App. 2025) (chancellor erred in sealing the entire record without balancing the need for privacy against the public interest in open records).

§ 19.08 Evidence

[1] Testimony of children

Page 715. Insert in text after sentence ending in footnote 248:

The court held that a chancellor erred in automatically refusing to allow a couple's children to testify and in failing to record an in-camera interview with the children. The court emphasized that calling children to testify in divorce proceedings is "highly disfavored." However, because of the due process right to call witnesses, a per se rule excluding children as witnesses is unconstitutional. The court also noted that the chancellor must make a record of the interview and, if testimony is not allowed, state the reasons, including the factual information gleaned from the interview that the chancellor would consider.[248.1]

[248.1] Denham v. Denham, 31 So. 3d 954, 960-61 (Miss. 2022) (also holding that the chancellor must make this determination with regard to older children); *see also* Daly v. Raines, 394 So. 3d 924, 931 (Miss. Ct. App. 2023) (chancellor erred in denying mother's request to call child without conducting in camera recorded interview).

[b] Statement for purpose of medical diagnosis

Page 716. Add to footnote 256:

But cf. Myers v. Myers, 324 So. 3d 808, 822 (Miss. Ct. App. 2021) (court properly excluded as hearsay a letter from son's counselor including the boy's statement related to abuse).

[c] Other hearsay exceptions

Page 717. Add to footnote 260:

But see Myers v. Myers, 324 So. 3d 808, 822-23 (Miss. Ct. App. 2021) (mother's recording of daughter saying her father hurt her was properly excluded as hearsay; the incident the girl discussed occurred two years earlier; statement was not admissible under the present sense impression or excited utterance exception).

[2] Expert testimony

Page 718. Add to footnote 268:

Cf. In re Adoption of M.R.H., 312 So. 3d 385, 390 (Miss. Ct. App. 2020) (rejecting father's argument that chancellor erred in considering hearsay such as medical and school records in the expert guardian ad litem's report).

Page 718. Insert in text after sentence ending in footnote 269:

A separate hearing is not required to qualify an expert witness, so long as the parties have an opportunity to address the witness' qualifications.[269.1]

[269.1] Baumann v. Baumann, 304 So. 3d 175, 180-82 (Miss. Ct. App. 2020) (chancellor properly admitted a licensed social worker as an expert in child development).

Page 718. Add to footnote 271:

Cf. Stewart v. Stewart, 309 So. 3d 44, 72-73 (Miss. Ct. App. 2020) (rejecting mother's argument that chancellor erred in admitting testimony of family counselor as expert without review of her qualifications on the record; she was appointed with agreement of the parties to address a single incident and was qualified to be an expert); Baumann v. Baumann, 304 So. 3d 175, 180-82 (Miss. Ct. App. 2020) (chancellor properly admitted a licensed social worker with a master's degree and a decade of experience as an expert in child development).

[6] Attorney-client privilege

Page 722. Add to footnote 308:

See also Pace v. Pace, 324 So. 3d 369, 377 (Miss. Ct. App. 2021) (wife did not waive attorney-client privilege by a brief reference to emails between her and her attorney; she did not put the content of their communication at issue).

Page 724. Insert in text after section ending in footnote 323:

[12] Judicial notice [NEW]

A court may take judicial notice of matters commonly known in the community or which "can be accurately and readily determined from sources whose accuracy cannot reasonably be questioned" such as maps, tables, census data, or dates and times. A chancellor erred in taking judicial notice related to sexually transmitted diseases, a matter that required expert medical testimony.[323.1]

[323.1] Doe v. Doe, 341 So. 3d 953, 968 (Miss. Ct. App. 2021) (court took judicial notice that there are many types of HPV and inferred that there was no link between wife's previous HPV infection causing cervical dysplasia and her current infection causing genital warts, making it reasonable to assume that husband transmitted the current infection).

§ 19.10 Judgments

[1] Findings of fact and conclusions of law

[b] Requested findings of fact

Page 728. Insert in text after sentence ending in footnote 363:

A court was not required to provide findings upon a husband's request after hearing his post-trial motion for reconsideration. Whether to provide findings in post-trial matters is at the discretion of the court.[363.1]

[363.1] Roley v. Roley, 329 So. 3d 473, 499-500 (Miss. Ct. App. 2021).

[3] Consent judgments

Page 729. Insert in text after sentence ending in footnote 374:

In contrast, in other matters, a party is bound by an agreement read into the record and to which the party gives assent on the record.[374.1]

[374.1] Harrison v. Howard, 356 So. 3d 1232, 1245 (Miss. Ct. App. 2023).

§ 19.11 Post-judgment motions

[1] Notice of post-judgment motions

Page 731. Add to footnote 394:

See also Urban v. Urban, 411 So. 3d 1092, 1101 (Miss. Ct. App. 2023) (no Rule 81 summons required for Rule 59 hearing).

[3] Rule 60(a): Relief based on clerical mistakes

Page 733. Add to footnote 411:

See also Lockhart v. Lockhart, 324 So. 3d 777, 784-86 (Miss. 2021) (chancellor did not err in clarifying a vague property division judgment by providing for the manner of enforcing the order, specifying values for the properties involved, and defining gross profits; both parties complained that the order was ambiguous and failed to comply with its terms).

[4] Relief based on misconduct, mistake, newly discovered evidence

[a] Newly discovered evidence

Page 734. Add to footnote 420:

See also Pond v. Pond, 302 So. 3d 1236, 1240-41 (Miss. Ct. App. 2020) (chancellor was not required to consider statement showing value of husband's pension; he failed to disclose the pension or provide evidence of its value at trial; statement was available at the time of trial and not newly discovered evidence).

[5] Relief from judgment after six months

Page 736. Add to footnote 439:

Cf. Thornton v. Thornton, 322 So. 3d 485, 490-91 (Miss. Ct. App. 2021) (chancellor erred in finding a wife's motion to set aside under Rule 60(b) for fraud on the court untimely because it was not filed in sixty days; motions related to fraud on the court must be filed within a reasonable time). *See also In re* Adoption of D.A.S., 391 So. 3d 1181, 1187 (Miss. Ct. App. 2024) (mother's petition to set aside adoption for misrepresentations did not amount to fraud on the court; even if it did, five years was not a reasonable amount of time to delay challenging adoption).

Page 736. Add to footnote 441:

See Brister v. Martin, 413 So. 3d 636, 641-42 (Miss. Ct. App. 2025) (chancellor did not err in setting aside prior order of child support based on husband's misrepresentation of income).

[a] Void provisions

Page 736. Add to footnote 442:

See also Hodge v. Hodge, 2025 WL 2837224, at *5 (Miss. Ct. App. Oct 7, 2025). *But cf.* Rahman v. Lyons, 332 So. 3d 311, 316-17 (Miss. Ct. App. 2021) (parties who fail to appeal a challenge to subject matter jurisdiction may not collaterally attack jurisdiction).

Page 737. Insert in text after sentence ending in footnote 444:

In a 2023 case, the supreme court held that a paternity judgment, void for lack of proper service of process, could be set aside decades later. The court held that a void judgment can be set aside at any time – laches is not a defense to a void judgment. However, the father waived the objection by entering into a stipulated agreement to make payments under the judgment.[444.1] In contrast, a voidable order is waived if it is not appealed – a husband who objected that he did not agreed to a consent order could not attack the judgment collaterally.[444.2]

[444.1] Mississippi Dep't of Human Servs. v. Johnson, 396 So. 3d 1151, 1156 (Miss. 2024).

[444.2] Harrison v. Howard, 356 So. 3d 1232, 1244-45 (Miss. Ct. App. 2023) (also finding that husband agreed to order).

Page 737: Insert in text after section [a]:

[a1] Judgment should no longer have prospective application [NEW]

In a 2025 case, the court of appeals held that a chancellor had authority to set aside a child support judgment and hold a new trial because no evidence was presented by the pro se parties at the prior trial to support the award of child support. The court of appeals affirmed. A court may set aside a judgment if "it is no longer equitable that the judgment should have prospective application."[444.3]

[444.3] Brister v. Martin, 413 So. 3d 636, 641-42 (Miss. Ct. App. 2025).

[c] Fraud on the court

Page 738. Add to footnote 453:

Cf. Brister v. Martin, 413 So. 3d 636, 641-42 (Miss. Ct. App. 2025) (court did not err in setting aside order of child support based on husband's misrepresentation of income).

Page 738. Insert in text after sentence ending in footnote 454:

However, the fact that a wife decided to sign a joint complaint and agreement without her attorneys' involvement did not in itself prove duress or fraud to set aside the divorce.[454.1]

[454.1] Hodge v. Hodge, 2025 WL 2837224, at *8 (Miss. Ct. App. Oct 7, 2025).

Page 738. Add to footnote 457:

See also O'Steen v. O'Steen, 304 So. 3d 697, 700-01 (Miss. Ct. App. 2020) (rejecting husband's argument that wife's failure to file 8.05 was fraud on the court).

Page 739. Insert in text after sentence ending in footnote 458:

For example, a wife's failure to affirmatively disclose her PERS retirement account was not fraud on the court. The couple agreed to keep their own retirement accounts and to waive all rights to the retirement accounts of the other. They did not file financial statements. There was no indication that she intentionally concealed the account.[458.1]

[458.1] O'Steen v. O'Steen, 304 So. 3d 697, 700-01 (Miss. Ct. App. 2020). See also *In re* Adoption of D.A.S., 391 So. 3d 1181, 1186-87 (Miss. Ct. App. 2024) (mother's petition to set aside five-year-old adoption for misrepresentations about an "open" adoption did not amount to fraud on the court).

[6] Post-judgment motions after appeal

Page 739. Insert in text after sentence ending in footnote 461:

However, in a 2021 case the court rejected a father's argument that a chancellor lacked jurisdiction to hear a contempt petition filed while the case was on appeal, noting that the court retained continuing jurisdiction.[461.1] Similarly, the court of appeals stated that a chancellor could modify visitation while an appeal was pending, if the circumstances warranted it.[461.2]

[461.1] Stephens v. Stephens, 328 So. 3d 760, 770-72 (Miss. Ct. App. 2021).
[461.2] Roley v. Roley, 329 So. 3d 473, 508 (Miss. Ct. App. 2021) (but finding that circumstances did not).

§ 19.12 Appeals

[1] Appealable order

Page 739. Add to footnote 468:

See also Williams v. Williams, 415 So. 3d 1011, 1013 (Miss. Ct. App. 2025) (grant of divorce in bifurcated trial was not final judgment); Crocker v. Daves, 409 So. 3d 1188, 1189 (Miss. Ct. App. 2025) (award of custody that reserved issue of child support was not a final order); Banks v. Banks, 396 So. 3d 499, 501 (Miss. Ct. App. 2024) (judgment dividing property and awarding alimony, but not granting divorce, was interlocutory); Williams v. Williams, 347 So. 3d 178, 182 (Miss. 2022) (judgment styled as "final" that addressed custody and financial matters but not divorce was not a final judgment).

Page 740. Add to footnote 473:

But cf. Shandy v. Davis, 423 So. 3d 717, 719 (Miss. Ct. App. 2025) (order recognizing prenuptial agreement as valid, although certified under Rule 54(b), was not appealable; it did not resolve a claim between the parties).

[3] Time of appeal

Page 741. Add to footnote 485:

See McChester v. McChester, 300 So. 3d 1035, 1039-40 (Miss. 2020) (pro se litigant's Rule 60(b) motion filed twenty days after judgment did not toll time for appealing judgment of divorce).

Page 741. Add to footnote 489:

See also In re Interest of M.M., 319 So. 3d 1188, 1203-04 (Miss. Ct. App. 2021) (court had no discretion to extend time based on request made more than 180 days after judgment; rule is strictly enforced).

[6] Appeal of consent judgment

Page 744. Insert in text after sentence ending in footnote 509:

For example, a wife could not challenge as unfair a property division to which she agreed, in the absence of a showing of duress.[509.1]

[509.1] Montgomery v. Montgomery, 339 So. 3d 819, 829 (Miss. Ct. App. 2022).

[7] Briefs on appeal

[b] Lack of citation

Page 745. Add to footnote 516:

See also Green v. Green, 349 So. 3d 1187, 1200-01 (Miss. Ct. App. 2022) (wife waived arguments related to grant of divorce by failing to cite authority); Reading v. Reading, 350 So. 3d 1195, 1200-01 (Miss. Ct. App. 2022) (pro se prisoner husband's appeal dismissed for failure to cite legal authority to support his argument); Montgomery v. Montgomery, 339 So. 3d 819, 829 (Miss. Ct. App. 2022) (wife waived challenge to grant of divorce to her husband by failing to cite authority to support her position); Carter v. Carter, 324 So. 3d 327, 333 (Miss. Ct. App. 2021) (a pro se father's appeal of a visitation modification was procedurally barred because he cited no authority for his arguments).

[c] Waiver of argument

Page 745. Add to footnote 517:

See also Luse v. Luse, 992 So. 2d 659, 662-64 (Miss. Ct. App. 2008) (husband who failed to respond, appear in action, or file post-trial motions barred from challenging decision on appeal).

Page 745. Add to footnote 518:

See also Colbert v. Colbert, 403 So. 3d 729, 734 (Miss. Ct. App. 2025) (husband who failed to argue at trial that prenuptial agreement barred separate maintenance could not make the argument on appeal); *cf.* McFall v. Osborne, 424 So. 3d 286, 292-93 (Miss. Ct. App. 2025) (husband could not make collateral attack on judgment that he argued divided military disability benefits in violation of federal law; he should have appealed).

Page 745. Insert in text after sentence ending in footnote 518:

However, a party who fails to appear at trial may appeal an issue that they challenged sufficiently during pretrial proceedings or in post-trial motions. In a 2022 case, the court of appeals held that a wife who did not appear for a divorce trial was permitted to appeal the court's property division because she challenged the husband's requests for division through her pleadings and in pretrial hearings. However, she waived appeal of the court's grant of divorce because she did not address the issue in pretrial proceedings.[518.1]

[518.1] Green v. Green, 349 So. 3d 1187, 1200-01, 1203-04 (Miss. Ct. App. 2022) (wife's attempts to argue divorce grounds through an unsworn letter to the court and in a hearing on another issue did not constitute evidence). *See also* Speights v. Speights, 270 So. 3d 968, 972, 975 (Miss. Ct. App. 2018) (husband who failed to appear at trial waived argument that court should have made findings of fact regarding divorce but did not waive challenge to property division findings of fact; his answer denied his wife's requests for property division).

Page 745. Add to footnote 521:

See also Myles v. Lewis, 388 So. 3d 598, 605 (Miss. Ct. App. 2024) (mother was not procedurally barred from challenging child support award; a motion for new trial is not necessary to challenge matters addressed in rulings during trial); Thompson v. Thompson, 380 So. 3d 945, 957 (Miss. Ct. App. 2024) (husband did not waive his objections to the chancellor's failing to make findings of fact because he did not file a post-trial motion).

[d] Record on appeal

Page 746. Add to footnote 524:

See also Scott v. Rouse, 348 So. 3d 345, 350 (Miss. Ct. App. 2022) (husband waived arguments related to motions by failing to designate transcripts of motions as part of the record on appeal).

Page 746. Add to footnote 526:

See Schaubhut v. Schaubhut, 373 So. 3d 802, 808 (Miss. Ct. App. 2023) (to support his argument that wife made fraudulent statements, defendant who did not appear should have used this procedure; without it, the appellate court could not review his claim).

[8] Effect of reversal

[b] Reversal of financial award

Page 747. Add to footnote 531:

See also Thompson v. Thompson, 380 So. 3d 945 (Miss. Ct. App. 2024).

Page 747. Insert in text after sentence ending in footnote 531:

And in one case, the court of appeals reversed all financial awards because it reversed for additional findings with regard to a boat.[531.1]

[531.1] Chapman v. Chapman, 395 So. 3d 447, 457 (Miss. Ct. App. 2024).

[c] Remand

Page 748. Add to footnote 540:

Cf. Gossett v. Gossett, 313 So. 3d 1063, 1072-73 (Miss. Ct. App. 2021) (rejecting mother's argument that court used "stale" evidence from 2016 hearing to make temporary award of custody in 2018; a party is not necessarily entitled to a new hearing on remand unless mandated by the appellate court).

Page 748. Insert in text after sentence ending in footnote 540:

However, the fact that a chancellor is instructed to determine custody based on circumstances at the time of the remand does not prevent them from considering facts in evidence in the trial of the matter.[540.1]

[540.1] Riley v. Heisinger, 302 So. 3d 1243, 1253-54 (Miss. Ct. App. 2020) (mother's long history of denying visitation was relevant to custody award).

Page 748. Insert in text after sentence ending in footnote 542:

An award made on remand may be made retroactive to the date of the parties' divorce. A chancellor did not err in awarding a wife 45% of her husband's pension, retroactive to the date of divorce.[542.1]

[542.1] Johnson v. Johnson, 376 So. 3d 362, 371 (Miss. Ct. App. 2023); *see also* Monroe v. Monroe, 745 So. 2d 249, 253 (Miss. Ct. App. 1999) (chancellor should have made award of alimony on remand retroactive to date of divorce).

[12] Right to appeal *in forma pauperis*

Page 749. Add to footnote 552:

See also Roley v. Roley, 329 So. 3d 473, 503-04 (Miss. Ct. App. 2021) (husband who lost custody not entitled to appeal *in forma pauperis*).

[13] Dismissal of appeal

[a] Fugitive dismissal rule

Page 749. Add to footnote 553:

See also Gillen v. Gillen, 375 So. 3d 681, 686-87 (Miss. Ct. App. 2023) (court declined to hear appeal of contempt order by husband who removed himself from the state to avoid incarceration).

[b] Dismissal for mootness

Page 749. Add to footnote 554:

See also Wise v. Broome, 416 So. 3d 148, 152 (Miss. Ct. App. 2022) (father's appeal of custody modification denial was moot; daughter was twenty-three years of age at the time of the appeal).

§ 19.14 Mediation and collaborative divorce

Page 751. Insert in text after sentence ending in footnote 567:

The Mississippi Supreme Court on July 26, 2024, granted the petition of the Mississippi Bar to approve the Mississippi Collaborative Law Rules allowing parties and their lawyers to resolve family law matters through a collaborative law process. The rules provide that parties in a collaborative law process agree to forego court intervention during the process except in certain emergencies, to hire neutral experts, and to make "timely, full, candid, and informal" disclosure without formal discovery. They also commit that if the process is terminated, a collaborative lawyer or his or her firm cannot continue as the lawyer in litigation except in defined emergencies. The rules contain detailed provisions discussing the information a lawyer must provide to a party considering collaborative law as an option.[567.1]

[567.1] *In re Rules for Collaborative Law,* No. 89-R-99044-SCT (Miss. July 26, 2024).

XXIII
MARITAL AGREEMENTS

§ 23.02 Requirements

[1] Consideration

Page 786. Add to footnote 15:

See Estate of Bell v. Estate of Bell, 372 So. 3d 1008, 1018 (Miss. Ct. App. 2023).

[6] Substantive fairness and unconscionability

Page 790. Add to footnote 51:

See also Estate of Bell v. Estate of Bell, 372 So. 3d 1008, 1017-18 (Miss. Ct. App. 2023) (agreement fair even though husband's estate was smaller; agreement included mutual waivers).

[7] Specific provisions
[b] Waiver of rights upon death

Page 791. Add to footnote 59:

See also Estate of Bell v. Estate of Bell, 372 So. 3d 1008, 1017-18 (Miss. Ct. App. 2023) (rejecting husband's argument that agreement waived election to renounce will but not automatic renunciation; parties clearly intended to waive all rights to inheritance).

Page 793. Insert in text after section [f]:

[g] Continued joint ownership [NEW]

A chancellor properly declined to address division of a couple's only significant asset, the marital home, based on their premarital agreement that any assets held as joint tenants with rights of survivorship would remain in joint title and pass to the survivor. The court declined to award exclusive possession of the home to either party based on their agreement that neither would do anything to affect the joint tenancy unless agreed upon by both.[66.1]

[66.1] Hatton v. Hatton, 323 So. 3d 1149, 1153 (Miss. Ct. App. 2021).

Page 794. Insert in text after sentence ending in footnote 77:

§ 23.06A Construction [NEW]

The court of appeals affirmed a chancellor's interpretation of a couple's ambiguous premarital agreement, applying canons of construction to harmonize conflicting provisions. Section 2 of the agreement stated that assets purchased during the marriage with premarital assets would remain separate. Section 4 provided that jointly titled assets acquired during marriage would be marital property. At issue were three properties acquired with the husband's premarital funds but titled in both parties' names. The court of appeals noted that in the event of an ambiguity, courts should first apply the canons of construction to resolve the ambiguity. Two canons supported the chancellor's decision: First, an ambiguity should be read more favorably for the non-drafting party, in this case the wife. Second, a specific provision should be given more weight than a general provision. Both supported a finding that section 4 controlled. Applying those rules, jointly titled property purchased during marriage with the husband's premarital funds should be classified as marital.[77.1]

[77.1] Bowman v. Bowman, 332 So. 3d 317, 322-23 (Miss. Ct. App. 2021).

§ 23.07 Settlement agreements

[3] Formalities

[a] In general

Page 796. Add to footnote 89:

See also Hardin v. Hardin, 335 So. 3d 1088, 1093 (Miss. Ct. App. 2022) (parties' oral agreement dictated into the record by the chancellor in a separate maintenance action was binding on the parties).

§ 23.08 Enforceability: Binding effect on parties

[1] General rule

Page 796. Add to footnote 93:

See Montgomery v. Montgomery, 339 So. 3d 819, 829 (Miss. Ct. App. 2022) (wife was bound by agreed property division in the absence of a showing of duress).

[3] Mississippi: Withdrawal of consent to other agreements

Page 797. Add to footnote 100:

Cf. Harrison v. Harrison, 385 So. 3d 804, 808-09 (Miss. Ct. App. 2023) (interpreting ambiguous agreement as one for fault-based, rather than irreconcilable differences divorce; rejecting husband's argument that his withdrawal of consent negated the agreement).

§ 23.09 Court approval and incorporation into decree

[1] Court approval

[a] Property division

Page 798. Add to footnote 101:

But cf. Gerty v. Gerty, 296 So. 3d 704, 707 (Miss. 2020). The supreme court held that a chancellor was not bound by a couple's property division agreement which included a provision that "this Agreement shall be made a part of the Judgment and that such Judgment shall not conflict with the terms of the Agreement except to the extent disapproved" and that "each mutually submits to the personal jurisdiction of [the court] so that said Court has the power to decide any and all matters and questions concerning the dissolution of the parties' marriage, and the division of the parties' property." *Id.* at 707.

[b] Child custody and support

Page 798. Add to footnote 108:

Cf. Bryant v. Bryant, 348 So. 3d 309, 316-317 (Miss. 2022) (chancellor may override educational choice of designated decision-maker if decision is not in child's best interest).

§ 23.10 Defenses to and alteration of agreed judgments

[2] Duress, undue influence, or overreaching

Page 801. Insert in text after sentence ending in footnote 130:

A couple's property settlement agreement was signed under duress and was unenforceable when an incarcerated, unrepresented husband signed an agreement beyond his means so that he would not be returned to jail pending divorce. He had lost his job, filed for bankruptcy, and could not pay the $105,470 in arrears required to obtain his release. Facing reincarceration for months, he agreed to pay his wife $1,400 a month in support, deed her the marital home and a condominium, pay all debts on both properties, pay $900,000 in lump sum payments, obtain $1 million in life insurance, pay all the court-appointed expert's fees, the expert's and his wife's attorneys' fees and transfer to his wife one-half of any business interest that he acquired within the next five years.[130.1]

[130.1] Lindsay v. Lindsay, 303 So. 3d 770, 785-87 (Miss. Ct. App. 2020).

Page 801. Add to footnote 135:

See also Harrison v. Harrison, 385 So. 3d 804, 814 (Miss. Ct. App. 2023) (refusing to set aside agreement even though husband was distraught when he signed the agreement and had difficulty reading; he could have obtained an attorney to explain the terms) (wife had no obligation to explain terms to him).

[3] Unconscionability

Page 802. Add to footnote 141:

See also Harrison v. Harrison, 385 So. 3d 804, 814-15 (Miss. Ct. App. 2023) (agreement in which wife took most assets was not unconscionable; husband signed agreement; he stated that he wanted her to "have everything").

§ 23.12 Construction

Page 805. Insert in text after sentence ending in footnote 170:

The court of appeals applied the canons of contract construction to reconcile conflicting provisions of a premarital agreement, noting that agreements are construed more strictly against the drafter and that in case of conflicts, more specific provisions control over more general ones.[170.1]

[170.1] Bowman v. Bowman, 332 So. 3d 317, 322-23 (Miss. Ct. App. 2021).

Page 806. Insert in text after sentence ending in footnote 175:

Similarly, a father's payment of basic support past the age of majority for his oldest child supported the mother's argument that he agreed to pay basic support during six years of college.[175.1]

[175.1] Stewart v. Stewart, 382 So. 3d 531, 540 (Miss. Ct. App. 2024).

§ 23.13 Specific provisions

[2] Child support

[a] Agreements expanding support obligations

Page 808. Add to footnote 197:

See Stewart v. Stewart, 383 So. 3d 531, 540 (Miss. Ct. App. 2024) (looking at the four corners of the agreement, parents intended basic support to extend past majority).

Page 808. Insert in text after sentence ending in footnote 203:

Parents should consider the possible impact of unlimited agreements for large-ticket items such as tuition. A father whose children attended private school in Jackson agreed at divorce to pay one-half of the costs of any private school that his children "may later attend." After divorce, his daughter was diagnosed with dyslexia and other learning disabilities. The mother, with his permission, enrolled her in a special school in Memphis. The mother then enrolled the girl in a more expensive school in Nashville. The father objected to the mother's choice as unreasonable. The court of appeals acknowledged the reasonableness requirement but found no abuse of discretion in the chancellor's approval of the mother's choice. The court noted that the agreement did not limit the costs of private education and that the mother presented evidence that the school provided advantages over the girl's current school.[203.1]

[203.1] Smith v. Smith, 318 So. 3d 484, 491-92 (Miss. Ct. App. 2021). See § 13.07[5] *supra* for a discussion of the reasonableness of custodial parents' decisions regarding education.

[e] Provisions regarding extracurricular activities

Page 811. Add to footnote 218:

See also Myles v. Lewis, 388 So. 3d 598, 613 (Miss. Ct. App. 2024) (traveling team did not qualify as an extracurricular activity; mother did not present evidence of circumstances to qualify the activity for a deviation).

Page 811. Insert in text following sentence ending in footnote 218:

A provision for payment of extracurricular activities may be modified. In a 2021 case, the court of appeals affirmed a chancellor's modification of a provision that he found was "unworkable." The father agreed at divorce to pay 100% of the activities "mutually agreed upon by the parties in advance." After the parents disputed the father's obligation for certain activities, the chancellor modified his obligation to a maximum of $6,000 a year per child. The court of appeals affirmed, based on the chancellor's finding that the provision was unworkable because the parties could not agree on activities.[218.1]

[218.1] Smith v. Smith, 318 So. 3d 484, 496-97 (Miss. Ct. App. 2021).

[4] Property division

Page 815. Insert in text after section [b]:

[b1] Division of jointly titled assets [NEW]

A divorcing couple's agreement to divide jointly titled assets is effective without a transfer by deed if their intent is clear. The court of appeals held that a couple's joint tenancy with right of survivorship in two mineral interests was severed by their agreement to "divide equally all mineral rights" in one field and that the husband "shall have exclusive rights to" the other field. When the husband died, his will leaving the mineral interests to his son was effective even though title was never changed. Their intent to divide the property was clear.[252.1] To avoid litigation, however, the better practice is to ensure that the provision is also memorialized by a transfer of title from joint tenancy to tenancy in common.

[252.1] *In re* Estate of Callender, 309 So. 3d 131, 137-38 (Miss. Ct. App. 2020).

[7] General release and waiver provisions

Page 817. Add to footnote 267:

See also Woodard v. Miller, 326 So. 3d 439, 449-51 (Miss. 2021) (wife's tort action against husband for transmitting STD may have been waived by general release of claims; however, husband waived defense by delaying to assert a claim).

CASE NAME	MARRIAGE	AGE & CHILDREN	FAULT	INCOME	DIVISION	ALIMONY	SUPPORT	APPEAL	COMMENTS
I. Marriages over 20 years									
A. Permanent alimony awarded									
Williamson v. Williamson, 296 So. 3d 206 (Miss. Ct. App. 2020)	21	2 minor children (wife)	Irreconcilable differences	Husband: $8,617./mo; Wife: $1,384/mo	Wife: Approx $230,000	$1200/mo 22% of disparity	$1,720	Husband, aff'd	Wife unable to meet expenses; marriage ended with his affair; Husband had $180,000 in separate property
Phang v. Phang, 350 So. 3d 1154 (Miss. Ct. App. 2022)	34	Adult children; Wife 62	Irreconcilable differences	Husband: $7,997/mo; Wife: $0/month	Both: $606,000	$2,700/mo (34% of disparity)	NA	Husband, aff'd	Long marriage, great disparity in incomes
Lewis v. Lewis, 360 So. 3d 298 (Miss. Ct. App. 2023)	20	2 Adult children: Wife 51 Husband 52	H: Adultery	Husband: $125,000/yr; Wife: $3,470/mo		$2,000/mo (29% of disparity)	NA	Husband, aff'd	Husband's ongoing affair; disparity; marriage length supported award.
Howard v. Howard, 2025 WL 1741634 (Miss. Ct. App. June 24, 2025)	20	Wife: custody of 20-year-old disabled son	W: Adultery	Husband: $7,500/mo; Wife: $2,500/mo	Small estate	$2,000/mo (40% of disparity)	H: $1,050/ 10 mos	Husband, aff'd	Wife had custody and support of 20-year-old disabled son; child support would soon end; disparity in incomes
B. Rehabilitative alimony awarded									
Baird v. Baird, 2025 WL 2962388 (Miss. Ct. App. Oct. 21, 2025)	20	5 children (husband)	Irreconcilable differences	Husband: $8,562/mo Wife: $1,000/mo	Wife: Approx $300,000 plus $52,000 temp alimony	$1,000/mo for 6 mos/ (13% of disparity)	W: $275/mo	Wife, aff'd	Husband had custody 5 children; she chose not to work at full capacity
D. All alimony denied									
Coleman v. Coleman, 324 So. 3d 1204 (Miss. Ct. App. 2021)	20	Husband: disabled; No children	Irreconcilable differences	Husband: $1,500 Soc. Sec./mo; Wife: $2,781/mo	Equal	Denied	NA	Husband, aff'd	Property division provided adequately for both
Neely v. Neely, 305 So. 3d 164 (Miss. Ct. App. 2020)	42	Children emancipated	Irreconcilable differences	Unclear; incomes equal	Unclear	Denied	NA	Husband, aff'd	Equal incomes; neither had debt; parties kept finances separate during marriage
II. Marriages 10 - 19 years									
A. Permanent alimony awarded									
Oates v. Oates, 291 So. 3d 803 (Miss. Ct. App. 2020)	16	Wife, disabled; No children	H: Adultery	Husband: $33,000/yr; Wife: disabled	Unclear	$504/mo (18% of disparity)	NA	Husband, aff'd	Wife unable to work; could not meet expenses
Gaskin v. Gaskin, 304 So. 3d 641 (Miss. Ct. App. 2020)	18	Wife; disabled; 2 minor children (wife)	H: Adultery	Husband: $12,085; Wife: $500/mo	Equal; Wife received $786,521	$1,000/mo (11% of disparity)	$2,417	Husband, aff'd	Wife disabled; substantial disparity
Ewing v. Ewing, 301 So. 3d 709 (Miss. Ct. App. 2020)	15	4 children (wife)	Irreconcilable differences	Husband: $4,752; Wife: $3,115/mo	Wife: $44,000	$500/mo (71% of disparity)	$938/mo	Husband, aff'd	Wife unable to meet expenses; custody of four children
Descher v. Descher, 304 So. 3d 620 (Miss. Ct. App. 2020)	17	2 children (wife)	Irreconcilable differences	Husband: $71,377/mo; Wife: $2,000/mo earning capacity	Equal: $1.5 million	$7,500/mo (12% of disparity)	$7,500/mo	Husband, aff'd	Extreme income disparity; standard of living of marriage
Wildman v. Wildman, 301 So. 3d 787 (Miss. Ct. App. 2020)	15	H: 39: Wife: 38; 2 children (wife)	Irreconcilable differences	Husband: $10,049; Wife: $1,726/mo higher earning capacity	Equal: $198,277	$3,000/mo (46% of disparity)	$1,800/mo	Husband, rev'd	Affirming permanent alimony but reversing amount as excessive; wife could increase earnings by working full-time
Anderson v. Grabmiller, 394 So. 3d 493 (Miss. Ct. App. 2024)	14	H: 41; W: 39; 2 children (wife)	Irreconcilable differences	Husband: $2,995; Wife: $12,969.mo	Equal: $140,000	$1,000/mo (11% of disparity)	H: $600/mo	Wife; aff'd	Physician wife had significantly higher income; marriage was long; husband cared for children and home during marriage
B. Rehabilitative alimony awarded									
Warren v. Rhea, 318 So. 3d 1187 (Miss. Ct. App. 2021)	15	1 child (husband)	W: Habitual cruelty	Husband: $4,795; Wife: $2,115	Unclear	$750/mo for 4 yrs (28% of disparity)	None	Husband; rev'd on other grounds	Disparity in incomes
Case v. Case, 339 So. 3d 796 (Miss. Ct. App. 2022).	14	H: 40; Wife: 40; 2 children (husband)	H: Adultery	Unclear	Unclear	$2,500/mo for 4 yrs	NA	Wife; aff'd	Rehabilitative alimony appropriate for wife in 40s returning to school; husband had custody and wife's support for children was suspended for four years
McKenzie v. McKenzie, 397 So. 3d 510 (Miss. Ct. App. 2024)	13	Wife: 36; 3 children (wife)	Irreconcilable differences	Husband: $13,654/mo; Wife: homemaker	Equal: $1,700,000	$5,000/mo for 3 yrs	H: $3,000/mo	Wife; aff'd	Wife was young and had worked previously; she received substantial property, including $1 million in cash assets
Denham v. Denham, 2022 WL 290890 (Miss. Ct. App. Feb. 1, 2022), reversed in part, 354 So. 3d 954 (Miss. 2022)	15	3 children (wife)	H: Adultery	Unclear	Wife: 60%; Husband: 40%	$350/mo for 2 yrs	$1,736/mo	Husband, aff'd	Husband's income was greater; wife had greater share of debt; reversed on other grounds
Thornhill v. Thornhill, 421 So. 3d 626 (Miss. Ct. App. 2025)	15	H &W: 60: 1 child (husband)	W: Desertion	Unclear	No equity; debt divided equally	$250/mo for 3 yrs	W: $160/mo	Wife, aff'd	Wife had $362,000 while husband had primarily debt; she received four years of temporary alimony.
D. All alimony denied									
Pace v. Pace, 324 So. 3d 369 (Miss. Ct. App. 2021)	14	Wife: 43; 1 child (wife)	H: Adultery	Both currently unemployed; both with earning capacity	Wife: $720,000	Denied	$1,200	Wife; aff'd	Wife was young with earning capacity as Dietician; physician husband relinquished license after treatment for addiction
III. Marriages under 10 years									
B. Rehabilitative alimony awarded									
Garner v. Garner, 343 So. 3d 1097 (Miss. Ct. App. 2022).	8	2 children (wife)	Irreconcilable differences	H: $42,000; W: $600,000	H: 48%; W: 52%	$508/mo for 2 yrs (.1% disparity)	H: $508/mo	Husband, aff'd	Husband could earn more; Wife had care of children; Husband's abuse ended the marriage
Gussio v. Gussio, 371 So. 3d 734 (Miss. Ct. App. 2023)	9	4 children (wife); Wife 35	Husband: HCI	H: $9,000/mo imputed; W: homemaker	Prenuptial - most to husband	$250,000 lump sum $1,500 rehabilitative for 30 mo	H: $2,000/mo	Husband, aff'd	Husband had higher income and $4 million in separate property; divorce based on his abuse

CASE NAME	LENGTH OF MARRIAGE	AGE & CHILDREN	FAULT	INCOME	PROPERTY DIVISION	ALIMONY	CHILD SUPPORT	APPEAL	COMMENTS
C. Lump sum alimony awarded									
Shannon v. Shannon, 357 So. 3d 1043 (Miss. Ct. App. 2022)	1	None	W: Habitual cruelty			$26,000 lump sum alimony	NA	Wife, aff'd	Elderly man with Alzheimers granted divorce against wife based on habitual cruelty; award would support her for 13 months, the length of the marriage
IV. Reversals; type required not clear									
Hammond v. Hammond, 327 So. 3d 173 (Miss. Ct. App. 2021)	25	Wife: 47; 1 child (wife)	Husband: Adultery	Husband: $12,150/mo plus bonus; Wife: $646/mo	Wife: 55%	$500/mo for 2 years (5% of disparity)	$1167/mo	Wife, rev'd	Grossly inadequate considering marriage length, great disparity in incomes; husband's affair ended marriage

Made in the USA
Monee, IL
11 October 2026

65488117R00131